Climate Change Litigation in Japan

NIHU Studies in the Humanities

VOLUME 1

The titles published in this series are listed at *brill.com/nihu*

Climate Change Litigation in Japan

Cases, Challenges, and Opportunities for Environmental Law

By

Masako Ichihara

BRILL

LEIDEN | BOSTON

Cover illustration: Unit 3 of the coal-fired power plant, newly constructed and commenced operation by Kobe Steel in 2022. Photographed by attorney Shunsuke Sugita of the Kobe Climate Cases' Attorney Team.

The Library of Congress Cataloging-in-Publication Data is available online at https://catalog.loc.gov
LC record available at https://lccn.loc.gov/2025051026

Typeface for the Latin, Greek, and Cyrillic scripts: "Brill". See and download: brill.com/brill-typeface.

ISSN 3050-8126
ISBN 978-90-04-75629-8 (hardback)
ISBN 978-90-04-75703-5 (e-book)
DOI 10.1163/9789004757035

This book is printed on acid-free paper and produced in a sustainable manner.

Contents

Preface

Since the completion of my doctoral research on Japanese climate change litigation in September 2021, both domestic and global landscapes have undergone marked transformation. At the time, the Sabin Center's database at Columbia Law School recorded 1,398 climate change litigation cases in the United States and 447 in other jurisdictions. By May 2025, those numbers had risen to 1,990 and 1,071 respectively, underscoring the rapid proliferation of climate-related legal action. In Japan, other developments signaled growing momentum, such as the 2023 establishment of the Japan office of Client Earth, a globally recognized environmental legal charity, and the increasing engagement of prominent law firms in climate risk assessments.

A major international milestone occurred in July 2022, when the United Nations General Assembly recognized access to a clean, healthy, and sustainable environment as a universal human right. This resolution, grounded in the cumulative influence of climate litigation worldwide, affirmed a human rights–based approach to environmental degradation and litigation, and is likely to catalyze further legal action globally.

On August 6, 2024, sixteen young Japanese citizens initiated legal proceedings against ten major electric utilities. They alleged that the defendants' continued operation of coal-fired power plants violated their duty of care under tort law and contravened international public order, especially in line with the carbon budgets established by the Intergovernmental Panel on Climate Change. This case, the fifth climate case in Japan to date, marks the first instance in Japan where youth formed the sole plaintiff group in climate litigation – a notable development in Japan's historical experience in pollution and environmental lawsuits, as described in greater detail in following chapters.

Japan's experience with industrial pollution in the late twentieth century resulted in significant citizen-initiated lawsuits and spurred progressive environmental legislation. Consequently, Japan came to be regarded as a leader in environmental governance (Schreurs 2004). In contrast, its recent performance in climate mitigation has been widely criticized. As an indication of its flagging international reputation, Japan has received the "Fossil of the Day" award at four consecutive UN Climate Change Conference COPs since COP25, held on December 2–13, 2019.

It is not too late for Japan to realign with global efforts. By drawing on its past achievements in environmental regulation, Japan has the potential to meaningfully contribute to the preservation of a stable international climate regime. The timing of this publication coincides with a moment of significant change in Japan's legal response to climate change, despite the limited number of cases. In capturing and documenting this critical transitional phase, I hope this book will prove useful both as an academic endeavor and as a contribution to future generations.

Acknowledgments

This book arises from my doctoral research in legal studies undertaken at Kyoto University. After successfully defending my dissertation, I was fortunate to be able to deepen and refine my thinking while working in the Kyoto Climate Change Adaptation Center, a joint endeavor supported by Kyoto Prefecture, Kyoto City and the Research Institute for Humanity and Nature (RIHN), where I took my first position. This position at RIHN, which is one of the six institutes forming Japan's National Institutes for the Humanities (NIHU), provided several unusual advantages that enabled the publication of the present volume. RIHN's particular cultural approach to environmental study and deeply transdisciplinary research structure brought me into communication with a wide range of scholars interested especially in the human dimensions of environmental change. Through NIHU, in addition, RIHN's studies are framed at the national level by the humanities, underlining the challenge of climate change to human cultural beliefs and institutions in Japan and beyond. In this context I hope this study is most engaging, as the reader understands how climate change is challenging Japan's civil society and legal system in unprecedented ways. While there is much discussion of climate and environmental change within Japan, very little of it is known or understood by non-Japanese speakers. NIHU's newly established book series with Brill therefore provides a precious platform for international discussion of the Japanese perspective on the human and environmental changes that define our time. It is a particular honor and privilege to publish my research within it.

Looking back over my research career, I am deeply grateful to my dissertation supervisor Professor Makoto Usami for his insightful guidance and sustained encouragement. At Kyoto University, I also thank Associate Professor Gregory Patrick Trencher for his valuable suggestions and Professor Jane Singer for her detailed and constructive feedback on Chapter 4.

My research, including the surveys and interviews, would not have been possible without the collaboration of Professor Koichi Hasegawa, president of Morioka University, nor the lead plaintiff in the *Sendai* case. I also benefited greatly from the advice of Professor Jusen Asuka at Tohoku University. I am indebted to Mr. Rikuro Suzuki, the lead plaintiff of *Yokosuka* case and Ms. Takako Momoi (Kiko Network, Tokyo Office) for their consistent support and cooperation.

I wish to acknowledge the attorneys and plaintiffs involved in the *Kobe* cases; their openness allowed me to observe hearings and participate in meetings. Thanks also go to Mr. Naoki Ikeda, lead attorney in both *Kobe* cases; Ms. Mie

Asaoka, attorney in the *Kobe* and *Yokosuka* cases and president of the Kiko Network; and Mr. Hajime Yamamoto of Kiko Network's Kyoto Office. Moreover, I am grateful to Mr. Yutaka Hirooka, the lead plaintiff of both *Kobe* cases, as well as all survey participants for their time and input.

In preparing this manuscript for publication, I was fortunate to receive generous support from many individuals and institutions. Professor Takahiro Hattori facilitated my postgraduation enrollment as a research trainee at the Kyoto University School of Law, and Professor Keisuke Kondo kindly accepted my candidacy. Professor Koichi Hasegawa, the president of Morioka University, who supported my initial survey, once again provided indispensable assistance in the design and implementation of follow-up surveys. I also extend my gratitude to Professor Daniel Niles and Ms. Nozomi Kawabata of RIHN for their patient, generous support throughout the publication process. Furthermore, I express my heartfelt gratitude to Mr. Jon Wilcox, who patiently and meticulously adjusted and revised my manuscript within an extremely limited timeframe.

On a personal note, I owe much to my close friends Dinita Setyawati, Bahareh Ghafouri, Kumie Hattori, and Lilia Shahar Griffin for their unwavering friendship. Finally, I thank my husband and three daughters, whose love and support have sustained me throughout this journey. This work would not have been completed without them.

This study was generously supported by the Sumitomo Life Women Researchers Encouragement Prize and the Asahi Glass Foundation. I gratefully acknowledge receipt of a Publication Grant for Early Career Researchers provided by the Institute for the Future of Human Society, Kyoto University. Support for Open Access publication was generously provided by the National Institutes for the Humanities, Japan.

Figures and Tables

Figures

Tables

Abbreviations

ACLA	Administrative Case Litigation Act
APA	Administrative Procedure Act
CAA	Clean Air Act
CCL	climate change litigation
CCS	carbon capture and storage
CFPP	coal-fired power plant
CO_2	carbon dioxide
COP	Conference of the Parties
EBA	Electricity Business Act
ECtHR	European Court of Human Rights
EDI	Environmental Democracy Index
EIA	environmental impact assessment
EPA	Environmental Protection Agency
FDA	Food and Drugs Administration
FFF	Fridays For Future
GHG	greenhouse gas
IEA	International Energy Agency
IPCC	Intergovernmental Panel on Climate Change
LOS	Legal Opportunity Structure
METI	Ministry of Economy, Trade, and Industry
MEXT	Ministry of Education, Culture, Sports, Science, and Technology
MOE	Ministry of Environment
TAI	The Access Initiative
UNEP	United Nations Environment Programme
U.N.T.S.	United Nationals Treaty Series
U.S.	US Supreme Court [in legal citations]
U.S.C.	United States Code
WRI	World Resources Institute

Introduction

In recent decades, climate change litigation (CCL) has rapidly increased worldwide. Japan is no exception, with the first climate change case (*Sendai*) occurring in 2017 and three additional cases in 2018 and 2019 (two *Kobe* cases and *Yokosuka*), each of which filed for injunctions against the operation and construction of coal-fired power plants (CFPP). A fifth case (*Youth*) began in 2024. Despite these filings, CFPPs still produce about 30 percent of all electricity generated in Japan. Such reliance on coal suggests several significant obstacles to the further development of Japanese CCL.

This book expands on the author's PhD research, which used questionnaire surveys and semi-structured interviews with key actors in the first four Japanese CCL cases (the doctoral dissertation was completed in 2021, before the emergence of the *Youth* case). It maps out the historical precedents, novel features, parallel trends, challenges, and opportunities for CCL in Japan.

Chapter 1 reviews the historical background in which early CCL arose globally, including Japan, setting the stage for consideration of the key obstacles that remain. It examines the early development of CCL and introduces key cases filed in Japan. It then reviews the existing literature on CCL and coal phase-out, before discussing studies identifying obstacles to litigation more generally in Japan. Finally, it lays out the key objectives and methodologies used in the present study.

Chapter 2 provides an overview of the Japanese legal system as essential background for understanding CCL in the local context. Although modeled on Western legal frameworks, Japan's system is distinctive, having adapted foreign principles and procedures to its own social and cultural conditions. This chapter sets the stage for analyzing how CCL interacts with Japanese society and jurisprudence in the chapters that follow.

Chapter 3 examines how earlier waves of environmental litigation, concerning both pollution and climate change, has shaped present-day CCL and highlights the ways contemporary CCL differs from earlier experiences. Two core features of Japanese CCL emerge: first, its continuity with the expansive scope of earlier environmental cases; second, its novel legal features arising from the unique character of climate change itself. In other words, while pollution lawsuits and CCL share issues such as causation and distributed responsibility, they diverge sharply in temporal and spatial scale. These twin characteristics underpin the book as a whole and inform the analysis in subsequent chapters.

Chapter 4 provides detailed accounts of all five Japanese climate change cases, which have received scant attention in international scholarship. It shows how plaintiffs and their attorneys sought to persuade judges by deliberately framing these cases as extensions of past air pollution litigation. The defendants' rebuttals, in turn, clarified key legal issues – plaintiffs' standing, causal proof, and justifiability – that mirror challenges seen in CCL worldwide. The chapter also highlights how arguments in Japanese CCL are dominated by disputes over standing, infringement of human rights, and causation.

Chapter 5 investigates institutional barriers to CCL, drawing on the background in Chapters 2 and 3. Using the Legal Opportunity Structure framework, it assesses the likelihood of legal mobilization by social activists through three adapted indicators: (1) access to courts, including rules on standing and access to available resources (financial support, donations, legal expertise); (2) existing law and legal bases, covering favorable statutes and precedents, especially antipollution cases; and (3) judicial receptiveness, examining how Japanese courts have historically handled environmental and pollution claims.

Chapter 6 explores the cognitive barriers to CCL. It draws primarily on survey and interview data collected from key actors in the first four cases. The motivations and expectations of plaintiffs in the cases are identified, showing how they overcame such hurdles. Plaintiffs did not necessarily recognize either the strategic differences between past air pollution litigation or climate change cases and the potentially lengthy duration of legal proceedings. These insights highlight how Japan's history of environmental litigation, especially landmark antipollution cases that spurred pre-environment legislation, assists plaintiffs to overcome cognitive obstacles. The findings show that these obstacles stem from low public awareness of climate urgency and uncertainty about the costs, duration, and outcomes of litigation.

Chapter 7 considers how these barriers might evolve and how Japanese CCL could develop, including possible areas of improvement. It first reassesses the three types of institutional obstacles identified in Chapter 5. Regarding access to courts, reforms such as relaxing strict standing rules, adopting alternative pathways (as in Germany), increasing the number of attorneys engaged in public interest litigation, expanding the loser-pays rule, and improving access to judicial information may enhance litigation opportunities. In terms of available laws, further legislation on climate mitigation and adaptation and insights drawn from foreign cases – though not directly applicable – may guide Japanese courts. Finally, in the area of judicial receptiveness, expanding case categories covered by lay judges and strengthening legal education may encourage more openness to climate claims. The chapter then returns to the cognitive obstacles identified in Chapter 6 and discusses strategies of overcoming them in future cases. It highlights the role social networks and global communications in disseminating legal information and increasing awareness of climate change, and points to potential strategies to reduce the length (and thereby the financial burden) of case trials.

The second half of the chapter traces a possible trajectory for Japanese CCL by comparing it to US tobacco litigation. After outlining the three historical waves of US tobacco cases, it maps similar periodic patterns in US CCL and applies this framework to Japan. The analysis suggests that current Japanese CCL, as illustrated by the five cases studied, resembles the first wave of US tobacco litigation.

Chapters 2 to 7 each close with a summary section, and the book itself concludes with a chapter summarizing the study's key findings, limitations, and directions for future research. Three main implications emerge: First, this study provides the most detailed analysis to date of the five Japanese climate cases litigated so far, offering valuable empirical data from East Asia, where scholarship has been scarce and largely focused on Western nations. Second, by positioning Japanese CCL within the historical trajectory of environmental litigation, this research connects climate cases to a broader sociolegal tradition in Japan. Finally, by drawing parallels with US tobacco litigation, it identifies the potential for Japanese CCL to drive future shifts in climate policy.

CHAPTER 1

Research Background and Existing Scholarship

This chapter introduces the research background to the study and the current state of CCL worldwide and in Japan. It then reviews the existing literature on CCL, coal phase-out, and obstacles to litigation in Japan, before detailing the objectives and methodologies used in the present study. As such, the chapter lays out the context and framework for the rest of the book.

1.1 Research Background

1.1.1 *Development of Climate Change Litigation*

Over the past four decades, climate change litigation (CCL) has expanded substantially worldwide. While definitions of CCL vary, the United Nations Environment Programme describes it as encompassing cases brought before judicial or quasi-judicial bodies that raise material issues related to climate change science, policy, or law (UNEP 2023, 10). As of August 2024, approximately 1,796 climate change cases have been filed in the United States and 939 in other jurisdictions (Figures 1–3).[1]

Approximately 70 percent of these cases were filed after the adoption of the Paris Agreement in 2015,[2] which, though a framework treaty, imposed a legal obligation on signatory countries to implement climate measures (Preston 2021, 3; Setzer and Higham 2024, 2). Globally, filings peaked in 2021 and have since declined, possibly reflecting reduced fossil fuel infrastructure development in the United States and a growing diversification of CCL targets elsewhere – some of which now fall outside UNEP's definition.

To date, CCL has been pursued in fifty-five countries (Setzer and Higham 2024, 11). Initially concentrated in the Global North, filings have increasingly emerged in the Global South (Lin and Peel 2024).[3] The number of cases

1 Data from the Sabin Center database, https://climatecasechart.com/non-us-climate-change-litigation, accessed May 5, 2025. The development of climate litigation in the United States is described in more detail in Section 7.3.3.

2 Paris Agreement to the United Nations Framework Convention on Climate Change, December 12, 2015, T.I.A.S. No. 16–1104.

3 One exception is Lliuya v. RWE AG, in which a Peruvian farmer sued Germany's largest electricity producer. Lliuya v. RWE AG, 5 U 15/17 OLG Hamm, Case No. 2 O 285/15 Essen Regional Court, https://climatecasechart.com/non-us-case/lliuya-v-rwe-ag.

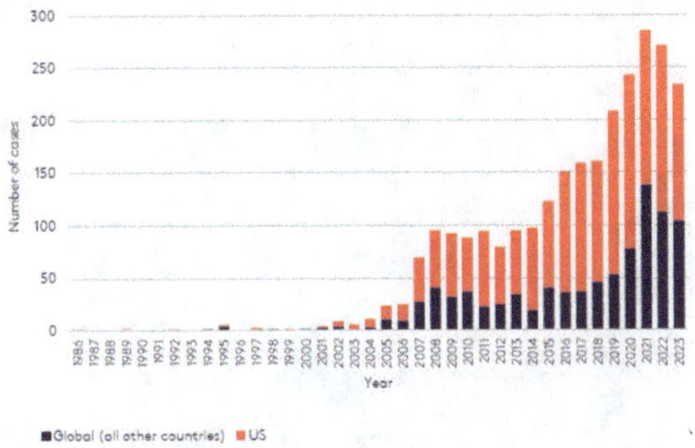

FIGURE 1 Total global climate change cases over time, 1986–2023
SOURCE: REPRODUCED FROM SETZER AND HIGHAM (2024, 10)

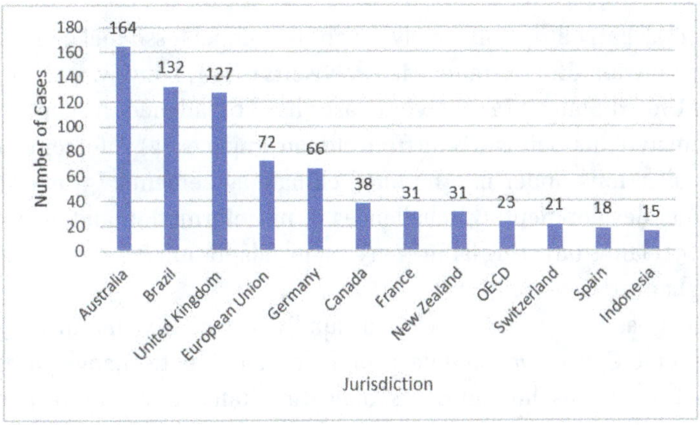

FIGURE 2 Top ten non-US jurisdictions by number of climate change cases, 1986–2025. Note: OECD = Organisation for Economic Co-operation and Development
SOURCE: CREATED BY THE AUTHOR BASED ON DATA FROM THE SABIN CENTER DATABASE

before international courts, as well as requests for advisory opinions, has also increased (Setzer and Higham 2023, 13).

CCL provides civil society and individuals with a legal avenue to demand adequate climate action by both states and private actors (UNEP 2023, 7), a role emphasized by the Intergovernmental Panel on Climate Change in its Sixth Assessment Report (IPCC 2023, 63). Nongovernmental organizations (NGOs) and individuals are plaintiffs in more than 70 percent of global cases, while governments and corporations are the most common defendants (Setzer and

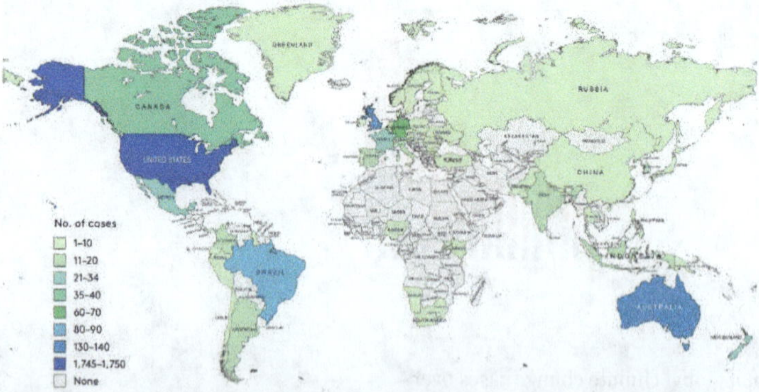

FIGURE 3 Geographical distribution of climate change cases, included in the Climate Change Litigation Database as of May 2024, https://climatecasechart.com/non-us-climate-change-litigation
SOURCE: REPRODUCED FROM SETZER AND HIGHAM (2024, 11)

Higham 2023, 18).[4] Early litigation largely sought to compel fossil fuel companies to reduce emissions, for example, Massachusetts v. EPA, Lliuya v. RWE AG, and Juliana v. United States.[5] More recent cases have broadened in scope to include: (1) human rights claims arising from climate impacts; (2) enforcement of domestic obligations under international climate agreements; (3) efforts to ban fossil fuel development; (4) challenges to misinformation and greenwashing; and (5) claims targeting failures in climate adaptation (UNEP 2023, 4; Setzer and Higham 2024, 3–4).

Human rights-based CCL has developed rapidly in recent years. In 2019, the Dutch Supreme Court's *Urgenda* decision held that climate change poses a serious threat to citizens' human rights, obligating states to take protective action.[6] Specifically, the court ruled that the adverse effects of dangerous climate change violate the right to life (Article 2 of the European Convention on Human Rights) and the right to respect for private and family life (Article 8), and that the state must adopt adequate measures to prevent such violations. This was the first time a national supreme court explicitly recognized climate change as a human rights issue. The judgment triggered a wave of similar

4 In 2023, governments were the plaintiffs in more than 70 percent of cases registered in the Sabin Center database.

5 Massachusetts v. EPA, 549 U.S. 497 (2007), https://climatecasechart.com/case/massachusetts-v-epa; *Luciano Lliuya* (supra note 3); Juliana v. United States, 947 F.3d 1159 (9th Cir. 2020), https://climatecasechart.com/case/juliana-v-united-states.

6 Urgenda Foundation v. State of Netherlands, HR, December 20, 2019, ECLI:NL:HR:2019:2007, https://climatecasechart.com/non-us-case/urgenda-foundation-v-kingdom-of-the-netherlands.

cases, including *Friends of the Irish Environment v. Ireland, Do-Hyun Kim et al. v. South Korea,* and *Citizens' Committee on the Kobe Coal-Fired Power Plant v. Japan* (hereafter, *Kobe administrative* case).[7]

The German Constitutional Court followed with its 2021 decision in *Neubauer et al. v. Germany,* holding that insufficient greenhouse gas (GHG) regulation violated the constitutional rights of future generations.[8] In the same year, the Hague District Court ordered Royal Dutch Shell to reduce its emissions, citing the company's duty to respect the human rights of Dutch citizens.[9] These rulings helped pave the way for the United Nations' 2022 declaration recognizing access to a healthy environment as a universal human right.[10]

In 2024, the European Court of Human Rights (ECtHR) ruled in *Klima-Seniorinnen* that the Swiss government had failed to adequately protect elderly women from climate harms, thereby infringing their human rights.[11] Notably, the plaintiffs had previously lost in Swiss domestic courts, in 2020. ECtHR affirmed that while states retain discretion in shaping climate policy, they must adopt transparent, structured decision-making processes.

This human rights trend is also evident in litigation against corporate greenwashing. In 2024, a Dutch court held that fifteen of nineteen environmental advertisements by KLM misled the public in violation of consumer protection law.[12]

7 Friends of the Irish Environment v. Ireland, 2017 No. 793 JR, https://climatecasechart.com/non-us-case/friends-of-the-irish-environment-v-ireland; *Do*-Hyun Kim et al. v. South Korea, https://climatecasechart.com/non-us-case/kim-yujin-et-al-v-south-korea; Citizens' Committee on the Kobe Coal-Fired Power Plant v. Japan, Osaka Koto Saibansho [Osaka High Ct.] April 26 2022 1513 Hanrei Taimuzu [Hanta] 98 (second judgment), https://climatecasechart.com/non-us-case/citizens-committee-on-the-kobe-coal-fired-power-plant-v-japan.

8 Neubauer et al. v. Germany, B VerfG, Beschluss des Ersten Senats vom März 2021-BvR 2656/18, https://climatecasechart.com/non-us-case/neubauer-et-al-v-germany.

9 Milieudefensie et al. v. Royal Dutch Shell plc. Rechrbank Den Haag, May 26, 2021, ECLI:NL:RBDHA:2021:5337, https://climatecasechart.com/non-us-case/milieudefensie-et-al-v-royal-dutch-shell-plc.

10 G.A. Res. 76/300, The human right to a clean, healthy and sustainable environment, July 28, 2022, https://docs.un.org/en/A/RES/76/300g.

11 KlimaSeniorinnen v. Switzerland, (ECtHR) Application no. 53600/20, https://climatecasechart.com/non-us-case/union-of-swiss-senior-women-for-climate-protection-v-swiss-federal-council-and-others. For the 2020 Swiss court decision, see https://climatecasechart.com/non-us-case/union-of-swiss-senior-women-for-climate-protection-v-swiss-federal-parliament.

12 FossielVrij NL v. KLM, Rechtbank Amsterdam, March 20, 2024, ECLI:NL:RBAMS:2024:1512, https://climatecasechart.com/non-us-case/fossielvrij-nl-v-klm.

1.1.2 *Japanese Cases*

Despite being a signatory to the Paris Agreement, Japan has continued to expand its reliance on coal. Following the Great East Japan Earthquake in March 2011, which severely damaged the Fukushima Daiichi Nuclear Power Plant, the government promoted the construction of new coal-fired power plants (CFPPs) as an alternative energy source.

In April 2013, the Ministry of the Environment (MOE) and the Ministry of Economy, Trade, and Industry (METI) jointly established the Director-General Meeting Agreement,[13] which relaxed approval criteria for new CFPPs. Rather than applying the original standards contemplated under the Environmental Impact Assessment Act (EIA Act), the agreement allowed all applications that satisfied generation-efficiency requirements under the Energy Conservation Act, coupled with voluntary emissions-intensity targets.[14] Notably, the Electricity Business Act (EBA) contains no provisions on carbon dioxide (CO_2) emissions.[15] This deregulatory framework spurred a surge in coal plant construction. As of May 2025, Japan operated 165 CFPPs, with one additional facility under construction.[16] In 2022, per capita CO_2 emissions were approximately 9.41 metric tons, with total national GHG emissions of 1,182 million tons, placing Japan eighth in global emissions at 2.2 percent of the world share (EDGER 2023, 5).

Fossil fuels are a major driver of climate change, and coal is the most carbon-intensive of all. In 2018, coal-fired generation accounted for roughly 40 percent of global CO_2 emissions (IEA 2021, 4), releasing nearly twice as much CO_2 as natural gas.[17] At COP28, the international community agreed to accelerate the transition away from coal, underscoring its phase-out as an urgent prerequisite to achieving the Paris Agreement's 1.5 °C target (UNFCCC 2023). Consequently, litigation targeting coal use has become a major strand

13 For the terms of the agreement, see the official document at https://www8.cao.go.jp/kisei-kaikaku/kaigi/meeting/2013/committee/130502/item1.pdf (in Japanese). Unless otherwise stated (such as those available at www.japaneselawtranslation.go.jp cited throughout), translations from non-English sources are the author's.

14 Environmental Impact Assessment Act, Act No. 81 of June 13, 1997, https://www.japaneselawtranslation.go.jp/en/laws/view/3375; Act on Rationalization of Energy Use and Shift to Non-Fossil Energy (Energy Conservation Act), Act No. 49 of June 22, 1979, https://www.japaneselawtranslation.go.jp/ja/laws/view/4592.

15 Electricity Business Act, Act No. 170 of July 11, 1964, https://www.japaneselawtranslation.go.jp/en/laws/view/51.

16 Data according to the Beyond Coal Japan website, at https://beyond-coal.jp, accessed May 5, 2025.

17 On natural gas versus coal, see https://www.gasvessel.eu/news/natural-gas-vs-coal-impact-on-the-environment, accessed May 5, 2025.

of CCL worldwide, including in South Africa, Australia, the United States – and Japan.[18]

Amid Japan's CFPP construction boom, a new project by Sendai Power Station Company was announced in 2014 in Sendai City, Miyagi Prefecture. Concerned about potential harm to human health and the local environment, residents sought to negotiate cancellation of the plan but were unsuccessful. In 2017, 124 citizens – led by two university researchers – filed Japan's first climate lawsuit to halt the plant's operation (*Sendai* case).[19] The Kiko Network, a Japanese NGO dedicated to climate advocacy, supported the plaintiffs and publicized the case nationwide.[20]

In September 2018, forty citizens filed a similar civil suit in Kobe City, Hyogo Prefecture, opposing two planned CFPPs (*Kobe* civil case). Some plaintiffs also brought an administrative case in November 2018 against METI, challenging its issuance of the final EIA notice (*Kobe* administrative case).[21] In May 2019, another group of forty-five citizens in Yokosuka City, Kanagawa Prefecture, filed an administrative case seeking to revoke METI's EIA approval for a CFPP there (*Yokosuka* administrative case).[22] Finally, in August 2024, sixteen young people from across Japan jointly filed a civil case seeking an injunction against ten major electric power companies to prevent them from exceeding emission-reduction targets consistent with the IPCC's Sixth Assessment Report (IPCC 2023) and the 1.5 °C temperature goal (*Youth* case).[23] Attorneys involved

18 For example, in South Africa: EarthLife Africa Johannesburg v. Minister of Environmental Affairs and Others, Case no. 65662/16, https://climatecasechart.com/non-us-case/4463; in Australia: Gloucester Resources Limited v. Minister for Planning, [2019] NSWLEC 7; 234 LEGRA 257, https://climatecasechart.com/non-us-case/gloucester-resources-limited-v-minister-for-planning, and Youth Verdict v. Waratah Coal, [2020] QLC 33; [2021] QLC 4; [2021] QLC 36; [2022] QLC 3; [2022] QLC 4, https://climatecasechart.com/non-us-case/youth-verdict-v-waratah-coal; in the United States: Montana Environmental Information Center v. U.S. Office of Surface Mining, 274 F.Supp.3d 1074 (D. Mont. 2017), https://climatecasechart.com/case/montana-elders-for-a-livable-tomorrow-v-us-office-of-surface-mining, Levin Richmond Terminal Corp. v. City of Richmond, 482 F.Supp.3d 944 (N.D. Cal. 2020), https://climatecasechart.com/case/levin-richmond-terminal-corp-v-city-of-richmond, and Held v. Montana, Case No. CDV-2020-307, https://climatecasechart.com/case/11091.

19 The trajectory of the *Sendai* case is explained on the website of the plaintiff group: https://stopsendaips.jp (in Japanese). See Sec. 4.2.1 for the facts of the case.

20 The website of the Kiko Network is available at https://www.kikonet.org (in Japanese).

21 On the *Kobe* case, see https://kobeclimatecase.jp/en. See Secs. 4.2.2 for the civil case and 4.2.3 for the administrative case.

22 On the *Yokosuka* case, see https://yokosukaclimatecase.jp/en. See Sec. 4.2.4.

23 The facts of the *Youth* case can be found on the website of the plaintiff group: https://youth4cj.jp (in Japanese). See Sec. 4.2.5.

in the *Kobe* cases shared strategies with those in the *Yokosuka* case, and one lawyer participated in the *Kobe*, *Yokosuka*, and *Youth* cases. The Kiko Network supported all three cases through nationwide information dissemination.

International criticism of Japan's coal dependence intensified after the Paris Agreement. UN Secretary-General António Guterres repeatedly urged all countries, including developing economies, to eliminate CFPPs by 2040 (Reuters 2022) and singled out Japan for its continued reliance on coal (Takahiro 2024). Japan also received the "Fossil of the Day" award for four consecutive years after COP25 (Kyoto News 2019). These external pressures prompted some Japanese corporations to divest from fossil fuels, shift their supply chains to renewable energy, and join international renewable energy platforms.[24]

In response to both domestic and international pressure, the Japanese government revised its energy policy to pursue carbon neutrality. On July 2, 2020, METI announced plans to phase out 90 percent of inefficient CFPPs by 2030 (Reuters 2020). On October 26, 2020, Prime Minister Yoshihide Suga pledged that Japan would achieve net-zero emissions by 2050,[25] followed by an April 22, 2021 announcement of a 46 percent reduction target in GHG emissions by 2030 compared to 2013 levels (Kyoto News 2021). At the same time, the government continued to emphasize coal's role in Japan's energy mix, citing the efficiency of advanced CFPP technologies and the anticipated deployment of carbon capture and storage (CCS) systems. However, CCS remains highly contested, with assessments ranging from optimism (IEA 2023) to skepticism (Abreu 2023), and Japan's ongoing reliance on coal appears increasingly at odds with global decarbonization trends (Rowling 2021).

In 2021, the Japanese government introduced a policy to reduce CO_2 emissions by co-firing ammonia with coal, enabling the continued operation of existing CFPPs.[26] However, large-scale production of "green ammonia" – which emits no GHGs across its lifecycle – remains prohibitively expensive. In practice, the policy is expected to rely on "gray ammonia," produced from coal and associated with significant CO_2 emissions, making its contribution to global-emissions reduction negligible.

Despite mounting international criticism and accelerating global momentum toward decarbonization, Japan's coal policy remains misaligned with

24 For example, the RE100 platform: https://go100re.jp/portfolio/re100.

25 PM Suga's speech was accessed on August 4, 2024, at https://mainichi.jp/english/articles/20201026/p2g/00m/0na/081000c (in Japanese, link no longer active); see also McCurry (2020).

26 See the interim summary of the Public-Private Council for the Introduction of Fuel Ammonia, https://www.meti.go.jp/shingikai/energy_environment/nenryo_anmonia/pdf/20200208_1.pdf (in Japanese).

climate goals. Notably, only a handful of climate lawsuits have been filed in Japan to date, despite the large number of operational CFPPs. Japan is known for its exceptionally low litigation rates, explained by factors such as strict standing requirements, lengthy proceedings, and a shortage of attorneys (Kidder and Miyazawa 1993, 618), and these conditions may discourage many citizens from pursuing legal action, an issue we will return to.

Nevertheless, Japan has a history of impactful environmental litigation, particularly in response to pollution. After World War II, the government prioritized rapid economic development over environmental protection (Otsuka 2020a, 5, 9), delaying regulatory measures and prompting citizens to seek judicial remedies (Upham 1987, 211–223; Kidder and Miyazawa 1993, 610–613; Otsuka 2020a, 3–26). Lawsuits were often coordinated with broader social movements, and in several instances courts issued pro-environment rulings that spurred legislative reform, especially during the 1970s and 1980s. Some attorneys involved in current CCL have explicitly framed their cases as building on this legacy.[27]

However, climate change fundamentally differs from traditional pollution disputes, requiring new legal strategies. Past cases typically addressed localized harms – such as river contamination – caused by clearly identifiable polluters. By contrast, climate change involves diffuse sources, global impacts, and harms that are less immediate and more abstract. Establishing legal causation is far more difficult, as extreme weather events such as heatwaves and droughts cannot be traced to individual emitters in the same way as industrial pollutants. Whether CCL in Japan can meaningfully be understood as a continuation of its historical environmental litigation trajectory remains uncertain and will be discussed further in Section 3.4.

1.2 Literature Review

1.2.1 *Climate Change Litigation* (CCL)

As noted above, CCL initially emerged and developed primarily in Western jurisdictions, and early scholarship reflected this focus. A systematic review of 130 English-language articles published between 2000 and 2018 found that approximately 76 percent analyzed CCL in the Global North, 26 percent

27 In a statement responding to the Osaka District Court decision on March 15, 2021, attorneys in the *Kobe* case criticized defendants' enormous CO_2 emissions as "global environmental disruption." See https://kobeclimatecase.jp/en/blog/2021/03/16/administrative_litigation_judgement20210315.

addressed international dimensions, and only five examined cases in the Global South (Setzer and Vanhala 2019, 4). The review also noted that three Japanese cases from this period (*Sendai* and the two *Kobe* cases) were entirely overlooked, underscoring Japan's limited visibility in global CCL research.

Within this body of literature, many studies addressed recurring legal hurdles such as standing, causality, and justiciability (Gerrard and Freeman 2007; Burns and Osofsky 2009; Humphreys 2009; Carlarne 2010; Markell and Ruhl 2010; Lord et al. 2011). Others examined how legislation, regulation, and litigation interact (Vanhala 2013; Peel and Osofsky 2015; Preston 2016; Setzer and Nachmany 2018), while a smaller group considered how domestic litigation could reinforce international climate law (Carnwath 2016; Butterfield 2018).

More recent scholarship reflects the global expansion of CCL, particularly in the Global South. Studies increasingly analyze how institutional contexts in these regions shape litigation strategies, contrasting them with high-profile cases in the Global North (Peel and Lin 2018; Setzer and Benjamin 2020; Lin and Peel 2024). Some provide cross-jurisdictional comparisons (Alogna, Bakker, and Gauci 2021; Sindico and Mbengue 2021), while others focus on single-country studies, including China (Zhao, Shuang, and Zhu 2019) and, more recently, Japan (Linden 2023; Nishikawa 2023; Otsuka 2023).

1.2.2 *Coal Phase-Out*

In all five Japanese climate cases, plaintiffs sought partial or total injunctions against CFPPs, situating these lawsuits within the broader global trend toward coal phase-out. A substantial literature examines coal phase-out policies in coal-dependent countries such as Germany (Heinrichs and Markewitz 2017; Oei et al. 2020) and the United Kingdom (Littlecott 2016). In Japan, numerous studies address strategies for coal reduction, including policy recommendations,[28] analyses of corporate practices (Trencher et al. 2020), and social movement strategies (Yamamoto 2020). However, despite this attention to coal policy, Japan's five climate lawsuits have received little to no consideration in international academic literature.

1.2.3 *Obstacles to Litigation in Japan*

As mentioned earlier, Japan is widely recognized for its relatively low litigation rates. A 2010 Japan Federation of Bar Associations survey found that,

28 For example, see the calls of the European Business Council in Japan (2025) and Japan Climate Initiative (2024) for Japan to set a 2035 emissions reduction target of at least 66 percent.

relative to population size, Japan's civil litigation rate was only one-eighth that of the United States, one-fourth that of England and France, and one-third that of Germany and South Korea (reported in Nikkei 2020). This disparity has prompted extensive scholarship on the barriers suppressing litigation in Japan.

Institutional explanations include the availability of alternatives to litigation – such as mediation and informal administrative remedies – which are often preferred for their expedience and simplicity (Haley 1979, 378–379; Upham 1979, 218–268; 1987, 16–18). Other obstacles are frequent judicial rotations that disrupt case continuity, the limited number of legal professionals (Haley 1979, 381–383; Kidder and Miyazawa 1993, 618), and Japan's strict standing requirements (Upham 1979, 239–244; Takahashi 2013, 30–36; Okubo 2016, 498). Courts have also been reluctant to grant injunctive relief – critical in environmental disputes – viewing it as unduly restrictive of defendants' activities, while preferring monetary or declaratory remedies (Otsuka 2020a, 16). Additionally, judicial passivism, marked by deference to executive discretion, is frequently noted as a distinctive feature of Japan's judiciary (Urabe 2016, 394–395).

Cultural and cognitive factors also discourage litigation. A traditional emphasis on social harmony and communal solidarity renders legal rights less assertive and litigation socially undesirable (Kawashima 1967, 139–141; Haley 1979, 359–390; see also Takana 2005, 52). Individuals often avoid even minimal legal risk, particularly in cases with predictable outcomes such as traffic accidents (Ramseyer 1988, 116–117; 1990, 15–46). The 2016 Civil Litigation Survey discussed in more depth in Section 6.2, further reported that lengthy proceedings (78.4%) and high costs (75.3%) were major deterrents (Minji Sosyou Seido Kenkyu-kai 2018, 86–87).

Despite these well-documented institutional and cultural barriers, their specific implications for CCL remain largely unexplored and will form the basis of analysis in Chapters 5 and 6.

1.3 Research Objectives and Methods

This study investigates the obstacles to CCL in Japan. As previously noted, Japanese CCL has received little international scholarly attention; this study therefore represents the first detailed examination of its kind.

Environmental legislation has historically influenced Japanese judicial decisions and procedures (Otsuka 2020a, 26). Environmental activists have at times used litigation strategically to raise public awareness, despite procedural and institutional hurdles, leveraging Japan's generally low litigation rates to amplify visibility (Kidder and Miyazawa 1993, 609). However, whether similar strategies can succeed in CCL remains an open question.

CCL differs fundamentally from traditional environmental lawsuits. It addresses global harms adjudicated in domestic courts under national legal systems, and plaintiffs may even assert rights or protections for future generations – those not yet born. These features suggest that the legal barriers to CCL are distinct. Clarifying these obstacles not only illuminates how CCL diverges from earlier environmental litigation, but also yields insights relevant to other jurisdictions with comparable sociolegal contexts. Given the worldwide rise of CCL, such findings can inform broader legal strategies for CCL.

To analyze barriers to CCL in Japan, this study pursues two subobjectives focused on institutional and cognitive dimensions of litigation barriers. These reflect the challenges litigants face at different stages of the legal process: institutional obstacles typically arise in the information-gathering and claim-preparation phase, while cognitive barriers – such as risk aversion or social disincentives – tend to influence the decision to proceed with litigation. Examining both dimensions provides a fuller understanding of constraints on Japanese CCL.

Analytically, this study applies the Legal Opportunity Structure (LOS) framework developed by Chris Hilson (2002), widely used to evaluate when social movements engage in legal mobilization. Social movements are defined here using Charles Tilly's (1984, 306) broad formulation: "a sustained series of interactions between powerholders and persons successfully claiming to speak on behalf of a constituency lacking formal representation, in the course of which those persons make publicly visible demands for changes in the distribution or exercise of power and back those demands with public demonstrations of support." Legal mobilization is understood in collective rather than individual terms, following Lisa Vanhala (2020, 1): the process by which collective actors invoke legal norms, discourse, or symbols to influence policy or citizen behavior. This definition aligns with the structure of the Japanese climate lawsuits considered here, all initiated by citizen groups.

Practically, the LOS framework assesses the extent to which legal channels are available to ordinary citizens or citizen groups, compared with alternative avenues for collective action such as political lobbying, protests, or petitions. It evaluates three primary indicators to gauge whether social movements are likely to pursue legal mobilization (Hilson 2002, 11; De Fazio 2012, 3; Vanhala 2018, 1).

The first is access to the courts, typically reflected in standing requirements.[29] The second is existing law, including relevant statutes and judicial precedents. Precedents are particularly valuable because they show how laws have been applied in practice, helping citizens assess whether a legal provision can be used effectively to address a given issue. The third is judicial receptiveness – the likelihood that courts will admit, even partially, claims brought by social activists (Vanhala 2020, 1). Judicial receptiveness is shaped by the *trias politica* – the relationship between judiciary, executive, and legislature. Depending on the social movement examined, additional indicators may be relevant, such as the availability of legal and financial resources, familiarity with litigation, and the degree of "environmental democracy," meaning whether land and resource decisions adequately and equitably reflect citizens' interests.[30]

Applied to CCL, Setzer and Benjamin (2020) used LOS to analyze sociolegal conditions in the Global South, contrasting them with those of the Global North. They highlighted that scarce access to legal and financial expertise is a critical barrier to CCL in the Global South. This additional indicator underscores how resource constraints shape litigation strategies. In terms of existing law, their study found that explicit human rights provisions – such as rights to water and clean air – reduce hurdles for rights-based climate claims in many Global South jurisdictions (Setzer and Benjamin 2020, 91–92). By contrast, litigants in Global North cases often argue that existing constitutional rights (e.g., to life or due process, as in *Juliana*) implicitly encompass a right to a stable climate system or protection from climate-related harm.

In Japan, relevant features include low litigation rates and significant institutional and cognitive barriers. Japan's tradition in environmental litigation – particularly its judicial precedents – must also be considered. Accordingly, this study applies the LOS framework to Japanese CCL with two modifications: (1) Resources (access to legal professionals and funding) are explicitly included

---

29 Standing refers to a party's right to make a legal claim or seek judicial enforcement of a duty or right (Garner et al. 2014).

30 On environmental democracy, see the webpage on the website of the Center for International Environmental Law: https://www.ciel.org/issue/environmental-democracy-access-rights. In 2015, the World Resources Institute and the Access Initiative launched the Environmental Democracy Index, which uses a set of indicators to measure and rank countries' degree of judicial accessibility (https://www.environmentaldemocracyindex.org). The index functions similarly to the LOS framework. The EDI will be discussed at greater length in Sec. 5.2.1.

as an additional indicator to capture Japan-specific obstacles. (2) Judicial precedent is directly integrated into the analysis of existing law, as prior cases illuminate how courts have received similar legal arguments. These adjustments allow the framework to better reflect Japan's sociolegal landscape and clarify how established norms and precedents might be mobilized in domestic CCL.

CHAPTER 2

Overview of the Japanese Legal System Relevant to Climate Change Litigation

2.1 Overview

This chapter provides essential background for understanding CCL in Japan. CCL raises critical questions for judiciaries worldwide: How can a global problem be interpreted within a domestic legal framework, and how should courts respond within the limits of their authority? Nearly all jurisdictions recognize that existing laws and legal theories alone cannot deliver immediate solutions to what the ECtHR called in *KlimaSeniorinnen* a "common concern for humankind." While legal resources differ by country, many climate rulings – especially those driving national policy change – draw on shared values such as human rights, the precautionary principle, and intergenerational equity.

Courts have often sought to interpret existing laws creatively, while still respecting institutional boundaries. Many have cited foreign climate judgments to justify progressive decisions.[1] The British Institute of International and Comparative Law has examined legal issues and rulings in seventeen countries, producing comparative studies and conceptual diagrams illustrating the evolution of climate-related legal theory.[2] By contrast, courts that take a conservative view of accumulated jurisprudence tend to avoid addressing novel challenges like climate change. Japanese courts largely display this cautious approach, though a few rulings have advanced innovative human rights interpretations in climate contexts, as will be discussed later.

The sections that follow compare Japanese climate cases with those from countries such as the United States and South Korea, situating each within its judicial system and its approach to CCL. Section 2.2 explains the structure of Japan's judiciary through the lens of the separation of powers (*trias politica*). Section 2.3 examines the legal status of public access to justice in environmental litigation. Section 2.4 introduces major climate-related laws cited in previous cases. Section 2.5 summarizes the legal foundations and constraints shaping CCL's prospects in Japan.

1 E.g., *KlimaSeniorinnen* (Chapter 1, supra note 11); *Milieudefensie* (Chapter 1, supra note 9).

2 See the Institute's Global Toolbox on Corporate Climate Litigation at https://www.biicl.org/global-toolbox-corporate-climate-litigation.

2.2 Japanese Judiciary

2.2.1 *Trias Politica*

Japan's first modern Constitution, adopted in 1889 during the imperial era and heavily influenced by German legal thought, was abolished during the US occupation after World War II. The current Constitution, effective from 1947, redefined judicial power along US constitutional lines. The judiciary is tasked with protecting human rights and authorized to conduct judicial review, serving as a check on legislative and executive power.[3]

Courts, however, are expected to respect the roles of the legislature and executive in making laws and policies through democratic processes. This limit is reflected in Article 76(1), which precedent interprets as confining judicial power to "adjudicating concrete disputes by applying and declaring the law" (Arai et al. 2021, 179; see also Sato 2021, 630).[4] A "concrete dispute," defined as the scope of justiciability, is one involving the existence or nonexistence of specific rights, obligations, or legal relationships between parties. As a result, judicial decisions are generally considered binding only on the litigants and do not establish broad rules for third parties.

2.2.2 *Judicial Passivism*

This constitutional design underscores the judiciary's delicate relationship with democratic governance. Because judges lack a direct electoral mandate, a central question arises: To what extent may courts overturn laws enacted by a democratically elected bodies? If democratic legitimacy is the overriding principle, judicial review must be exercised sparingly and deferentially – a position known as judicial passivism.

Judicial activism, by contrast, emphasizes the courts' role in safeguarding minority rights and public goods that may not be adequately protected through political processes. Japanese courts have largely adopted a passive model, limiting judicial review within the boundaries of adjudicating specific cases (e.g., the case concerning the unconstitutionality of the National Police

3 Per Article 81 of the Japanese Constitution, "The Supreme Court is the court of last resort with power to determine the constitutionality of any law, order, regulation or official act." Nihonkoku Kenpo [Kenpo] [Constitution], https://www.japaneselawtranslation.go.jp/ja/laws/view/174.

4 Article 76(1) reads: "The whole judicial power is vested in a Supreme Court and in such inferior courts as are established by law." The Constitution of Japan, supra 3.

Reserve Corps[5]). Under this "incidental review system," courts review constitutionality only to the extent necessary for resolving the case at hand. This approach is reinforced by the principle of avoiding constitutional judgments not essential to a case's disposition. Consequently, Japan's Supreme Court has struck down only thirteen laws as unconstitutional as of May 2025 – far fewer than peer courts worldwide. This conservatism has drawn international criticism, with some scholars characterizing Japan as an example of extreme judicial passivism (Tonami 2015, 4).

Judicial passivism has also discouraged doctrinal innovation – an issue particularly salient in CCL, where traditional doctrines often fall short. In jurisdictions lacking explicit constitutional climate rights, courts frequently ground claims in general rights such as rights to life, privacy, or family life (Setzer and Higham 2024, 17). Yet converting these abstract rights into concrete legal obligations on governments or private actors is difficult. Climate harms typically resemble public goods – like clean air or water – rather than discrete injuries, making them hard to frame as "concrete disputes." Japanese courts have thus been reluctant to recognize such emerging legal interests.

2.2.3 *Judicial Passivism in Private Human Rights Issues*

Many alleged human rights violations in CCL stem from large-scale GHG emissions by private corporations. In several countries, systemic lawsuits have targeted both regulatory failures and individual firms, seeking court-mandated emission limits or policy reforms. Private actors thus often play a central role in climate-related human rights claims.

When such entities are defendants, courts face two major hurdles: proving causation and reconciling legal duties with economic freedoms. In jurisdictions like Germany, where private entities are recognized as having obligations to protect fundamental rights,[6] courts can directly restrict harmful corporate conduct. In Japan, however, constitutional rights are generally interpreted as constraints only on the state. Courts therefore rely on an "indirect application" doctrine, incorporating constitutional values into private law norms (Sato 2021, 138). This approach limits the judiciary's capacity to enforce human rights protections in disputes between private parties.

---

5 Saiko Saibansho [Sup. Ct.], October 8, 1947, no. 6, 9 Saiko Saibansho Minji Hanreisyu [Minshu] 783.

6 "Grundrechts-Schutzpflicht-Theorie", Chapter 1 of the German Constitution. Basic Law for the Federal Republic of Germany, adopted in 1949, available in English translation at http://www.fitweb.or.jp/~nkgw/dgg.

2.3 Public Access to Justice in Environmental Litigation

Access to justice in environmental contexts – specifically regarding access to information, public participation in decision-making, and access to justice – is guaranteed under the 1998 Aarhus Convention.[7] Some of the most influential climate rulings – such as those in the Netherlands, Germany, and the United Kingdom – have come from Aarhus signatories. These jurisdictions grant standing to environmental NGOs to represent public interests. Under Article 2(5) of the Aarhus Convention, qualified environmental organizations are deemed "interested public," and Article 9(2) obliges member states to grant such entities legal standing. Furthermore, Article 9(4) mandates that access to justice must be "fair, equitable, timely, and not prohibitively expensive," and must provide "effective remedies."

Japan, by contrast, provides little opportunity for such litigation. Even environmental organizations with legal personhood struggle to claim that environmental harm directly violates their rights. Japanese jurisdictional doctrine requires showing a specific, legally protected interest impaired by administrative action – something most NGOs cannot demonstrate. As a result, they generally lack standing in both civil and administrative suits.

2.4 Laws Mobilized in Japanese CCL

Because Japan's Constitution does not expressly recognize environmental rights – and courts have not affirmed such rights in precedent – this section reviews the actual legal provisions invoked by plaintiffs or considered by courts in the five Japanese climate change lawsuits analyzed in Chapter 4. In each case, plaintiffs alleged that climate change violated their human rights or exposed them to concrete risks of such violations. They sought judicial orders requiring the state or companies to eliminate these infringements. The following laws were invoked to substantiate claims and illustrate how litigants have framed climate harms within Japan's existing legal framework.

7 Officially, the United Nations Economic Commission for Europe (UNECE) Convention on Access to Information, Public Participation in Decision-Making and Access to Justice in Environmental Matters, adopted on June 25, 1998, 2161 U.N.T.S. 447, https://unece.org/environment-policy/public-participation/aarhus-convention/text. For an overview: https://environment.ec.europa.eu/law-and-governance/aarhus_en.

2.4.1 *Basic Law*

Three civil cases (*Sendai, Kobe, Youth*) sought injunctions for alleged rights violations, with plaintiffs arguing that climate change poses a tangible threat to rights protected by the Japanese Constitution. They invoked *jinkakuken* (health-related personal rights), understood as the rights necessary for personal autonomy and self-determination. However, although well recognized in case law, *jinkakuken* has no explicit constitutional basis. Scholars typically derive it from Article 13 (pursuit of happiness) and Article 25 (right to life), and these articles provided the legal bases of claims in the *Sendai* and *Kobe* cases.[8]

In administrative litigation, courts have examined whether the statutory provisions underlying the contested administrative decisions – such as those in the EIA Act – confer plaintiffs a specific and individualized legal interest in preventing climate-related harm. A further question is whether CO_2 emissions fall within the scope of environmentally hazardous substances regulated under these statutes.

2.4.2 *Civil Law*

In the *Kobe* civil case, plaintiffs sought relief under tort law, citing Articles 709 and 719 of the Japanese Civil Code.[9] They claimed that large-scale GHG emissions by electric utilities constituted unlawful acts against international public order (as in the *Youth* case). While these provisions clearly allow claims for damages, plaintiffs argued that they should also permit injunctions when international public order is at stake.

8 Article 13 of the Japanese Constitution states: "All of the people shall be respected as individuals. Their right to life, liberty, and the pursuit of happiness shall, to the extent that it does not interfere with the public welfare, be the supreme consideration in legislation and other governmental affairs." Article 25 reads: "All people shall have the right to maintain the minimum standards of wholesome and cultured living. In all spheres of life, the State shall use its endeavors for the promotion and extension of social welfare and security, and of public health." Jap. Const. (supra note 3).

9 Article 709 of the Civil Code (Compensation for Loss or Damage in Torts) reads: "A person that has intentionally or negligently infringed the rights or legally protected interests of another person is liable to compensate for damage resulting in consequence." Article 719(1) (Liability of Joint Tortfeasors) states: "If more than one person has inflicted damage on another person by a joint tort, each of them is jointly and severally liable to compensate for the damage. The same applies if it cannot be ascertained which of the joint tortfeasors inflicted the damage." Japanese Civil Code, Act No. 89 of April 27, 1896, https://www.japaneselawtranslation.go.jp/en/laws/view/3494.

2.4.3 *Environment Impact Assesment Act*

In the two administrative cases (*Kobe*, *Yokosuka*), plaintiffs challenged the legality of final and binding notices issued by METI, the competent authority that had approved the construction of CFPPs. They alleged violations of the EIA law, arguing that the assessments were inadequate. Because Japan's EIA Act allows certain exceptions for power plant-related procedures under the EBA, plaintiffs disputed the validity of the procedures under both statutes. Although the EIA law requires quantification of GHG emissions, it does not mandate assessment of their cumulative environmental impact – a key issue in both administrative cases.

2.4.4 *Climate Change Law*

In 1998, Japan passed the Act on the Promotion of Global Warming Countermeasures (APGWC).[10] A 2022 amendment codified the national carbon-neutrality target for 2050 (Article 2–2), consistent with the 2 °C to 1.5 °C goal of the Paris Agreement (Otsuka 2020a, 754). The Act obliges the central government to develop a Global Warming Countermeasure Plan (Article 8) and local governments to adopt similar plans. Both levels of government must establish Action Plans for GHG reduction (Article 20), and emissions reporting is mandatory (Article 26).

The Climate Change Adaptation Act (CCAA) was adopted in 2018.[11] Like the APGWC, it is a framework statute specifying responsibilities for various actors. Under the Act, the national government must prepare a Climate Change Adaptation Plan (Article 7), and local governments are encouraged to do likewise.

In 2023, the Hydrogen Society Promotion Act was enacted to accelerate early-stage development and use of low-carbon hydrogen.[12] It requires the national government to establish basic policies, implement approval schemes for business plans, introduce regulatory and financial support measures for approved enterprises, and formulate technical standards for hydrogen

10 Act on the Promotion of Global Warming Countermeasures, Act No. 117 of October 9, 1998, https://www.japaneselawtranslation.go.jp/ja/laws/view/4479.

11 Climate Change Adaptation Act, Act No. 50 of June 13, 2018, https://www.japaneselawtranslation.go.jp/ja/laws/view/3212.

12 Act on Promotion of Supply and Utilization of Low-Carbon Hydrogen and Its Derivatives for Smooth Transition to a Decarbonized, Growth-Oriented Economic Structure, https://www.japaneselawtranslation.go.jp/outline/146/905R618.pdf.

supply businesses. Additionally, a domestic emissions trading scheme targeting high-emitting companies is scheduled for launch in 2026.[13]

2.5 Summary: Key Legal Constraints to CCL in Japan

Taking into account Japan's judiciary, public access to justice, and existing legal framework, three major limitations shape the prospects for contemporary CCL in Japan.

First, restricted standing. Climate harms are typically diffuse, cumulative, and slow to manifest, with uncertain timing, location, and form, yet environmental groups generally lack standing to sue. Individual plaintiffs face heavy time and cost burdens in proving concrete rights violations, and they typically cannot represent the rights and interests of future generations. Although environmental organizations are better positioned conceptually, their inability to qualify as plaintiffs remains a major barrier to access to justice.

Second, procedural and evidentiary hurdles. Japan does not permit abstract or systemic constitutional challenges. Plaintiffs must identify specific actors, prove causation, and document individualized harm. These strict requirements impose high evidentiary and procedural burdens, limiting the ability to pursue climate claims.

Third, judicial passivism. Climate policy is viewed primarily as the domain of the executive branch, and legislative action is the responsibility of the National Diet. Courts conduct constitutional review only in the context of concrete disputes, and climate harms rarely fit this framework. Even when plaintiffs allege threats to life or health, it is difficult to meet the evidentiary threshold required to prove an imminent and specific danger. This difficulty is further compounded by the doctrinal requirement of justiciability, which restricts the scope for judicial intervention in climate matters.

13 METI, "Cabinet Decision on the Bill for the Act for Partially Amending the Act on the Promoting Transition to the Decarbonized Growth Economic Structure and the Act on the Promotion of Effective Utilization of Resources," https://www.meti.go.jp/english/press/2025/0225_001.html.

CHAPTER 3

From Environmental to Climate Change Litigation

3.1 Overview

This chapter traces the trajectory of environmental litigation in Japan, highlighting the historical influences, continuities, and divergences between earlier environmental lawsuits – including antipollution cases – and current CCL. Section 3.2 outlines this historical background, identifying four key waves of litigation following the prewar period. Section 3.3 discusses six structural causes of environmental degradation, while Section 3.4 considers CCL as a continuation of environmental litigation. Section 3.5 summarizes the chapter. By situating the five climate cases within this broader history, the chapter clarifies how they build on prior legal strategies while also exhibiting novel features that arise in response to the unique legal challenges posed by climate change.

3.2 Historical Background

3.2.1 *Prewar Era (Before 1945)*

Japan has a long history of industrial pollution and insufficient environmental controls. Following the period of national isolation ("Sakoku," 1639–1854), the Meiji government pursued rapid industrialization to catch up with Western powers. This accelerated development, taking place in a densely populated country with limited territory and rich biodiversity, often produced severe environmental degradation (Miyamoto 2010, 1).

One of the earliest and most infamous cases was the *Ashio Copper Mine* pollution in Gunma Prefecture, which began around 1890 (Morinaga 1982; Sugai 1983; Otsuka 2020a, 4). Operations at the mine, which started in 1877, discharged toxic effluent into the nearby Watarase River, devastating fisheries, agriculture, and residents' health throughout the basin. Local residents, led by Shozo Tanaka, a member of the House of Representatives, organized protests, pursued negotiations with the company, petitioned the government, and sought relief for victims. Despite these efforts, the movement failed to secure adequate compensation. Some protestors were arrested and prosecuted, though later acquitted by the Supreme Court. Ultimately, the government forcibly relocated the affected village and buried contaminated land to prevent

 | DOI:10.1163/9789004757035_005

further flooding damage, while the mining company provided only minimal compensation and few meaningful countermeasures.

A contrasting outcome occurred in the contemporaneous *Hitachi Copper Mine* case (beginning in 1906), involving severe air pollution. There, the Hitachi company provided significant compensation, including building what was then the world's tallest chimney (156 meters) to disperse emissions (Seki 1963). The differing outcomes in these cases illustrate that, in the absence of legal regulation, the extent of compensation ultimately depends on each company's voluntary response (Sugai 1983, 23–25; Arahata [1970] 1999, 57–63; Otsuka 2020a, 4).

Despite the *Ashio* case's notoriety, the government continued to prioritize industrial growth over environmental protection, leading to widespread problems such as land subsidence,[1] river contamination, and air pollution. In cases such as *Hitachi*, citizens and companies negotiated pollution control agreements, while litigation also began to play a role.[2] In the *Osaka Alkali* case (1916), for example, the plaintiffs, landowners in the affected areas and farmers who had been farming that land, successfully sued a chemical company for damage to agricultural products, receiving a favorable verdict from the Taishin-in, as the Supreme Court was then called.[3] These early legal and social efforts helped lay the groundwork for later compromises between civil society and industry on pollution issues (Koyama 1973; Miyamoto 2010, 2–4; Otsuka 2020a, 4–5).

3.2.2 *First Wave (1950s to Mid-1970s)*

Japan's industry and urban infrastructure were devastated during World War II. In the postwar period, national policy focused on economic recovery

1 One such subsidence case occurred in the North Kita Kyusyu coal mine area in the early 1900s (Otsuka 2020a, 4; Miyamoto 2010, 1–2). During World War II, intensive coal mining in Fukuoka Prefecture – where mines extended beneath flatlands – caused significant land subsidence, severely damaging farmland and residential areas (Miyamoto 2017, 66).

2 Another important control agreement arose from the 1939 *Shisaka-Jima* air pollution case involving Sumitomo Metal Mining Co. This dispute began in 1893, when waste gas from copper smelting at the Besshi Copper Mine in Ehime Prefecture allegedly damaged rice paddies, sparking a conflict between farmers and the operator. Sumitomo relocated the smelter to the then uninhabited Shisakajima Island in 1904, but smoke carried by Seto Inland Sea air currents continued to damage crops in other areas of Ehime. A strict settlement was eventually reached, including compensation payments and limits on copper production. See Environmental Restoration and Conservation Agency, "Ehimeken Besshi Douzan ni okeru Engai (1900 Nengoro)," https://www.erca.go.jp/yobou/taiki/rekishi/01_01.html (in Japanese). See also Hiratsuka (1941).

3 Daishin-in [Sup. Ct.], December 22, 1916, 22 Minji-Hanrei Roku [Minroku] 2474.

and growth, reversing the modest pro-environmental trends that had emerged before the war (Miyamoto 2010, 4). Reindustrialization brought widespread and severe pollution (Tsuru 1968; Shoji and Miyamoto 1975), to the point that foreign observers described Japan as a "developed country in the field of environmental pollution," suffering from nearly every form of environmental damage (Miyamoto 2017, 5).

Grassroots movements emerged throughout the country, particularly in regions hardest hit by pollution. These citizen groups occasionally spurred local governments to adopt environmental measures, such as the Tokyo Factory Pollution Control Ordinance of 1949, which regulated soot, smoke, noise, vibration, foul odors, and water pollution.[4] National authorities, however, were reluctant to shift priorities from growth to regulation, as most pollution effects were seen as local (Otsuka 2020a, 8). In rural areas – where governments often depended on industry and hesitated to enforce controls – citizen groups increasingly turned to litigation as a last resort (Miyamoto 2017, 11).

A handful of landmark lawsuits from this era became known as the "Big Four."[5] Two concerned methylmercury poisoning: the *Minamata* disease case (beginning in the 1950s)[6] and the *Niigata Minamata* disease case (starting in 1965).[7] Another involved respiratory illnesses caused by industrial emissions: the *Yokkaichi* asthma case (1972).[8] And the fourth addressed cadmium poisoning: the *Itai-Itai* disease case (1960s).[9] Among these, *Yokkaichi* had especially broad national impact. It was the first case to use epidemiological data to establish a causal link between emissions and asthma, and it prompted regulation of harmful substances such as sulfur oxides (SOx) and nitrogen oxides (NOx), which were shown to cause bronchial diseases. The decision also recognized joint tort liability, permitting courts to apportion responsibility among multiple actors according to their contributions, provided the harm displays sufficient unity to be treated as a single act under generally accepted social norms

4 For an excerpt of the 1949 Ordinance text, see https://www.toshiseibi.metro.tokyo.lg.jp/kenchiku/kijun/boushijyorei.pdf (in Japanese).

5 Several studies have investigated the "Big Four," including in English. On all four cases, see Upham (1975). On *Minamata*, see Harada (1982). On *Niigata Minamata*, see Harada (1982). On *Yokkaichi*, see Kitagawa (1984); Feng (2021). On *Itai-Itai*, see Kaji (2012).

6 Saiko Sainahsho [Sup. Ct.], October 15, 2004, no. 58, 7 Saiko Saibansho Minji Hanreishu [Minshu] 1802.

7 Niigata Chiho Saibansho [Niigata Dist. Ct.], March 31, 1992, Hanrei Jihou [Hanji] 1422, 39.

8 Tsu Chiho Saibansho Yokkaichi Shibu [Tu Dist. Ct. Yokkaichi Branch], July 24, 1972, Hanrei Jihou [Hanji] 672, 30.

9 Nagoya Koutou Saibansyo Kanazawa Shibu [Nagoya High Ct. Kanazawa Branch], August 9, 1972, Hanrei Jihou [Hanji] 674, 25.

(Shiomi [2005] 2020, 182). Notably, attorneys in the *Kobe* case have sought to extend these legal principles established in *Yokkaichi*.[10]

The increasing use of litigation to address environmental conflicts in the early postwar period – often supported by social movements – highlighted the need to shift from ex post remedies to ex ante prevention of pollution. In response, the Basic Law for Environmental Pollution Control was enacted in 1967 as Japan's first comprehensive environmental policy legislation.[11] Though industry initially resisted, it relented under public pressure. The law included a provision requiring environmental measures to "harmonize with economic development," reflecting continued ambivalence in practice.[12] As a result, many new regulations following from the Basic Law largely focused on preventing harm to life and property, while broader environmental degradation persisted. By 1970, pollution had become so severe that public concern surged, promoting the passage of fourteen environmental laws during the so-called "Diet of Environmental Disruption" (Mori 2013; Otsuka 2020a, 11) – a major turning point in Japan's legal response to environmental harm.

This period, from the 1950s through the mid-1970s, is widely recognized as the "first wave" of Japan's antipollution movement, including many cases that were litigated in the courts (Awaji 2012, 26; Otsuka 2020a, 9–14; Miyamoto 2010, 4–8). Its defining characteristic was robust civil society action, which followed two main paths: local governments collaborating with citizen movements and political parties to promote environmental conservation regulations, and citizens filing lawsuits with support from lawyers and researchers. This latter strategy was often pursued when polluting companies exerted strong influence over local authorities (Miyamoto 2017, 6).

3.2.3 *Second Wave (Mid-1970s to 1980s)*

The immediate postwar experience of industrial pollution gave way to a second wave of environmental litigation in the mid-1970s and 1980s. Whereas the first wave focused on specific regional pollution incidents, the second wave emphasized the conservation of public goods more broadly (Awaji 2012, 27; Miyamoto 2017, 12; Otsuka 2020a, 14). As environmental degradation can to be perceived as pervasive rather than localized, more actors recognized the need

10 Further explanation is provided in Sec. 5.3.2.

11 Basic Law for Environmental Pollution Control, Act No. 132 of 1967. The outline is available at, https://www.env.go.jp/en/laws/policy/basic/leaflet2.html.

12 Article 1(2) stipulates, "Harmonization with sound economic development shall be considered in environmental preservation."

for comprehensive regulation instead of piecemeal administrative measures (Otsuka 2020a, 12).

This recognition spurred the creation of the Environmental Agency in 1971 (later reorganized as the Ministry of the Environment). Its enactment of the Nature Conservation Act in 1972 filled a gap in the Basic Law for Environmental Pollution Control, which lacked a nature conservation perspective.[13] Together, these initiatives laid the groundwork for Japan's modern environmental law (Otsuka 2020a, 12).

International developments reinforced these domestic shifts. The United Nations Conference on the Human Environment, held in Stockholm in 1972, adopted the Stockholm Declaration, which affirmed the duty of the present generation to protect the environment for future generations.[14] It also articulated the precautionary principle, later a core tenet of international environmental law (Matsui 2010, 82; Otsuka 2020a, 14).

Litigation imitated this broader orientation. Whereas first-wave cases mainly sought compensatory damages for identifiable victims, second-wave lawsuits increasingly pursued injunctive relief and systemic protection of the environment itself. With rapid economic growth and nationwide urbanization, environmental problems shifted from regionally concentrated industrial pollution to more diffuse nuisances affecting everyday urban life. Between 1960 and 1975, Japan's three biggest cities (Tokyo, Nagoya, Osaka) had grown significantly (Table 1), as had sulfur and nitrogen oxide levels between 1955 and 1971 (Table 2), suggesting an increase in air pollution from highway traffic (Shoji, Yamamoto, and Nishida 1966).[15] Other, more diffuse environmental issues

13 Nature Conservation Act, Act No. 85 of June 22, 1972, https://www.japaneselawtranslation.go.jp/en/laws/view/3745/en.

14 Principle 2 states: "The natural resources of the earth, including air, water, land, flora and fauna, and especially representative samples of natural ecosystems, must be safeguarded for the benefit of present and future generations through careful planning or management, as appropriate." Report of the United Nations Conference on the Human Environment, Stockholm, June 5–16, 1972, UN Doc. A/CONF.48/14/Rev.1 (1973), https://digitallibrary.un.org/record/523249, p. 4.

15 Many highway air pollution lawsuits were brought, including the *National Highway No. 43* case: Saiko Saibansyo [Sup. Ct.], July 7, 1995, no. 49, 7 Saiko Saibansho Minji Hanreishu [Minshu] 1870. In this case, residents living along the highway sued the national government and the Hanshin Expressway Authority in 1976, alleging harm from noise and exhaust emissions caused by traffic.

included vibrations and noise from newly constructed airports in cities such as Osaka and Niigata.[16]

These harms were less visible and severe than earlier industrial disasters but also more widespread and ambiguous.[17] Accordingly, the focus of litigation gradually evolved – from seeking narrowly targeted antipollution measures to defining and preserving more comprehensive conception of environmental protection.

Addressing this new form of urban environmental harm required novel litigation strategies. Because such diffuse and previously unrecognized forms of damage were not explicitly protected as human rights, victims, their attorneys, and legal scholars sought to construct new legal theories to safeguard interests that merited protection. These included environmental rights to enjoy nature, scenic rights, and rights to silence and sunshine. Such claims were often derived from existing constitutional guarantees, such as the right to maintain a minimum standard of living and *jinkakuken*[18] – personal rights related to health and dignity (Upham 1979, 249).

However, these novel claims often failed to satisfy the legal thresholds for obtaining remedies, particularly when they concerned harms to the urban public sphere. Instead of invoking clear individual rights, the lawsuits addressed infringements of collective public interests – such as clean air, clean water, and the right to quiet – that were not formally recognized as conferring legal standing (Awaji 2012, 26–27). Consequently, courts rarely upheld the plaintiffs' claims.

Even so, environmental activists continued to bring such cases, viewing litigation as a vehicle for institutional and societal change. Even when unsuccessful, these lawsuits raised public awareness and amplified environmental concerns. In this way, litigation during the second wave gradually evolved from a mechanism for direct legal redress to a strategic tool within a broader social movement (Osawa 1988, 15; Awaji 2012, 26–27).

---

16 For the Osaka case, see Saiko Saibansyo [Sup. Ct.], December 16, 1981, no. 35, 10 Saubanjo Minji Hareisyu [Minshu] 1369. For Niigata, see Saiko Saibansyo [Sup. Ct.], February 17, 1989, no. 43, 2 Saubanjo Minji Hareisyu [Minshu] 56.

17 Asthma is a good example. It is often caused by air pollution, but not all those exposed to such pollution have such symptoms – and asthma also has many other causes, some of them genetic.

18 For the relevant text of Articles 13 and 25 of the Japanese Constitution, see Chapter 2, supra note 3.

TABLE 1 Population increase in the three largest urban areas in Japan, 1960–1975

	Population (thousands)				Percentage of national population			
Year	1960	1965	1970	1975	1960	1965	1970	1975
Tokyo area	17,864	21,017	24,113	27,042	19.1	21.4	23	24.
Nagoya area	5,691	6,313	6,929	7,550	6.1	6.4	6.6	6.
Osaka area	11,404	14,538	14,538	15,696	12.2	13.3	13.9	14
Areas combined*	34,959	41,868	45,580	50,288	37	41	44	45
National total	93,419	98,275	104,665	111,937	100	100	100	100

Notes: *Data for Tokyo, Nagoya, and Osaka combined
SOURCE: REPRODUCED WITH SLIGHT MODIFICATIONS FROM MIYAMOTO 2017, 10

TABLE 2 Sulfur and nitrogen oxide concentration levels in three Japanese coastal regions, 1995 and 1971

	Sulfur oxides (SOx)		Nitrogen oxides (NOx)	
Year	1955	1971	1955	1971
Kanto coastal area	18.3	165.2	2.3	68.3
Tokai	8.4	71.7	1	27.4
Kinki coastal area	27.8	188.2	3	61.1
Areas combined*	16.2	131.3	1.9	49.8
National total	6.6	45.6	0.6	17

Notes: SOx and NOx are pollutants whose amounts are stochastic (random or unpredictable) because they vary significantly based on human activities like industrial and traffic emissions, natural sources, and environmental conditions.
SOURCE: REPRODUCED WITH SLIGHT MODIFICATIONS FROM MIYAMOTO (2017, 9)

3.2.4 *Third Wave (1990s–2000s)*

From the 1990s to 2000s, a third wave of environmental litigation emerged, focused on securing environmental amenities and redressing accumulated or "stocked" harms such as asbestos and industrial waste – issues largely absent from the earlier waves (Miyamoto 2010, 19–20; Awaji 2012, 3; Otsuka 2020a, 23). "Amenities" refers to desirable environmental features or qualities – pleasantness, comfort, or aesthetic quality. Litigation during this period pursued

Population increase (thousands)			**Percentage of population increase**		
960–65	1965–70	1970–75	1960–65	1965–70	1970–75
,153	3,096	2,929	17.7	14.7	12.1
622	616	621	10.9	9.8	9
,666	1,468	1,158	14.5	11.2	8
,441	5,180	4,708	16	13	10
,856	6,390	7,272	5.2	6.5	6.9

two overlapping goals: first, to promote institutional reform, and second, echoing the second wave, to secure individual compensation for harm caused by long-term exposure to industrial waste (Awaji 2012, 28; Miyamoto 2017, 16–18).

Growing attention to environmental amenities was reflected in the enactment of the Basic Environmental Act in 1993, which replaced the 1967 Basic Law for Environmental Pollution Control.[19] This law was partly influenced by international developments, notably the 1992 United Nations Conference on Environment and Development (UNCED) in Rio de Janeiro, which introduced the concept of sustainable development as a global priority.[20] Domestically, three factors shaped Japan's evolving environmental governance (Miyamoto 2017, 6–10, Otsuka 2020a, 19; cf. Miyamoto 2010, 15). First, new forms of environmental harm arising in densely populated urban areas required regulation to preserve shared social amenities. Second, diffuse sources of harms, often linked to citizens' everyday activities rather than large industrial actors, called for a comprehensive environmental management system to reduce total environmental burdens. Third, global environmental challenges, such as climate change, highlighted the need for internationally coordinated regulation. Despite these developments, plaintiffs struggled to obtain favorable

19 Basic Act on the Environment, Act No. 91 of 1993, https://www.japaneselawtranslation.go.jp/en/laws/view/3850/en.

20 Rio Declaration on Environment and Development, Report of the United Nations Conference on Environment and Development, June 3–14, 1992, A/CONF.151/26 (Vol. I), https://www.un.org/en/development/desa/population/migration/generalassembly/docs/globalcompact/A_CONF.151_26_Vol.I_Declaration.pdf.

court rulings, as the alleged harm often failed to meet established thresholds for legal remedy.

Cases involving accumulated harm and industrial waste frequently centered on asbestos. Because the health effects of asbestos exposure typically manifest after 15–45 years, proving causation, identifying responsible parties, and assigning liability posed serious obstacles. As a partial policy response, the Act on Asbestos Health Damage Relief was enacted in 2006 to provide financial assistance to affected individuals.[21] However, the relief provided under this law remains limited, and the number of asbestos-related cases continues to rise (Ishiwata Higai Kyusai Seido Kenkyu-kai 2021).

3.2.5 *Fourth Wave (2000s–Present)*

The defining features of the fourth wave of environmental litigation are still emerging. Nevertheless, developments in the previous three waves suggest several likely directions (Miyamoto 2010, 19–25, Awaji 2012, 44–45; Miyamoto 2017, 16–18; Otsuka 2020a, 25–26).

First, there is growing recognition that sustainability demands a systemic break from mass-production, mass-consumption, and mass-disposal models. The legal basis for advocating this transition, however, remains unsettled.

Second, environmental harms have become even more geographically and chronologically diffuse than in earlier periods, making causal links between victims and contributors increasingly difficult to establish. As a result, determining liability – particularly identifying responsible parties – has become critical. This challenge gained urgency following the Fukushima Daiichi nuclear disaster (2011), where many victims required timely and comprehensive relief. Similar issues arise in climate-related damage claims.

Third, it has become increasingly apparent that citizen participation is indispensable in managing environmental risk, defined as the possibility that human activities disrupt environmental processes in ways that threaten sustainability and human well-being (Otsuka 2020a, 24). Risks related to chemical substances illustrate this problem: both their harms and benefits may be only partially understood, and unlike point-source pollution, risk is inherently uncertain, making it more difficult to address at the policy level. Effective management therefore requires broad public consensus, and where participation is lacking, courts may question whether due process has been adequately observed.

21 Act on Asbestos Health Damage Relief, Act No. 4 of February 2006, https://www.japaneselawtranslation.go.jp/en/laws/view/3797/en.

3.3 Structural Causes of Japanese Environmental Damage

From a political and economic systems perspective, six structural factors underlie the onset and intensification of environmental degradation in Japan (Miyamoto 2010, 14–19; cf. Miyamoto 2017, 6–15; Otsuka 2020a, 25–26). First, industrial sectors failed to invest real capital in preventive environmental measures during periods of rapid economic growth. Second, Japan's economy was highly dependent on heavy chemical, fossil fuel–based industries and nuclear power, all with large environmental footprints. Third, a rapid increase in automobile ownership and use led to significant pollutant emissions. Fourth, the combination of concentrated urbanization and intensive industries created high environmental risks to local inhabitants. Fifth, Japanese lifestyles in the postwar Americanized context shifted toward mass consumption, fueled by rapid product turnover in consumer appliances. This cycle generated large volumes of waste and harmful by-products such as dioxins during disposal. Sixth, the strong political influence of industrial sectors impeded environmental protection and prioritized economic growth.

These structural conditions produced three defining characteristics of environmental degradation in Japan. First, vulnerable populations – the elderly, infants, and the chronically ill – bear disproportionate harm. Second, these harms fall mainly on socially marginalized groups with limited capacity for self-protection. Third, unlike economic losses, environmental damage is frequently irreversible and best prevented rather than remedied.

Litigation has therefore become an important tool for addressing systemic environmental problems. Lawsuits have spurred the enactment of pro-environmental legislation, curbed harmful industrial practices, and heightened public awareness. Importantly, they also give socially vulnerable populations a venue to be heard, provided that meaningful access to justice is ensured.

3.4 CCL as an Extension of Environmental Litigation

As we have seen, Japanese environmental litigation following World War II can be grouped into four waves, with distinct tendencies. In the first wave (1950s–mid-1970s), the focus was on regional industrial pollution, individual harm was obvious, and causality relatively clear. In the second wave (mid-1970s–1980s), the focus shifted to urban and regional environmental problems, harm became more diffuse, legal claims weak, and causality unclear. In the third wave (1990s–2000s), attention shifted to nationwide and partly global issues, harm and causality became increasingly vague, with a new emphasis on environmental amenities and long-term harm. The fourth wave (2000s–present) is characterized by global environmental problems, claims based on individual harm are legally very weak, and causality highly uncertain.

CCL shares key features with this fourth wave of environmental litigation. Climate change is global in scope, yet both its causes and damages are often uncertain or difficult to trace.[22] These factors create major hurdles for litigation. Even so, structural similarities with earlier environmental problems have informed new strategies. A majority of cases examined in the next section, for example, argue that air pollutants such as PM2.5, SOx, and NOx linked to climate change pose direct threats to public health.[23] Their outcomes illustrate how Japanese courts are responding to climate-related claims.

3.5 Summary

This chapter traced Japanese environmental litigation from its origins in the late nineteenth century to the present, highlighting periodic characteristics and chronological shifts. In the first era, environmental lawsuits primarily targeted industrial polluters, with relatively straightforward causal links. In the second era, during rapid urbanization, harm became more diffuse and legal claims more complex, with a diversification of pollutants. In the third era, litigation broadened from targeted antipollution measures to efforts to preserve the environment as a whole. In the current fourth era, CCL has emerged, combining elements of earlier cases with new challenges rooted in the global, uncertain, and systemic nature of climate change. This dual nature of Japanese CCL – part continuation, part innovation – provides the framework for the next chapters.

---

22 For example, heatstroke has been regarded in Japan as a symptom caused by climate change.

23 PM refers to particulate matter (also called particle pollution), a mixture of solid particles and liquid droplets in the air. Some particles – such as dust, dirt, soot, or smoke – are visible to the naked eye, while others are so small they can only be detected with an electron microscope. See https://www.epa.gov/pm-pollution/particulate-matter-pm-basics.

CHAPTER 4

Five Climate Change Cases in Japan

4.1 Overview

This chapter examines the five climate change lawsuits filed in Japan since 2017.[1] Although these cases have received limited attention in international scholarship, they provide valuable insight into how climate-related claims are framed and litigated within Japan's legal system. These cases demonstrate how plaintiffs have adapted legal arguments from earlier air pollution and environmental litigation and sought new strategies to address unique challenges and negotiate both institutional and cognitive obstacles.

The five cases, first introduced in Section 1.1.2, are:

1. *Sendai* case (2017)
2. *Kobe* civil case (2018)
3. *Kobe* administrative case (2018)
4. *Yokosuka* case (2019)
5. *Youth* case (2024)

All five challenge the construction or operation of CFPPs and represent efforts to align domestic litigation with the global trend of climate change lawsuits. While they share important features, each also reflects distinct legal strategies, procedural choices, and regional circumstances.

The analysis highlights the main legal and procedural hurdles faced by Japanese plaintiffs, including issues of standing, causation, justiciability, and the framing of human rights-based claims. These are familiar challenges in comparative CCL but take on unique dimensions within Japan's institutional and cultural setting.

This chapter is structured as follows: Sections 4.2.1 through 4.2.5 provide detailed descriptions of each case. Section 4.3 compares them, identifying commonalities and differences. Section 4.4 examines the extent to which these lawsuits inherit and adapt principles from past antipollution and environmental litigation. Section 4.5 examines the distinctive features of Japanese CCL. Section 4.6 summarizes the chapter.

---

1 As noted earlier, the PhD monograph which this book expands upon includes four cases but was completed too early to include the *Youth* case. In the present book, I include *Youth* and treat the dual case of *Kobe* as separate cases, included with *Sendai* and *Yokosuka* to comprise the five cases. All five cases are consistent with the definition of CCL introduced in Sec. 1.1.1.

4.2 Details of the Cases

This section provides a detailed account of each of the five Japanese CCL cases. Table 3 prefaces this account by giving summary facts the section proceeds to explain further.

4.2.1 Sendai *Case*

Sendai, a coastal city with a population of one million in Miyagi Prefecture, was heavily damaged by the Great East Japan Earthquake and tsunami of March 2011. The disaster also destabilized the Fukushima Daiichi Nuclear Power Plant, creating fears of a nuclear meltdown and electricity shortages,

TABLE 3 Summary features of the five CCL cases in Japan

	Sendai	*Kobe* (civil)	*Kobe* (administrative)	*Yokosuka*	*Youth*
Proceedings	civil	civil	administrative	administrative	civil
Date filed	September 2017	September 2018	November 2018	June 2019	August 2024
Plaintiffs	124 residents	40 residents	12 residents	45 residents (+ 3 added later)	16 young people from around Japan
Defendants	Sendai Power Station Co.	Kobe Steel Ltd., KOBELCO Power Kobe No. 2, Kansai Electric Power Co.	METI	METI	10 major thermal power companies operating CFPPS
Capacity (per 10,000kW)	112MW	1.3GW (2 × 650MW)	1.3GW (2 × 650MW)	1.3GW (2 × 650MW)	undefinable (whole facilities targeted)
Type	subcritical	ultra-supercritical	ultra-supercritical	ultra-supercritical	undefinable
Relief sought	injunction against CFPP operation	injunction against CFPP construction/operation and direction of electricity generation	(1) revocation of final notice of CFPP construction (2) illegality of lack of GHG regulations aligned with Paris Agreement	revocation of final notice of CFPP construction	injunction against CO_2 emissions beyond IPCC-defined international public order

TABLE 3 Summary features of the five CCL cases in Japan (*cont.*)

	Sendai	*Kobe* (civil)	*Kobe* (administrative)	*Yokosuka*	*Youth*
Justifications	(1) Health damage; (2) Breach of *jinkakuken* by climate change; (3) Biodiversity damage at nearby mudflats	(1) Health damage; (2) Breach of *jinkakuken* by climate change	(1) Illegality of final notice to construction plan; (2) Illegality of lack of GHG regulations aligned with Paris Agreement	Illegality of final notice given to construction plan	Human rights infringements (life, health, property, development, self-determination) and climate justice

Notes: kW = kilowatts (1,000 watts); MW = megawatts (1,000,000 watts); GW = gigawatts (1,000,000,000 watts)
SOURCE: CREATED BY THE AUTHOR

particularly in the Tokyo metropolitan area. In response, the national government urgently sought to reinforce power supply nationwide, turning primarily to fossil fuel, and especially coal-based power generation.

In 2013, the MOE and METI adopted the Director-General Meeting Agreement,[2] which relaxed EIA requirements for CFPPs. This policy triggered plans for approximately fifty new CFPPs nationwide, including one in Sendai. Announced in September 2014, the Sendai project – undertaken by the Sendai Power Station Company – had a planned output of 112 MW, just below the 112.5 MW threshold requiring a mandatory EIA.[3]

Local residents opposed the project, raising concerns about potential health and environmental damage caused by plant emissions. They also identified two broader objections. First, the perceived lack of local benefit. The plant was financed by Kansai Electric Power Company, based 700 kilometers away in Osaka, and its electricity was reportedly destined for an undisclosed Tokyo client. This business model drew sharp criticism from local residents and

2 See Chapter 1, supra note 13.

3 Enforcement Order of the Environmental Impact Assessment Act, Cabinet Order No. 346 of December 3, 1997, item 5 in Table 1, relating to Article 2(2) of the Order, https://www.japaneselawtranslation.go.jp/en/laws/view/3376.

gave rise to the slogan: "Electricity to Tokyo, money to Kansai, and pollution to Sendai?"[4]

The second objection pertained to the project's timing. Sendai was then undergoing reconstruction following the 2011 disaster, and while the Sendai Power Station Company claimed the project would aid recovery by creating jobs and spurring economic growth, many residents criticized it as a "recovery business," accusing the company of profiteering under the guise of disaster relief. Plaintiffs were also frustrated by Japan's carbon accounting rules, which attribute emissions to the location of consumption rather than production.[5] Under this framework, GHG emissions from the Sendai plant would be recorded in Tokyo, enabling the operator to deny responsibility to Sendai residents despite the plant's local environmental impact.

When plans for the Sendai plant were first announced, local residents requested detailed explanations of its potential environmental impacts and urged the company to reconsider. The company did not respond.[6] In September 2015, the Kiko Network – supporting the residents – filed a request with the Tohoku branch of the Industrial Safety and Inspection Department for full disclosure of the plant construction plan. However, only limited information was released.

In August 2016, residents asked the Sendai City's environmental department to arrange a direct meeting with company representatives. The city had signed a Pollution Control Agreement with the Sendai Power Station Company in March 2016, which provided for voluntary communication with local residents.[7] At the city's urging, the company eventually held an explanatory meeting in March 2017, though it initially preferred written communication.[8] At the meeting, the company stressed its compliance with all relevant laws and regulations but proposed no additional countermeasures.

4 The slogan appears on the website of the citizen group (https://sendaisekitan.wordpress.com [in Japanese]). The Kansai area comprises Osaka, Kyoto, Hyogo, Nara, Shiga, and Wakayama Prefectures.

5 Outlined in MOE's "Guidelines for the Calculation of Total Emissions of GHG" (2017), p. 5, http://www.env.go.jp/policy/local_keikaku/data/guideline.pdf (in Japanese). One interviewee expressed her frustration at the guidelines (March 6, 2020).

6 The process of negotiation was summarized by the Kiko Network: https://sekitan.jp/wp-content/uploads/2016/12/20161218sendaisiryo-webver5.pdf (in Japanese), p. 29.

7 Article 20 of the Pollution Control Agreement, https://www.pref.miyagi.jp/uploaded/attachment/346450.pdf (in Japanese).

8 *Asahi Shimbun* (Tohoku version), November 18, 2016 (link no longer available). See also http://www.sendai-ps.co.jp (in Japanese).

In February 2017, the company launched an official website, releasing information about its operations and announcing a test run of the nearly completed plant for June 2017. Full operation began in July 2017, despite repeated citizen appeals and without further action from Sendai City.

In September 2017, 124 residents living near the plant filed a lawsuit against the Sendai Power Station Company. The group, led by two Tohoku University professors – one a specialist international CCL – decided to pursue Japan's first ever climate lawsuit following discussions with the Kiko Network.[9] Together with supporters, the two professors organized public lectures and outreach, successfully recruiting several residents as plaintiffs.[10]

The defendant, Sendai Power Station Company, was established in 2014 to construct and operate the CFPP. It was jointly funded by Kanden Energy Solution Corporation (a Kansai Electric Power Company subsidiary) and ENEX Electric Power Corporation (an Itochu Corporation subsidiary), both based in the Kansai region, far from the Tohoku site.

As noted earlier, the company signed a Pollution Control Agreement with Sendai City in 2016, obligating it to disclose information on plant emissions (Article 14). Plaintiffs argued that this duty was not met, as the company refused to provide details beyond its limited disclosures. Some residents also complained that the plant operated intermittently and without notice, making it necessary to check for chimney emissions to determine whether it was running.[11]

The plaintiffs advanced three main claims: (1) air pollution from the plant would harm their health, (2) its GHG emissions would contribute to climate change, and (3) it would damage biodiversity in nearby mudflats. The first two claims were tied to *jinkakuken* (Upham 1989, 249). In coordination with the defendants and court, however, the plaintiffs narrowed the case to health impacts alone, judging arguments based solely on climate change or biodiversity less likely to succeed.[12]

Even with this narrowed scope, proving harm remained difficult. Most health effects from plant emissions had not yet materialized or were scientifically uncertain. In particular, Japan had not reached a consensus on the health impacts of PM2.5 exposure, and PM2.5 was not among the indicators

9 Interview, March 5, 2020.

10 Many interviewees confirmed that they had made up their minds to join the lawsuit after attending the lectures (March 3–6, 2020).

11 Participant interviews, March 3–5, 2020.

12 Sendai Chiho Saibansho [Sendai Dist. Ct.], October 28, 2020, Hei 29 (wa), no. 1175, p. 2. Several interviewees mentioned this point (March 4–7, 2020).

required by the EIA system. To support their case, the plaintiffs worked with Lauri Myllyvirta, a Finnish professor and analyst of Greenpeace, to develop a simulation model of PM2.5 dispersion showing statistically significant adverse health effects. The defendant challenged the model as unreliable because it relied on European (not Japanese) physiological data, and the court ultimately agreed, dismissing it as evidence.

In parallel, the plaintiffs and their legal team sought more detailed information on the company's pollution control measures. They succeeded in summoning the company president to testify – a rare event in Japanese environmental litigation, where corporate executives seldom appear in court personally in pollution lawsuits.

The Sendai District Court dismissed the lawsuit on October 28, 2020. However, it criticized the company for breaching its Pollution Control Agreement with the city. Following the ruling, one plaintiff appealed while the others accepted the decision. Those who did not appeal viewed the court's criticism as a partial victory and shifted strategy toward direct negotiations with the company – a pattern seen in earlier Japanese antipollution cases.[13]

On appeal, the appellant reiterated the climate change dimension of the case. On April 27, 2021, the Sendai High Court dismissed the appeal but acknowledged the broader climate issue, stating that in light of global trends and Japan's 2050 carbon-neutrality pledge, "there is a negative view of CFPPs." However, it added:

> Given Japan's current national energy policy and the need to ensure a stable energy supply in a resource-limited country, the utility and public value of CFPPs, which constitute a significant portion of the energy supply, cannot be immediately denied.[14]

Addressing the project's post-disaster reconstruction context, the court noted: "The facility employs subcritical pressure technology and has an output slightly below the EIA threshold. Overall, the project appears to have prioritized low cost and swift completion." Subcritical pressure plants were already outdated

13 For example, in a 1981 Kochi District Court case, local residents sought damages from a poultry farmer for odor pollution from chicken coops. The court held that the odor exceeded the regulatory standards of the Odor Prevention Act and violated the local pollution prevention ordinance, which required the farmer to make best efforts to mitigate odor. It further affirmed that Pollution Control Agreements are legally binding, thereby upholding the claim. Kochi Chiho Saibansho [Kochi Dist. Ct.], December 23, 1981, 471 Hanrei Taimus [Hanta] 179.

14 Sendai Koto Saibancho [Sendai High Ct.] April 27, 2021, 2510 Hanrei Jihou [Hanji] 22.

at the time, offering lower efficiency in power generation and heavier environmental impacts. Nevertheless, the court concluded that the plant qualified as necessary public infrastructure under prevailing national conditions. The appellant accepted the ruling and did not seek review by the Supreme Court.

4.2.2 Kobe *Civil Case*

Kobe, a major coastal city in Hyogo Prefecture with a population of about 1.5 million, has a long history of air pollution linked to industrial activity and national highways. Since the 1970s, residents have repeatedly organized plaintiff groups and pursued litigation. For example, in the *Nishi-Yodogawa* case (1978), 112 individuals sued ten companies, the government, and a highway corporation, seeking both an injunction against excess emissions and monetary compensation.[15] In 1991, the court ordered the companies to pay 360 million yen for health damage. Similarly, in 1976, 152 plaintiffs filed suit over pollution from *National Highway No. 43*, and in 1995 the court awarded partial compensation.[16] In the *Amagasaki* case (1988), 483 plaintiffs sued nine businesses, the government, and a highway corporation; after nearly twenty years of proceedings, the court granted a partial injunction.[17] Since these cases, air quality in Kobe has gradually improved due to emissions reductions, and the region remains subject to stringent pollution regulations today.

Kobe Steel Ltd began operating its first CFPP in 2002 and a second in 2004, despite resident opposition over air quality concerns.[18] In 2013, The company decommissioned part of its blast furnace in response to business pressures. Kansai Electric Power Company auctioned off the site, which Kobe Steel Ltd. subsequently acquired, announcing plans for two new ultra-supercritical CFPPs. Ultra-supercritical plants generate electricity at higher temperatures and pressures than the critical point of water by utilizing steam generated from burning coal,[19] improving thermal efficiency and reducing CO_2 emissions compared to conventional plants.[20] Each unit was designed with a capacity of 650 MW, comparable to the existing facilities.

15 Nishi-Yodogawa Sosho, Osaka Chiho Saibansho [Osaka Dist. Ct.], March 29, 1991, 1383 Hanrei Jihou [Hanji] 22.

16 Kokudo 43 gousen soshou, Saikou Saibansyo [Sup. Ct.], July 7, 1995, no. 49, 7 Minji Hanreishu [Minsyu] 1870.

17 Amagasaki Kogai soshou, Kobe Chihou Saibansyo [Kobe Dist. Ct.], January 31, 2000, 1726 Hanrei Jihou [Hanji] 20.

18 The plaintiff's complaint can be consulted at https://drive.google.com/file/d/1prCs6vWCLpfgUM51oOKMYQO47757WllC/view (in Japanese).

19 METI classifies CFPPs with an ultra-supercritical system as high-efficient (see Sec. 1.1.2).

20 Shin- Denryoku-Net, https://pps-net.org/glossary/106761 (in Japanese).

In compliance with legal requirements, Kobe Steel initiated the EIA process. However, residents, having experienced decades of air pollution, expressed serious concern. They repeatedly requested disclosure of data related to health impacts, including total air pollutants and CO_2 emissions, but an explanatory meeting held by Kobe Steel in July 2017 left many unsatisfied, as the company provided limited and evasive answers.[21] Further concerns about the EIA process subsequently emerged, including allegations of data manipulation and inappropriate evaluation methods. In response, residents established the Citizens' Committee for the Kobe CFPP in August 2017, submitting petitions to Hyogo Prefecture and Kobe City calling for stricter regulation.[22] More than 1,100 citizens questioned the credibility of the operator's draft environmental impact statement.[23]

In October 2017, Kobe Steel was revealed to have shipped products with falsified inspection data.[24] The EIA process was temporarily suspended during the ensuing investigation. In December 2017, 255 citizens petitioned the Hyogo Prefectural Pollution Examination Board for environmental pollution conciliation[25] against Kobe Steel and Kansai Electric Power Company, requesting an injunction against the planned CFPPs. The number of petitioners eventually rose to 481, with strong backing from the Citizens' Committee. While arbitration was still ongoing, METI issued a final notice approving the EIA assessment report in May 2018. On this basis, KOBELCO Power Kobe No. 2 submitted its construction plan to METI, allowing the project to proceed.

21 A summary of these negotiations can be found at the Citizen's Committee's website at https://kobesekitan.jimdoweb.com (in Japanese).

22 The Citizen's Committee's press release was originally accessed on August 4, 2024, at https://kobesekitan.jimdo.com/press-release2018-8-01 (in Japanese; link no longer active).

23 A statement required under Article 14 (Preparation of Draft Environmental Impact Statement) of the EIA Act requires the project operator to state their views on opinions received from residents and others (paragraphs 2 and 4 of item 1). See EIA Act (Chapter 1, supra note 14).

24 Kobe Steel's admission was originally accessed on August 4, 2024, at https://www.kobelco.co.jp/progress/report.html (in Japanese; link no longer active).

25 Environmental conciliation is provided for under Article 31 of the Act on the Settlement of Environmental Pollution Disputes, Act 108 of June 1, 1930, https://www.japaneselawtranslation.go.jp/en/laws/view/3897. It is a form of mediation in which a three-member committee from the Pollution Dispute Resolution Agency facilitates negotiations between parties to resolve disputes through mutual concessions. Proceedings are closed to the public to allow candid exchanges of views. See Ministry of Internal Affairs and Communications, *Cho-tei Tetsuzuki no Gaiyou* [Overview of conciliation procedure], https://www.soumu.go.jp/kouchoi/knowledge/how/summary_conciliation.html (in Japanese).

Consequently, forty citizens, including some of the original conciliation petitioners, filed a lawsuit.[26]

The conciliation petition by 486 residents thus preceded the civil lawsuit. Attorneys for the civil case recruited around forty plaintiffs from the larger group. Due to legal constraints, some applicants were denied standing, though many continued to support the movement and attend hearings.[27] A number of plaintiffs and supporters had connections to earlier pollution litigation, particularly the *National Highway No. 43* and *Nishi-Yodogawa* cases.[28]

The primary defendant, Kobe Steel Ltd., founded in 1905, operates nationwide through ten branches and was directly responsible for constructing the CFPPs under subcontract to KOBELCO Power Kobe No. 2, a subsidiary founded in 2018 for power generation.[29] Kobe Steel already operated two CFPPs adjacent to the proposed site. Kansai Electric Power Company, founded in 1951 and comprising eighty affiliated firms, entered into a long-term agreement with Kobe Steel to purchase all electricity generated by the new plants for more than thirty years. The contract included a seven-year advance termination clause and required compensation for early withdrawal by either party. Given this close commercial relationship, plaintiffs and attorneys argued that the two companies jointly committed a tort, as discussed below.

Kobe Steel argued that the new CFPPs would incorporate CCS systems and comply with regulatory efficiency standards. Estimated CO_2 emissions were 6.92 million metric tons annually – approximately 0.02 percent of total global emissions.[30] A central point of contention was information disclosure. Plaintiffs accused the defendants of avoiding open dialogue, which deepened distrust during the prolonged prelitigation negotiations. The defendants countered that they had disclosed all information required by law. Despite this, on May 5, 2021, the company began test operations without notifying residents.

In court, the plaintiffs raised two principal claims: (1) that air pollution, particularly at PM2.5, posed serious health risks, and (2) that the plant's environmental impacts violated the human right to a stable climate. They argued that both interests were protected under *jinkakuken*, as aspects of the right to a peaceful life (*heion-seikatsuken*), encompassing safeguarding life, body, and

---

26 The litigation document including complaints can be found at: https://kobeclimatecase.jp/document (in Japanese).

27 Observed in interviews from November 26 to December 13, 2020.

28 Observed in interviews from November 26 to December 13, 2020.

29 Its official website can be accessed at https://www.kobelco.co.jp/about_kobelco/Kobe Steel Ltd. /profile/index.html (in Japanese).

30 According to the *Kobe* civil case complaint (supra note 26), p. 16. Total global CO_2 emissions are sourced from 2015 data.

health. Unlike in the *Sendai* case, climate change remained central to their arguments. Attorneys outlined a causal chain: CFPPs emit GHGs → global temperature rises → adverse climate impacts occur in plaintiffs' regions → these impacts infringe upon their rights.[31] While acknowledging natural variation and other emission sources, they contended that contemporary climate science supports this sequence.

This case was unusual in having three defendants: Kansai Electric Power Company, Kobe Steel Ltd., and its subsidiary subcontractor KOBELCO Power Kobe No. 2. Kansai Electric Power Company initially claimed it was not liable, as it neither operated the plant nor directly emitted GHGs. Plaintiffs countered that its long-term purchase agreement amounted to substantive participation in electricity generation. Kobe Steel denied causation, asserting that its emissions were minimal and compliant with regulations. In response, the plaintiffs' attorneys invoked the doctrine of joint tort, arguing for shared liability among all CFPP operators since 2014.[32] They contended that after the 2013 Director-General Meeting Agreement – which relaxed EIA requirements – a surge in CFPP construction followed, despite climate risks already well recognized through the Kyoto Protocol (1997) and IPCC's Fourth Assessment Report (2007). All such plants thus knowingly contributed to climate change and were collectively liable, based on the theory of causation in joint tort liability established in the *Yokkaichi* case (Shimamura et al. 2021, 82). Since CFPPs cannot operate partially, the plaintiffs sought an injunction based on collective responsibility through partial liability.[33]

On March 20, 2023 – five and a half years after the filing – the Kobe District Court dismissed the case. The court accepted a legal framework requiring a violation, concrete risk, or serious anxiety of *jinkakuken* infringement to justify an injunction. Regarding air pollution, the court found no violation, citing the absence of PM2.5 regulation in the EIA Act and no objective evidence of heightened health risks. On global warming, the court acknowledged that CO_2

31 The 2019 *Urgenda* judgment (Chapter 1, supra note 6) had held that real and imminent climate crisis constitutes an infringement of human rights, independent of whether that crisis in fact materializes. Considering the cautiousness of Japanese courts to admit unprecedented human rights (noted in the previous chapter), the attorneys' strategy here seems reasonable.

32 For the text of Article 719(1) on Liability of Joint Tortfeasors, see Jap. Civ. Cod. (Chapter 2, supra note 9). The invocation was made in Brief No. 19 (a preparatory document), submitted to the court on December 1, 2021, https://kobeclimatecase.jp/wp-content/uploads/2021/01/kobe-minji-junnbisyomen19.pdf (in Japanese).

33 This was explained to the court by the plaintiffs' chief attorney on December 8, 2020, after the ninth hearing at Kobe District Court.

emissions could, in principle, violate *jinkakuken*, but found no infringement in this instance due to uncertainties about climate disasters and the plant's minimal share of global emissions (0.02%). The court emphasized the need for a strong causal link and concluded that climate policy was better addressed through democratic processes.[34] Regarding *heion-seikatsuken*, the court characterized the plaintiffs' concerns as "anxiety about an indeterminate future danger," finding no present basis for legal protection.[35]

On April 1, 2023, thirty-four plaintiffs appealed. In proceedings beginning October 10, 2023, they advanced a new argument: that their rights were violated by ongoing exposure to harm in a world already exceeding 1.5 °C of warming, even absent a specific disaster. They contended that while not all CO_2 emissions are unlawful, emissions that render the 1.5 °C target unattainable should be considered so, and that the defendants' emissions fell within this category.

On April 24, 2025, the Osaka High Court dismissed the appeal. Addressing the claim that personal rights were infringed by emissions contributing to warming beyond 1.5 °C, the court acknowledged that the effects of climate change on life, health, and safety are indeed a matter of concern. However, it held that the link between global warming and individual harm remains indirect and abstract, and therefore such interests cannot be subsumed under personal rights without concrete, demonstrable damage sufficient to justify restricting others' conduct. On causation, the court found no legally sufficient connection between the defendants' emissions and the alleged harms, citing uncertainty in attributing specific social or economic impacts to the facility.

After deliberation, the plaintiffs and their attorneys elected not to appeal to the Supreme Court. Instead, they chose to transfer their efforts to the *Youth* case (Sec. 4.2.5), filed in August 2024.

4.2.3 Kobe *Administrative Case*

The *Kobe* administrative case arose from the same circumstance as the *Kobe* civil case, aiming to hold the government directly accountable for its coal-dependent policies rather than focusing solely on individual power plant operators. After METI issued its final notice in May 2018 authorizing construction of the CFPPs, the plaintiffs and attorneys from the civil suit pursued a parallel legal strategy by filing an administrative action. A group of twelve residents was assembled, some of whom were also plaintiffs in the civil case. Under the Administrative Case Litigation Act (ACLA), lawsuits must be filed

34 *Kobe* civil case (supra note 26), judgment, p. 99.

35 *Kobe* civil case (supra note 26), judgment, p. 102.

within six months of the relevant administrative disposition.[36] The plaintiffs and attorneys therefore expedited their preparations and filed the case in November 2018.

The plaintiff group included twelve individuals, two of whom lived more than twenty kilometers from the plant site. Because the ACLA imposes strict standing requirements[37] that courts have traditionally interpreted narrowly,[38] standing was a central issue. Plaintiffs argued that residents within twenty kilometers should be granted standing, citing the relevant ministerial ordinance on EIAs for power plants, which appears to adopt a twenty-kilometer zone as the standard area of impact.[39] They further contended that even those outside this radius (two plaintiffs in this case) should qualify, given that global climate impacts threaten them as well.[40]

Notably, the group included a Kobe University undergraduate and member of the Kobe branch of Fridays For Future (FFF). Her participation reflected

---

36 Article 14(1) (Statute of Limitations for Filing an Action) reads: "No action for the revocation of an administrative disposition may be filed for a period of six months has elapsed from the day on which the person who seeks revocation became aware of the fact that the original administrative disposition or administrative disposition on appeal was made; provided, however, that this shall not apply if there are justifiable grounds for failing to meet such a time limit." Administrative Case Litigation Act (ACLA), Act No. 139 of May 16, 1962, https://www.japaneselawtranslation.go.jp/en/laws/view/3781.

37 Per Article 9(1) (Standing to Sue): "An action for the revocation of an original administrative disposition and an action for the revocation of an administrative disposition on appeal (hereinafter referred to as 'actions for the revocation of administrative dispositions') may be filed only by a person who has a legal interest in seeking the revocation of the original administrative disposition or of the administrative disposition on appeal (including a person who has the legal interest to be recovered by revoking the original administrative disposition or administrative disposition on appeal even after it has lost its effect because of the expiration of a certain period or for other reasons)." ACLA (ibid).

38 For example, in the following cases: Syufuren Juice, Saiko Saibansho [Sup. Ct.], March 14, 1978, no. 32, 2 Minji Hanreisyu [Minshu] 211; Naganuma Naiki, Saiko Saibansho [Sup. Ct.], September 9, 1982, no. 36, 9 Minji Hanreisyu [Minshu] 1679; Iba Iseki, Saiko Saibansho [Sup. Ct.], June 20, 1989, 1334 Hanrei Jihou [Hanji] 201.

39 Article 16 of the Ministerial Ordinance on EIA for Electric Power contains such provisions; see https://elaws.e-gov.go.jp/document?lawid=410M50000400054 (in Japanese). In one 2005 case, the Supreme Court judged that residents within twenty kilometers of a particular facility have standing when making a legal claim relevant to it, based on the relevant provision of an ordinance: Citizen Group v. Japan, Saiko Saibansho [Sup. Ct.], December 17, 2005, 10 Minshu 56, 2645. In that case, the court referred to the Tokyo Environmental Impact Assessment Ordinance, interpreting some of its provisions as establishing the "affected area" as up to twenty kilometers from the polluting source.

40 See the *Kobe* administrative case complaint, https://drive.google.com/file/d/1PWjHOasLp82MXv7zFbF5wn4jgkgyXFx2/view, pp. 57–59 (in Japanese).

the growing involvement of younger generations in CCL internationally.[41] She explained that her decision to join the case was motivated by a desire to raise climate awareness among her peers.[42]

The defendant was the Minister of METI, who regulates electricity providers under the EBA, approves EIA outcomes,[43] and is obligated to consider the views of other relevant ministries.[44] In addition, the EBA requires the minister to take into account the views of local governors and consult with the environment minister regarding environmental conservation.[45]

---

41 For example, younger people appeared in *Juliana* (Chapter 1, supra note 5); *Do-Hyun Kim* (Chapter 1, supra note 7); Thomson v. Minister for Climate Change Issues, [2017] NZHC 733, https://climatecasechart.com/non-us-case/thomson-v-minister-for-climate-change-issues; Armando Ferrão Carvalho and Others v. The European Parliament and the Council (hereafter, the *People's Climate Case*), Case no. T-330/18, https://climatecasechart.com/non-us-case/armando-ferrao-carvalho-and-others-v-the-european-parliament-and-the-council.

42 Interview with the author, November 11, 2020.

43 While the Minister of MOE is generally responsible for EIA, including its approval, an exceptional procedure exists for electricity generation due to its importance to the economy. This exception is provided for in Article 46–2 (Environmental Impact Assessment on Electric Facilities for Business Use) of the EBA: "An environmental impact assessment as prescribed in Article 2, paragraph (1) of the Environmental Impact Assessment Act (Act No. 81 of 1997) on a construction project to install or modify electric facilities for business use that falls under the category of Class 1 projects prescribed in paragraph (2) of the Article or the category of Class 2 projects prescribed in paragraph (3) of the Article (hereinafter referred to as an 'Environmental Impact Assessment') and relevant procedures are as provided for by that Act and this Subsection." See EBA (Chapter 1, supra note 15).

44 Article 3–6 of the EIA Act (Opinions of the Competent Minister): "When receiving the submission specified in Article 3–4, paragraph (1), the competent Minister may state the opinions in writing to a person who intends to implement the class-1 project within the period designated by cabinet order from the standpoint of the environment conservation for the document on primary environmental impact consideration. In any event, where the Minister of the Environment has stated any opinions pursuant to the provisions of the preceding article, such opinions must be taken into consideration." See EIA Act (Chapter 1, supra note 14).

45 Article 46–14 of the EBA (Recommendations on Draft EIS):

"(1) When a draft EIS has been submitted pursuant to Article 46–11, and the Minister of Economy, Trade and Industry finds it necessary to examine the draft EIS and ensure that due consideration will be given to environmental preservation in the specified relevant project pertaining to the draft EIS, while taking into account the relevant municipal or prefectural governor's comments given under Article 20, paragraph (1) of the Environmental Impact Assessment Act or comments of a mayor specified by Cabinet Order set forth in paragraph (4) of the article and a relevant municipal or prefectural governor set forth in paragraph (5) of the article, if any, as well as the outline of the comments under Article 18, paragraph (1) of the Act and the proponent's views thereon, which are submitted pursuant to Article 46–12, the Minister may make, within a period specified

Plaintiffs requested disclosure of all documents related to the approval of the EIA, including internal memoranda. These documents revealed that both the MOE and Kobe City had expressed strong concerns about the serious negative impacts of the CFPPs. The MOE provided critical feedback to METI, and the two ministries engaged in extensive debate, yet the latter ultimately proceeded with approved unchanged.

In court, plaintiffs advanced two main claims: (1) that the final notice authorizing construction was unlawful because the EIA failed to meet its core purpose – predicting and evaluating the cumulative impacts of CO_2 emissions on the environment; and (2) that Japan lacked legislation consistent with its commitments under the Paris Agreement to reduce GHG emissions. Unlike the *Sendai* and *Kobe* civil cases, this first administrative climate case in Japan raised several unprecedented legal challenges specific to the nature of climate change. This section focuses on two procedural and one substantive issue related to claim (1), before moving on to claim (2).

The first procedural issue concerned the dispositive character of the EIA final notice, which allowed construction of the CFPPs to proceed. According to judicial precedent, some final notices issued by public authorities to specific applicants are considered administrative dispositions that determine the scope of the applicants' legal rights or interests. In prior case law, however, EIA-related final notices were not typically regarded as dispositive; that is, the final notice did not in itself confer legal status. In this case, the plaintiffs argued that the final notice effectively authorized construction and that revocation would have forced Kobe Steel to halt the project. On this basis, they contended that the final notice did indeed determine the scope of the company's legal rights or interests, that is, it was dispositive. The defendants, by contrast, denied that the notice had such legal force.

The second procedural issue concerned the plaintiffs' standing under Article 9 of the ACLA. To qualify, an administrative disposition must directly affect the plaintiff's legal rights or interests, and its cancellation must provide redress. Plaintiffs therefore had to demonstrate that the assessment processes described by the EIA Act protects individual legal rights, and that the EIA for

---

by Order of the Ministry of Economy, Trade and Industry from the day when the submission made under Article 46–11 is accepted, necessary recommendations to the specified business operator regarding an Environmental Impact Assessment on the specified relevant project.

(2) If the Minister of Economy, Trade and Industry conducts an examination pursuant to the preceding paragraph, the Minister must consult with the Minister of the Environment from the standpoint of preserving the environment." See EBA (Chapter 1, supra note 15).

the Kobe CFPPs failed to satisfy those standards. Defendants countered that the Act's purpose is to promote the *public* interests in environmental protection, not to safeguard *individual* legal rights. They also noted that PM2.5 is not currently among the items required for assessment under the Act and that the EBA, which governs EIAs for fossil fuel power plants, partially excludes CO_2 evaluation. Accordingly, they argued, the EIA contained no legal defect. Plaintiffs, in turn, countered that the framework was structurally inadequate to address modern environmental and climate harms. To support standing, attorneys submitted local hazard maps showing plaintiffs' residences in flood- and storm-surge-prone areas and emphasized plaintiffs' ages to demonstrate their heightened vulnerability to heat-related illnesses.

The key substantive issue was justiciability. The Minister of METI enjoys broad discretion in issuing final notices based on the submitted EIA statements.[46] Accordingly, the referred EIA is presumed lawful. Such a decision may be deemed unlawful only under certain limited circumstances – or example, if the factual basis is demonstrably false, the evaluation is clearly unreasonable, or significant facts were disregarded.[47] Defendants argued that none of these applied and that the minister's decision fell squarely within his discretion. Plaintiffs, however, insisted that in light of the urgency of the climate crisis, failure to consider alternative, noncoal energy sources was itself unreasonable.

On March 15, 2021, the Osaka District Court dismissed all claims in the Kobe administrative case. On claim (1), the court first recognized the dispositive character of the final notice. It also granted the plaintiffs standing, but only with respect to air pollution. Consistent with the defendants' arguments, the court found that the legal basis for the EIA notice did not provide individual

46 Article 46–17 of the EBA stipulates the Order of Revision. This article assigns, in turn, broad discretion to the Minister of METI:

"(1) If the Minister of Economy, Trade and Industry finds it necessary and appropriate to ensure that due consideration will be given to environmental preservation in the specified relevant project pertaining to the EIS submitted under the preceding article, the Minister may order, within a period specified by Order of the Ministry of Economy, Trade and Industry from the day when the submission made under the article is accepted, the specified business operator to revise the EIS within a reasonable time limit set by the Minister.

(2) If the Minister of Economy, Trade and Industry finds it unnecessary to issue an order pursuant to the preceding paragraph, the Minister must notify the specified business operator to that effect without delay." See EBA (Chapter 1, supra note 15).

47 This framework was indeed applied in this case. See Osaka Chiho Saibansyo [Osaka Dist. Ct.], March 15, 2021, https://kobeclimatecase.jp/wp-content/uploads/2021/03/20210315 judgment-document_kobe_climate_case.pdf (in Japanese).

protection against climate change impacts. It reasoned that standing must rest on a distinct legal interest rather than the magnitude of harm and concluded that the plaintiffs, as individuals, had not suffered climate-related injuries that differentiated them from the general public. Accordingly, it held that climate change affects society as a whole and is more appropriately addressed through policymaking, not individual litigation.

The court also dismissed the claim under Article 10(1) of the ACLA, which bars challenges to administrative actions unrelated to a claimant's legal interests. Nonetheless, in obiter dictum, the court reviewed the plaintiffs' abuse-of-discretion argument under the framework of broad executive discretion established in past decisions. It ultimately found no abuse in this case.

On claim (2), regarding the alleged illegality of the absence of legislation consistent with Japan's Paris Agreement commitments, the court dismissed on procedural grounds. Under Japanese administrative litigation, declaratory judgments are permitted only for public law–related actions specified in Article 4 of the ACLA. Article 4 requires a direct legal relationship between the plaintiff and defendant. Here, the court held that the missing emissions regulations implicated a relationship between the state and the operator, not between the plaintiffs and the operator.

Eleven plaintiffs appealed to the Osaka High Court, focusing on claim (1) and the question of standing. On April 26, 2022, the High Court upheld the lower court's dismissal but with revised reasoning. It examined whether Article 9(1) ACLA protects the plaintiffs' individual interests against global warming impacts and concluded that it does not, as no such clause currently exists. However, the court added an important caveat:

> The court does not deny the possibility that the substance of the interest not to be affected by CO_2 emissions may be determined and recognized as a personal interest in the future, according to social changes in Japan and abroad. The court issues this judgment on the basis of the current social situation, with immature recognition of climate crisis as human rights' issue both in and outside of Japan.[48]

Regarding the legality of the EIA final notice, the High Court applied the same framework as the District Court but with a stronger emphasis on the government's responsibility to take immediate and concrete measures to align Japan's regulations with Paris Agreement. It highlighted the absence

48 Osaka Koto Saibansho [Osaka High Ct.], April 26, 2022, 1513 Hanrei Taimuzu [Hanta] 98, citation from page 30 of the original decision.

of a concrete roadmap to achieve Japan's 2030 ten Nationally Determined Contributions (NDCs), which had become a critical issue at the time of judgment. Nevertheless, the court concluded that such challenges belong to the political, not judicial, arena.

The plaintiffs appealed to the Supreme Court. On 9 March 2023, the Supreme Court dismissed the appeal, also ruling out the possibility of a final appeal, stating only that the case did not meet the criteria for either procedure.[49]

4.2.4 Yokosuka *Case*

Yokosuka, a coastal city of 390,000 in Kanagawa Prefecture, lies along Tokyo Bay. As in Sendai and Kobe, following the Great East Japan Earthquake in March 2011, four new CFPPs were proposed for the prefecture's bay area. Local residents in each location formed opposition groups, which in 2016 merged into a single coalition, "No Coal, Tokyo Bay."[50] The coalition engaged in sustained negotiations with the project developers, taking into account the global shift toward coal divestment and arguing that new coal plants were no longer commercially viable. Their efforts succeeded in halting three of the four projects, but the Yokosuka plan proceeded. The group continued to organize explanatory meetings and submit petitions to the governor of Kanagawa Prefecture and the MOE.

The proposed site had previously hosted two CFPPs built in 1960 and 1962, followed by six additional units constructed by 1970.[51] Operated by Tokyo Electric Power Company Holdings (TEPCO Fuel and Power), four units ceased operation in 2000 due to depreciation, and three more followed in 2001. By 2010, all units had shut down, although some were briefly restarted after the 2011 earthquake before finally closing in 2014. In 2016, JERA, the company established for the purpose of replacing and constructing new thermal power plants, inherited the electricity business from TEPCO Fuel and Power, assumed the construction plan, and pursued a simplified EIA process under

49 Article 318(1) of the Japanese Code of Civil Procedure states: "If the Supreme Court is the court with which the final appeal should be filed, it may rule, upon petition, to accept as the final appellate court, a case in which a prior instance judgment reflects a determination that conflicts with Supreme Court precedent (or, if there is no Supreme Court precedent, conflicts with precedent of the former Great Court of Cassation or precedent of the high court acting as the final appellate court or the court of second instance) or to accept any other case that is found to involve matters of material import in the interpretation of laws and regulations." Code of Civil Procedure, Act No. 109 of June 26, 1996, https://www.japaneselawtranslation.go.jp/en/laws/view/2834.

50 For the coalition's official website, see https://nocoal-tokyobay.net (in Japanese).

51 Cited from the complaint issued by the plaintiffs; see https://nocoal-tokyobay.net/wp-content/uploads/2019/05/yokosuka_complaint_20190527.pdf (in Japanese).

the Simplified Replacement Assessment Guidelines (hereafter, Simplified Guidelines), which allows streamlined review where replacement facilities are expected to have limited environmental impacts, such as air pollutants and GHG emissions.[52] JERA submitted its EIA report to METI on November 15, 2018, and METI issued final approval on November 30. With demolition of the old facilities already completed, construction began on August 1, 2019.

Meanwhile, the Kiko Network encouraged the leader of the local citizens' group to initiate litigation and assisted in recruiting attorneys.[53] To comply with the six-month filing deadline required by Article 14 ACLA, the complaint was filed on May 27, 2020. The plaintiff group comprised forty-five individuals. Yokosuka was also the hometown of then-MOE minister Shinjiro Koizumi, son of former prime minister Junichiro Koizumi. The group leader lived near Koizumi, and many plaintiffs had interacted with Koizumi family at local community events such as summer festivals. These personal ties contributed to heightened local awareness of environmental issues. Several plaintiffs testified that Japan's coal policy was a central concern,[54] and younger FFF members held meetings with Koizumi to present petitions directly to the MOE.[55]

In December 2019, three fishers joined the lawsuit, alleging that the CFPP would damage the marine environment through seaweed community destruction, rocky denudation, loss of coastal vegetation, and a sharp decline in seafood catches. These trends, already observed in Yokosuka Bay and nearby waters, were linked to rising sea temperatures associated with climate change (IPCC 2019, 478–481). The new plant was expected to discharge large volumes of thermal wastewater, further increasing local sea temperatures and potentially exacerbating ecosystem harm. The fishers aimed to demonstrate both ongoing and anticipated impacts from the project.

JERA was established in 2015 with Tokyo Electric Power Company Holdings (TEPCO Fuel & Power) and Chubu Electric Power Co. each holding a 50 percent stake. As with Sendai Power Station Company and Kobe Steel Ltd., JERA proceeded with demolition and construction without prior notice to residents,

52 In full, the Guidelines on the Simplification of Environmental Impact Assessment for Replaced Power Plants, originally accessed on August 4, 2024, at https://www.meti.go.jp/committee/kenkyukai/sangi/kankyo_assessment/pdf/009_02_00.pdf (in Japanese; link no longer active).

53 Leader of the citizen group, interview with the author, March 5, 2020.

54 Interviews with the author, March 3–6, 2020.

55 As reported, e.g., in *Asahi Shimbun*, June 26, 2020, originally accessed on August 4, 2024, at https://www.asahi.com/articles/ASN6T7WH9N6TULBJ01C.html (in Japanese; link no longer active).

fueling community resentment.[56] As construction began in August 2019, JERA launched a website posting monthly updates, claiming to mitigate impacts on air and sea.[57] The company also promoted its plan for "zero-emission fossil fuel power generation" by co-firing ammonia with coal.[58]

Court proceedings were significantly delayed by the COVID-19 pandemic. Filed in the Tokyo District Court – already burdened with a heavy caseload – the case moved slowly, with COVID-related restrictions further hampering scheduling.[59] Plaintiffs insisted on holding hearings in the grand courtroom to maximize public access and media visibility, which also extended the timeline. As of April 2021, hearings were held only about once every six months.[60]

In court, the plaintiffs challenged the legality of the final notice permitting plant construction on four grounds. First, they argued that the Simplified Guidelines were inapplicable, since they intended to simplify the EIA process only when environmental impacts would be reduced. Because air quality had improved significantly after the old facilities closed in 2014, this condition could not reasonably be met by constructing new plants. Second, they criticized the Simplified Guidelines for failing to assess the cumulative environmental impacts of CO_2 emissions, especially given their lack of consideration of alternative fuel sources and reliance on speculative CCS technologies. The new plant was expected to emit 7.26 million metric tons of CO_2 annually – roughly 1/5,000 of global emissions at the time. Third, they argued that the Simplified Guidelines inadequately evaluated thermal wastewater impacts on marine ecosystems, thereby threatening marine-based livelihoods. Fourth, as in *Sendai* and *Kobe*, they pointed to the omission of a PM2.5 impact analysis. As with the *Kobe* administrative case, the lawsuit was largely led by the Kiko Network and its president, who also served as lead attorney, with a legal strategy largely paralleling the *Kobe* case.

A notable distinction between the *Yokosuka* and *Kobe* administrative cases lay in the prioritization of claims. In *Kobe*, health and climate arguments

56 Interviews with the author, March 3–6, 2020.

57 The website can be viewed at https://www.jera.co.jp/en/corporate/business/thermal-power/list/yokosuka.

58 A short movie explains the process, available at https://www.jera.co.jp/notice/20210409_661 (in Japanese).

59 Some unhurried cases have been canceled or postponed. See https://www.courts.go.jp/tokyo/about/osirase/l4/Vcms4_00000616.html, originally accessed on August 4, 2024 (in Japanese; link no longer active).

60 On the trajectory of the *Yokosuka* climate case, see https://yokosukaclimatecase.jp/en/document.

were emphasized equally, whereas in *Yokosuka*, climate change became the primary focus.[61] The presiding judge requested evidence of specific harms to the plaintiffs from climate change, such as hazard maps showing flood or high-tide risks near their homes and data on age-based vulnerability to heat-stroke. Compared to *Sendai* and *Kobe*, *Yokosuka* attracted more young and middle-aged auditors,[62] some without personal ties to the plaintiffs, contrasting with the smaller auditor groups with stronger social ties to the plaintiffs observed in the other two cases.[63] Typically, courtroom auditors are directly connected to the plaintiffs or their supporters. The broader participation in *Yokosuka* thus suggests a growing generational interest in CCL.

On January 27, 2023, the Tokyo District Court dismissed the case. As in *Kobe*, it recognized the dispositive nature of the final notice and acknowledged standing only in respect to air pollution. It rejected standing on climate-related claims, again framing protection against climate impacts as a matter of public interest more appropriately handled through policy. The court also found no direct causal link between JERA's emissions and violations of the plaintiffs' claimed legal interests to be protected from climate-related harms. Notably, the ruling did not address the claims of the fishers, who argued that their right to a stable livelihood was threatened by thermal discharge and ecosystem damage.

In assessing the legality of the notice approving plant construction, the Tokyo District Court applied the same framework used in the *Kobe* administrative case, granting broad administrative discretion and limiting judicial intervention. It also upheld the use of the Simplified Guidelines, despite their arguably superficial application.

On February 22, 2024, the Tokyo High Court dismissed the plaintiffs' appeal of the District Court decision. The High Court acknowledged the seriousness of climate change, citing the IPCC Fifth Assessment Report (IPCC 2014) and the Special Report on Global Warming of 1.5 °C (IPCC 2018). It recognized that climate change is already driving weather disasters and altering ocean conditions worldwide, including in Japan, and noted the potential impacts on marine ecosystems raised by to appellants.

Nevertheless, on the issue of standing, the High Court noted that the Basic Matters and Ministerial Orders under the EIA Act treat GHGs differently from other evaluation items that involve health and environmental risks. It

61 Directly observed by the author at the second hearing on December 23, 2019, at Tokyo District Court.

62 Directly observed by this author at the second hearing on December 23, 2019, at Tokyo District Court. However, given that the survey only captured a proportion of plaintiff group members, respondent data may show a different result.

63 Observed through interviews with auditors, March 3–5, 2020.

concluded that CO_2-related harms do not qualify as individual legal interests but fall within the scope of broader public interests. The court also rejected the argument that the assessment should have considered alternative fuel sources, holding that regulations require only an evaluation of structural layout, location, and scale – not fuel type.

Regarding the exclusion of CO_2 emissions at the planning stage, the court cited the plant's estimated output of approximately 7.26 million metric tons per year, noting that this represented about 1/5,000 of global emissions in 2015 and 0.64 percent of Japan's total in 2006. It held that such emissions could not be regarded as significantly contributing to climate change–related harm. The court also noted the use of ultra-supercritical technology to improve efficiency and reduce emissions, and reaffirmed that CO_2 is not classified as a factor requiring individual evaluation under existing EIA guidelines.

Finally, the court upheld the application of the Simplified Guidelines rather than a full EIA, reasoning that emissions from the newly "rebuilt" plant could be compared with those of the former facility at its operational peak in 1970, rather than with the more recent period in which no plant was active.

On April 30, 2024, the plaintiffs appealed to the Supreme Court of Japan, alleging violations of human rights, due process, and procedural defects in the EIA process. On October 23, 2024, the Supreme Court summarily rejected the appeal, stating only that the case did not meet the requirements of Article 312 of the Code of Civil Procedure.[64] No further reasoning was provided.

4.2.5 Youth *Case*

On August 15, 2024, sixteen young people aged between fifteen and twenty-nine filed a lawsuit against ten major thermal power companies in Japan's electric power sector.[65] The plaintiffs alleged that the defendants' CO_2 emissions contribute to climate change and thereby infringe on their rights, creating liability under Civil Code Articles 709 and 719.[66] They sought an injunction requiring the companies to reduce emissions by 48 percent by 2030 and 65 percent by 2035, compared to 2019 levels. These targets mirror IPCC recommendations for limiting global warming to 1.5 °C and are consistent with the Paris Agreement.

The plaintiffs were motivated by escalating harms of climate change worldwide and by what they viewed as the persistent inaction of both the Japanese

64 Supra 49.

65 See https://youth4cj.jp. This case emerged too late to be included in the original PhD research (Ichihara and Nishikawa 2024) and is included in the present work for the first time.

66 See Jap. Civ. Cod. (Chapter 2, supra note 39).

government and the electric power sector. Japan's National Energy Policy still envisions coal providing 19 percent of electricity generation in 2030. Although the government promotes "decarbonized" coal through ammonia and hydrogen co-firing and through CCS systems, the plaintiffs argued that these measures are unlikely to deliver meaningful reductions. Ammonia and hydrogen, while carbon-free when burned, involve production and transport processes – often reliant on fossil fuels and long-distance shipping – that emit substantial CO_2. Japan has also pledged to convert about 20 percent of coal plants to ammonia co-firing by 2030, but large-scale commercial viability remains uncertain.

Unlike other G7 countries, Japan has not produced a concrete plan to phase out CFPPs, despite the growing feasibility of renewable alternatives. The plaintiffs therefore regarded the National Energy Policy as inconsistent with the 1.5 °C goal. The defendant companies – most of Japan's largest electric utilities – have also failed, according to the plaintiffs, to set credible interim targets. While they have pledged carbon neutrality by 2050, they continue to rely on unproven technologies such as CCS, without clarifying concrete pathways to near-term reductions.

According to the complaint, the plaintiffs argue that the defendants' actions violate a broad range of human rights. These include rights provided by the Japanese Constitution to life (Art. 13), health (Art. 13), property (Art. 29(1)), non-exposure to climate harm (Art. 13), and self-determination (Art. 13), and the right to development provided by the UN Convention on the Rights of the Child (Article 6(2)). The plaintiffs emphasize that these rights must be safeguarded not only for themselves and future generations, but also for those already disproportionately affected by climate change, particularly in developing countries across Asia, Africa, and South America. In this way, they explicitly ground their claims in a perspective of climate justice: as citizens of a nation consuming large volumes of fossil fuels and emitting significant GHG gases, there is a responsibility to avoid the climate crisis.

At the time of writing, the *Youth* case is pending before the Nagoya District Court. Hearings are being held in the court's largest chamber, which can accommodate around 100 auditors. Interest has exceeded capacity at every session, with entry determined by lottery.

4.3 Comparison of the Cases

4.3.1 *Similarities*

All five cases share a common feature: they seek to halt the construction or operation of CFPPs. Since CFPPs are among the largest sources of CO_2

emissions, it is understandable that they became the first targets of CCL in Japan.

Second, four of the five cases – excluding the *Youth* case – combine claims about air pollutants such as NOx, SOx, and PM2.5 with those concerning GHG emissions, particularly CO_2. This dual strategy, especially the inclusion of air pollution claims directly tied to individual health harms, was adopted to reduce the risk of early dismissal. Given the established approach of Japanese courts toward standing, as previously discussed, the attorneys in these cases anticipated that judges would be hesitant to recognize standing based solely on other harms caused by climate change.[67]

Third, all cases have been broadly supported by the Kiko Network. Because NGOs currently lack standing in environmental litigation in Japan, the Kiko Network cannot act as a plaintiff. Instead, it supports concerned citizens though various means, including financial assistance funded by membership fees, private donations, grants, and subsidies; assembling attorney teams; and facilitating communication between attorneys and plaintiff groups. As mentioned earlier, the president of the Kiko Network, who is also an attorney, served on the plaintiffs' legal teams in both the *Kobe* and *Yokosuka* cases. In the *Yokosuka* case, the Kiko Network even arranged bus transportation for plaintiffs and supporters, since jurisdiction required the trial to be held at the Tokyo District Court, about sixty-eight kilometers from Yokosuka. The organization also plays a central role in disseminating information about these cases to the public in order to raise awareness of climate change. Originally, the Kiko Network engaged in a wide range of climate-related activities, including divestment campaigns, awareness-raising, and environmental education. Today, CCL has become one of its most important tools.

---

67 It is worth noting that one conciliation case, known as the *Polar Bear* case, preceded the five CCL lawsuits in 2011. Details are available in a report issued by Kiko Network (https://www.kikonet.org/national/monitoring/shirokuma-saiban, in Japanese). The Act on the Settlement of Environmental Pollution Disputes (supra note 25) provides for alternative dispute resolution, including mediation, conciliation, arbitration, and adjudication. In this case, Kiko Network and the Japan Environmental Lawyers Association argued that CO_2 emissions should be recognized as a form of pollution and sought conciliation against eleven major electric companies. The Environmental Dispute Coordination Commission dismissed the claim. The plaintiffs subsequently brought the case before the Tokyo District Court, but the claim was dismissed both there (Osaka Chiho Saibansho [Osaka Dist. Ct.], September 10, 2014) and on appeal (Osaka Koto Saibansho [Osaka High Ct.], June 11, 2015, https://www.courts.go.jp/app/hanrei_jp/detail5?id=85481, in Japanese). From this experience, Kiko Network drew two key lessons: first, claims based solely on climate damage are likely to be dismissed by the judiciary; and second, suing all categories of electric companies at once is unlikely to succeed (Otsuka 2020b, 148).

4.3.2 *Differences*

The five cases differ in four main respects, as summarized in Table 4.

First, the type of judicial proceedings shifted from civil to administrative litigation up to the *Youth* case. This reflects a move away from seeking remedies (such as compensation or injunctions) against individual companies for specific damages toward broader challenges targeting emissions regulations. Notably, the plaintiffs and legal team in the *Kobe* administrative case explained that suing METI rather than the power companies aimed to provoke institutional reform and generate nationwide social impact.[68] This strategic orientation recalls the role of second- and third-wave antipollution lawsuits in Japan (Secs. 3.2.3 and 3.2.4), which similarly sought systemic change, an area of litigation the *Kobe* chief attorney was well aware of. The *Youth* case, by contrast, returned to civil litigation but named ten major thermal power companies – responsible for about 40 percent of Japan's total CO_2 emissions – as defendants. In doing so, it treats them as representatives of the entire sector, aligning with sectoral systemic litigation seen in other jurisdictions.

Second, the role of academics shifted. In the *Sendai* case, university professors specializing in environmental and energy policy played leading roles, marking a pioneering step in Japanese CCL. The *Kobe* cases also included professors, though in advisory rather than leadership positions: they served as consultants to attorneys, intermediaries between plaintiffs and legal teams, and authors of scholarly publications. The plaintiff group was led by a retired citizen. By contrast, no professors participated as plaintiffs in the *Yokosuka* or *Youth* cases, which were led instead by citizen groups and young plaintiffs. This suggests that academic leadership was important for initiating new types of litigation, once precedents existed, citizen-led groups could more readily carry forward the litigation model.

Third, youth participation increased progressively across the cases, culminating in the *Youth* climate case. The *Sendai* case involved only adult plaintiffs, while the *Kobe* and *Yokosuka* cases included several children, often through their parents, who were also plaintiffs. Many of these young people had a basic understanding of the importance of securing a stable climate for future generations.[69] In the *Kobe* administrative case, one plaintiff was an undergraduate student affiliated with FFF, serving as a link between courtroom litigation and

68 The team issued a press release stating that it was the state's responsibility to halt the construction and operation of new CFPPs. See https://kobeclimatecase.jp/wp-content/uploads/2019/03/181119kobe-administrative-law-suit-case.pdf (in Japanese).

69 Observed at the examination of plaintiffs during the eighth hearing of the *Kobe* administrative case, November 4, 2020.

TABLE 4 Differences among the five climate change cases in Japan

	Sendai	*Kobe* (civil)	*Kobe* (admin)	*Yokosuka*	*Youth*
Date filed	Sept. 2017	Sept. 2018	Nov. 2018	Jun. 2019	Aug. 2024
Proceedings	civil	civil	administrative	administrative	civil
Leading actors	attorneys, scholars, citizen group, Kiko Network	attorneys, scholars, citizen group, Kiko Network	attorneys, scholars, citizen group, Kiko Network	attorneys, citizen group, Kiko Network	attorneys, 16 young people, Kiko Network
Young people involvement	none	some children	some children, one university student	some children, young people as auditors	all plaintiffs
Prioritization of climate change issue	initially excluded; focus shifted to air pollution	balanced with air pollution	balanced with air pollution	climate change prioritized	climate change only

SOURCE: CREATED BY THE AUTHOR

the youth climate movement. By the *Youth* case, young plaintiffs themselves were the driving force, supported by broader generational engagement as auditors.

Fourth, the prioritization of climate change arguments evolved. In the *Sendai* case, legal claims were narrowed to focus primarily on air pollution. In the *Kobe* cases, climate arguments were presented alongside air pollution claims. In the *Yokosuka* case, climate change impacts became the central focus. Finally, the *Youth* case centers exclusively on climate change. This progression, from conventional air pollution to GHG emissions, reflects the broader transition in Japan from traditional environmental litigation to CCL, mirroring trends in the Global North.

4.4 Comparison of CCL and Earlier Antipollution/ Environmental Cases

Over decades, the processes of industrialization, urbanization, and globalization have altered both the patterns and the severity of environmental degradation in Japan. In parallel, the legal strategies used by plaintiffs to respond to

TABLE 5 Differences among antipollution, environmental, and climate change litigation

Litigation type	Individual damage observed	Regional scope	Generation	Causal relation	Adequacy of judicial solution
Related requirement	standing	standing	standing	causal proof	justification
Antipollution	clear and severe	local	current & near-future	fairly simple	fairly adequate
Environmental	partly clear	local-global	current & future	complicated	mostly adequate
Climate change	unclear	global	mostly future	complicated & overlapped	partly adequate

SOURCE: CREATED BY THE AUTHOR

these harms have also evolved. While CCL is often treated as a subcategory of environmental litigation (Perlman 2009, 1–58), it differs in important respects from earlier environmental lawsuits concerning, for example, nuclear power plants or asbestos. To clarify these differences, Table 5 compares antipollution, environmental, and CCL.

As Table 5 shows, environmental litigation in Japan incorporates characteristics of both antipollution and climate change cases. The following discussion highlights the distinctions.

First, antipollution litigation addressed severe and tangible health harms. Victims of pollution-related illnesses sought redress, supported by attorneys who dedicated their practice to these cases. By contrast, CCL plaintiffs – such as those on *Yokosuka* and *Youth* cases – seek to protect the stability of the climate system for future generations. In most CCL, the individual harms of climate change are either not yet realized, remain uncertain, or are less immediately severe than those from pollution in the 1960s and 1970s. This gap in immediacy partly explains both the reluctance of many attorneys to take on CCL cases and the courts' cautious or dismissive stance toward such claims.

Second, whereas pollution damage was typically confined to specific localities, the harms of climate change are inherently global. This creates particular challenges for Japanese courts in defining the geographic scope of standing. For example, in the *Kobe* administrative case, plaintiffs argued that residents within twenty kilometers of the CFPPs had standing because of exposure to conventional pollutants (Sec. 4.2.3). They also claimed that plaintiffs living farther away should have standing, on the grounds that climate-related harms – though more diffuse – still posed a credible risk.

Third, plaintiffs in antipollution cases typically sought redress for harms already suffered. Some also pursued injunctions or compensation to prevent likely future harm and to protect near-future generations. In contrast, CCL plaintiffs often aim not only to remedy climate-related harms already experienced but also to safeguard the global climate system for the indefinite future.[70] This raises a unique challenge: courts must assess standing for plaintiffs who, rather than asserting immediate legal rights, claim to represent the interests of future generations. Although such claims sit uneasily with existing legal frameworks, they align with the scientific consensus that future generations – who cannot represent themselves[71] – are already at risk due to present and ongoing climate threats.

Fourth, establishing causation in antipollution cases – for example, tracing pollutants in a river to specific health damage – was relatively straightforward.[72] CCL, however, involves a much more complex causal chain. GHG gases emitted from a facility disperse into the global atmosphere, contributing incrementally to rising temperatures. These changes in turn drive a wide range of adverse natural phenomena worldwide, only some of which may directly affect specific plaintiffs. Under conventional legal reasoning, each step in this chain must be demonstrated in court. Further complicating matters is the multiplicity of emitters worldwide and the interaction of anthropogenic emissions with natural climatic variability.

Fifth, in antipollution litigation plaintiffs typically suffered immediate and severe harm that required urgent remedies. Monetary compensation or injunctive relief often provided effective redress, making judicial intervention a meaningful solution. In CCL, however, harm is more diffuse, gradual, and difficult to substantiate in legal terms. Monetary compensation may be inadequate given the irreversible nature of many climate change impacts, while injunctions against individual emitters may have only limited effect on the overall problem. Although litigation can help stimulate institutional reform – as seen in earlier antipollution cases – the capacity of any single CCL case to remedy specific climate harms remains inherently constrained.

70 Observed throughout many interviews across all five cases.

71 Otsuka (2020b, 157) suggests that the right to a stable climate system should be admitted as a legal right of current and future generations.

72 Causation in such cases are nevertheless complicated compared with other areas of litigation, say, conflicts in sales contracts. However, it is still less complex than causation in climate change cases.

4.5 Uniqueness of CCL in Japan

Globally, the adverse impacts of climate change have given rise to a growing number of climate cases. As noted in Section 1.1.1, Western countries dominate this trend, with approximately 76 percent in the United States and 5 percent in Australia (Setzer and Byrnes 2020, 6). This imbalance has shaped a conventional understanding of CCL rooted largely in Western sociolegal systems (Sindico and Mbengue 2021, 6). Within this context, Japanese CCL displays several distinctive features, both in terms of the actors involved and the legal strategies advanced.

First, participation by younger generations remains strikingly limited compared to international examples. In Japan, only a single university student has appeared as a plaintiff (in the *Kobe* administrative case), alongside a number of children included through their parents. In contrast, youth-led litigation is a defining feature of many cases abroad, where young plaintiffs have played central roles, from individual claimants to large, organized groups.[73]

Second, Japanese cases generally involve relatively small plaintiff groups. The *Sendai* case, with 124 plaintiffs, remains the largest to date. In comparison, the *Urgenda* case in the Netherlands involved 886 citizens represented by the Urgenda Foundation, and thirty-seven plaintiffs in the *People's Climate Case* were supported by nearly 212,000 signatories.[74] The reasons for this limited public participation in Japan's climate cases are examined in Chapter 5.

Third, legal arguments in Japanese CCL have thus far been narrowly framed around injunctions against CFPPs. With only five CCL cases filed to date, litigation in Japan remains at an early stage. As the field develops, however, it may expand to include claims more commonly seen in other jurisdictions, such as attribution of responsibility for climate damages, enforcement of regulatory obligations, and challenges related to adaptation measures (UNEP 2020).[75]

---

73 For example, the landmark 2015 *Thomson* lawsuit was filed by a young law student. Meanwhile, twenty-one young plaintiffs appeared in *Juliana*, nineteen in *Do-Hyun Kim*, and ten families including children in the *People's Climate Case*. See Chapter 1, supra notes 5, 7, and Chapter 4, 107.

74 *Urgenda* (Chapter 1, supra note 6); *People's Climate Case* (supra note 41).

75 All varieties of legal arguments used in the United States, which are discussed in the next chapter.

4.6 Summary

This chapter examined five climate change lawsuits in Japan, providing case histories, similarities and differences, and comparisons with earlier environmental litigation. As of September 2025, the *Sendai*, *Kobe* (civil and administrative), and *Yokosuka* cases have all concluded with dismissals of the plaintiffs' claims, while *Youth* case remains ongoing. Together, these lawsuits reveal how plaintiffs and their attorneys have situated climate claims within Japan's longer tradition of antipollution litigation. At the same time, defendants' arguments and judicial reasoning have clarified a set of recurring legal issues – particularly those concerning standing, causation, and justiciability – that mirror challenges seen in CCL worldwide. Finally, this chapter highlighted the distinctive characteristics of Japanese CCL, especially its emphasis on standing and causal proof, which set it apart from developments in other jurisdictions.

CHAPTER 5

Institutional Obstacles

5.1 Overview

Chapter 3 outlined the historical background of environmental litigation in Japan, particularly antipollution cases that attorneys in the current climate lawsuits have consciously treated as legal antecedents. Chapter 4 then identified the key features of Japan's five climate cases and analyzed their progress through the courts. Building on those discussions, this chapter examines the institutional obstacles that hinder the development of CCL in Japan. In doing so, it offers a refined perspective on the significance and function of CCL within Japan's sociolegal context.

Like earlier forms of environmental litigation, CCL in Japan has been used by activists as a strategic tool to influence governance on climate and environmental issues. The LOS framework is therefore useful for analyzing the sociolegal conditions under which Japanese CCL unfolds. LOS has been widely used to assess the likelihood that a particular social movement will pursue legal mobilization, typically involving three core indicators: access to courts, existing law, and judicial receptiveness. Originally developed in studies of the Global North, the framework has also been adapted for the Global South. Setzer and Benjamin (2019, 2020) highlighted distinctive characteristics of Global South cases, including stronger reliance on human rights claims and more proactive judicial remedies for climate-related rights violations. Their work illustrates how LOS analysis can reveal contrasts between regions where CCL is more established (in the West) and those where it is still emerging (the Global South).

This study extends that comparative perspective by focusing on Japan – a country generally categorized as part of the Global North but whose CCL practice remains relatively undeveloped compared to Western counterparts. To properly assess Japan's sociolegal context, the LOS framework requires modification. Certain structural features – low litigation rates, widespread civic unfamiliarity with the judicial system, and limited experience with climate-related judgments – pose major obstacles. With only five major cases to date and no binding precedent, CCL in Japan faces both practical/institutional and cognitive barriers. At the same time, Japan's legacy of antipollution lawsuits provides important historical reference points.

Accordingly, this study adapts the LOS framework in three ways: First, the indicator of access to the courts (discussed in Section 5.2) is expanded to include not only legal standing but also the resources necessary for citizens to initiate litigation. These resources may be financial (e.g., funding, donations) or professional, particularly access to attorneys willing and able to support climate-related claims.

Section 5.3 examines posed by Japan's existing legal framework, including its statutes and case law. This second LOS indicator traditionally focuses on analysis of favorable statutory frameworks and legal precedents. In Japan, however, the absence of meaningful CCL precedents has led attorneys in the four major cases to rely heavily on environmental case law to bridge normative gaps in climate regulation. For this reason, the study places greater emphasis on precedents from environmental lawsuits.

In Section 5.4, the focuses switches to judicial receptiveness, the third LOS indicator, which concerns the characteristic tendencies of the Japanese judiciary. Here, too, past environmental rulings are particularly instructive, since judicial attitudes vary across different fields of law in Japan.[1]

For comparative purposes, these discussions primarily refer to the United States, which accounts for approximately 65 percent of all CCL globally and has generated case law that has shaped the conventional model of CCL. However, a secondary comparison is made with South Korea, whose experience is especially relevant as another East Asian country with a legal system and social conditions resembling Japan's. Section 5.5 concludes the chapter with a discussion of the procedural relationship and weight distribution between the three LOS indicators.

5.2 Access to the Courts

5.2.1 *Standing*

Standing – the right of a party to bring a claim – is the first major hurdle in initiating legal litigation. In most jurisdictions, including the United States, South Korea, and Japan, standing requirements are intended to ensure that only appropriate claims are adjudicated. However, when applied too strictly,

1 As we saw earlier, courts in Japan have generally taken a conservative approach on issues that may offend the government's discretion (Secs. 1.2.3 and 4.2.3). However, they have shown a readiness to protect human rights, for example in interpreting the provisions of the Constitution, especially Article 13 (Urabe 2016, 44–50).

these requirements can impede access to justice, particularly in environmental cases.

Internationally, various efforts have been made to loosen standing barriers. The Aarhus Convention (1998) operationalizes the participatory principles of Principle 10 of the 1992 Rio Declaration.[2] Article 9 calls for broad and flexible interpretations of standing to facilitate public participation in environmental litigation.[3]

Similarly, the UNEP Bali Guidelines (2010) provide further nonbinding guidance, establishing a normative standard for interpreting Principle 10 through twenty-six recommendations – twelve of which concern access to justice.[4] Guideline 18 recommends that states "should provide a broad interpretation of standing in proceedings concerned with environmental matters to achieve effective access to justice."

---

2 Principle 10 of the Rio Declaration reads: "Environmental issues are best handled with the participation of all concerned citizens at the relevant level. At the national level, each individual shall have appropriate access to information on the environment as held by public authorities, including information on hazardous materials and activities in their communities, and the opportunity to participate in decision-making processes. States shall facilitate and encourage public awareness and participation by making information widely available. Adequate access to judicial and administrative proceedings, including redress and remedy, shall be provided." Rio Declaration (Chapter 2, supra note 7).

3 Article 9(2) of the Aarhus Convention (Access to Justice): "Each Party shall, within the framework of its national legislation, ensure that concerned members of the public (a) Having a sufficient interest or, alternatively, (b) Maintaining impairment of a right, where the administrative procedural law of a Party requires this as a precondition, have access to a review procedure before a court of law and/or another independent and impartial body established by law to challenge the substantive and procedural legality of any decision, act, or omission subject to the provisions of Article 6 and, where so provided for under national law and without prejudice to paragraph 3 below, of other relevant provisions of this Convention. What constitutes a sufficient interest and impairment of a right shall be determined in accordance with the requirements of national law and consistently with the objective of giving the public concerned broad access to justice within the scope of this Convention. To this end, the interest of any nongovernmental organization meeting the requirements referred to in Article 2, Paragraph 5 shall be deemed sufficient for the purpose of subparagraph (a) above. Such organizations shall also be deemed to have rights capable of being impaired for the purpose of subparagraph (b) above." Aarhus Convention (Chapter 2, supra note 7), see https://unece.org/fileadmin/DAM/env/pp/documents/cep43e.pdf.

4 Bali Guidelines for the Development of National Legislation on Access to Information, Public Participation and Access to Justice in Environmental Matters, adopted by the UNEP Governing Council in 2010, https://www.unep.org/resources/publication/bali-guideline-implementation-guide.

Building on these developments, the Environmental Democracy Index (EDI) was launched in 2015 by the World Resources Institute (WRI) and The Access Initiative (TAI).[5] The EDI operationalizes the Bali Guidelines through seventy-five legal indicators and twenty-four practice indicators (Okubo 2017). Notably, Indicator 18 addresses standing through both a legal and a practice indicator (Table 6).

The EDI was the first systematic international assessment of environmental democracy, covering seventy countries with input from over 140 legal professionals. Each indicator, including standing (Indicator 18), was scored from 0 to 3 based to the level of public access to justice.[6] Both the United States and Japan were included in this assessment (South Korea was not). As of this writing, none of the three countries has ratified the Aarhus Convention. The EDI ranked the United States third overall, with a mean score of 2.2, while Japan ranked thirty-third, with a mean score of 1.5. Table 7 presents their scores on the issue of standing.

Both countries scored 1 on the legal indicator, reflecting relatively restricted standing in statutory terms. However, practice indicator 18-1 reveals a sharp divergence: the United States scored 2, while Japan scored 0.[7] This difference reflects the fact that, in practice, US law provides multiple pathways for citizen groups to obtain standing, leading to more active legal mobilization, despite the leniency of the statutory system. By contrast, Japanese citizens and NGOs face stricter barriers to participation. The following paragraphs examine how standing is established in each country, the role of group actions, and the relevant judicial precedents shaping these conditions.

In the United States, most environmental cases fall into two categories: judicial review and citizen suit (Hatakeyama 2008; Salzman 2019, 391–393). Judicial review is governed by the Administrative Procedure Act (APA), which establishes a general standing requirement for federal plaintiffs. Article 702 provides that: "A person suffering legal wrong because of agency action, or adversely affected or aggrieved by agency action within the meaning of a relevant statute, is entitled to judicial review thereof."[8]

---

5 EDI and its Technical Note, May 18, 2015, https://www.wri.org/environmental-democracy-index.

6 EDI Full Result Data, available for download via https://www.environmentaldemocracyindex.org/node/13967.html.

7 The scoring of the practice indicators was based qualitative methods due to the difficulty of achieving quantitative evaluations. EDI Technical Note (supra note 5), p. 7.

8 Administrative Procedure Act, 5 U.S.C. §§ 551–559.

TABLE 6 Guidance notes for EDI Indicator 18

Legal Indicators	Guidance Note
1. To what extent does the law recognize broad legal standing in proceedings concerned with environmental matters?	**The broadest standing** would allow challenges to a decision to be made by anyone acting in the public interest and out of a good faith sense of civic consciousness. **A less broad level** would allow all members of the public potentially affected, including environmental NGOs whose work encompasses the potentially affected geographical area, even if they are not necessarily located in that geographical area. **A more restrictive legal standing** would allow a challenge to be brought by anyone potentially affected by a decision, including NGOs located in the potentially affected area, but not those from outside it. **A still more restrictive legal standing** would allow standing only to persons with a proprietary interest in the decision. Where there are limitations on standing, make a note of them in the comment box. Where there are laws/decisions that broaden standing, note them in the comment box as well. **SCORING GUIDE** The law recognizes broad legal standing (e.g., any member of the public acting in the public interest) in all proceedings connected with environmental matters = 3 The law recognizes broad legal standing in **some** proceedings concerned with environmental matters but more restrictive legal standing (e.g., the potentially affected public) in others = 2 The law recognizes restrictive legal standing (e.g., potentially affected people) in most proceedings concerned with environmental matters = 1 The law restricts standing to those people who can show a proprietary interest in the decision = 0

SOURCE: REPRODUCED FROM EDI TECHNICAL NOTE, P. 38

This provision has often been read as enabling public actions in which private individuals act as "private attorneys general," representing broader public interests (Mashaw, Merrill and Shane 2009, 1101). Relying on this statute, numerous public interest lawsuits have gradually expanded the scope of

TABLE 7 Scores for EDI Indicator 18: United States and Japan

Countries	L1	P1
United States	1	2
Japan	1	0

Notes: L = legal indicator, P = practice indicator
SOURCE: REPRODUCED FROM EDI FULL RESULT DATA

standing in judicial practice.[9] The US Supreme Court has clarified four criteria for the admissibility of standing:[10]

> First, plaintiffs must prove that the questioned action has caused or will cause plaintiff injury in fact. Second, he or she must demonstrate that this injury is attributive to the action. Third, the plaintiff must show that the court can redress the injury by some form of available relief. Fourth, the judiciary prudentially tasks it by itself not to infringe on the legislative or executive domain. The injury must be within the zone of interest that the underlying substantive statute is designed to protect. (Hatakeyama 2008, 148–149; Salzman 2019, 393)

These requirements, designed to establish clear a cause-and-effect relationship, are particularly demanding in CCL, where traceability and redressability are often contested. A key turning point was the 2007 US Supreme Court decision in *Massachusetts v. EPA* – the first to officially recognize CO_2 as a pollutant subject to regulation under the Clean Air Act (CAA) – which has been viewed as substantially lowering these barriers in favor of climate action.[11]

The case, brought by twelve US states and thirteen environmental organizations, sought regulation of GHG emissions from new motor vehicles. Standing – especially the element of redressability – was a central focus.

9 The notion of public interest litigation has many diverse definitions. The tenth edition of *Black's Law Dictionary* (Garner et al. 2014) defines it as the "legal practice that advances social justice or other causes for the public good." See also Ramsden and Gledhill (2019, 425).

10 These four criteria have been consistently recognized across multiple court rulings as necessary for establishing standing. A typical example is *Lujan v. Defenders of Wildlife*, 504 U.S. 555 (1992).

11 *Massachusetts* (Chapter 1, supra note 5); Clean Air Act, originally established 1963, amended 1965, 1967, 1970, 1977, 1990, and 2022, 42 U.S.C. 85, 7401–7671q.

The court acknowledged that regulating vehicle emissions alone would not reverse global warming, given other domestic and international sources. Still, it rejected the argument that this limitation stripped courts of authority and affirmed the courts' jurisdiction to determine whether the Environmental Protection Agency (EPA) was obligated to act against air pollutants.[12] The court then modified precedent,[13] holding that plaintiffs can satisfy redressability by showing that a favorable ruling would relieve a discrete injury to themselves, even if it does not eliminate all harm. Notably, the court emphasized that the incremental nature of climate change does not negate the relevance of remedies. Measures such as phasing out older, higher-emission vehicles and replacing them with cleaner models could gradually address the harm, and this was sufficient to establish standing.

In 2015, eight years after *Massachusetts*, the case of *Juliana* was filed by twenty-one youth plaintiffs under the age of nineteen. The plaintiffs alleged that the federal government had violated their constitutional rights – under the Fifth and Ninth Amendments – to a climate system capable of sustaining human life.[14] They further argued that the government had breached its obligations under the public trust doctrine by failing to preserve a stable climate as a shared resource.

In November 2016, the US District Court for the District of Oregon denied the government's motion to dismiss, citing *Massachusetts*. The court held that

---

12 Per 42 U.S.C. 7602(g): "The term 'air pollutant' means any air pollution agent or combination of such agents, including any physical, chemical, biological, radioactive (including source material, special nuclear material, and byproduct material) substance or matter which is emitted into or otherwise enters the ambient air. Such term includes any precursors to the formation of any air pollutant, to the extent the Administrator has identified such precursor or precursors for the particular purpose for which the term 'air pollutant' is used." See https://www.law.cornell.edu/definitions/uscode.php?width=840&height=800&iframe=true&def_id=42-USC-1462657843-1186899448&term_occur=40&term_src=.

13 Established in Larson v. Valente, 456 U.S. 228, 244, no. 15, 102 Sup. Ct. 1673, 72 L. Ed. 2d 33 (1982).

14 Amendment 5 reads: "No person shall be held to answer for a capital, or otherwise infamous crime, unless on a presentment or indictment of a Grand Jury, except in cases arising in the land or naval forces, or in the Militia, when in actual service in time of War or public danger; nor shall any person be subject for the same offence to be twice put in jeopardy of life or limb; nor shall be compelled in any criminal case to be a witness against himself, nor be deprived of life, liberty, or property, without due process of law; nor shall private property be taken for public use, without just compensation." Per Amendment 9, "The enumeration in the Constitution, of certain rights, shall not be construed to deny or disparage others retained by the people." US Constitution, ratified in 1788, effective from 1789, https://www.senate.gov/civics/constitution_item/constitution.htm.

it was sufficient for plaintiffs to demonstrate that the requested remedy would slow or reduce the harm, thereby satisfying the redressability requirement. As discussed earlier, redressability is required to admit standing and generally assumed to involve a complete and timely remedy. However, in CCL, emissions reductions may take decades to manifest, and reductions from a single source may not yield sufficient mitigation. These factors have made redressability a recurring barrier to establishing standing.

The *Juliana* case proceeded through complex procedural steps until January 2020, when it was dismissed on the grounds that climate regulation was a matter of policy. In March 2020, plaintiffs petitioned for rehearing *en banc* ("on the bench") before the Ninth Circuit Court of Appeals, which was granted. In March 2021, they submitted a motion to amend their complaint.[15]

Since the 1970s, every major US environmental statute has included citizen suit provisions, which empower private parties to enforce environmental laws.[16] The first such provision appeared in the 1970 amended CAA,[17] granting citizens the right to sue violators for injunctive relief and penalties (Garner et al. 2014, 298). Environmental groups have widely relied on these provisions as tools of advocacy.

Citizen suit provisions enable both individuals and organizations to bring two types of claims not authorized under the APA. First, both may sue public or private entities for violating environmental laws – a strategy frequently used especially by environmental NGOs (Salzman 2019, 392). Second, they may sue government agencies such as the EPA for exceeding their discretion or failing to carry out mandatory duties, thereby enabling private actors to serve as "quasi-public prosecutors." Citizen suits most frequently invoke the Clean Water Act and the Resource Conservation and Recovery Act (Hatakeyama 2008, 295). For instance, between March 2019 and June 2010, sixty citizen suits were filed under the Clean Water Act in California alone, most initiated by environmental groups (California Environmental Protection Agency 2010).

Citizen suits, however, have limitations. To prevent abuse for personal gain, most statutes restrict them to injunctive relief, excluding claims for monetary compensation. Certain violations are exempted for political reasons, and suits are typically permitted only for ongoing violations, not past actions. These

15 Our Children's Trust, the organization supporting the plaintiffs, provides detailed information about the case at https://www.ourchildrenstrust.org/juliana-v-us.

16 See 42 U.S.C. 7604 (Citizen Suits). The only exception is the Federal Insecticide, Fungicide, and Rodenticide Act or FIFRA (Salzman 2019, 392).

17 CAA (supra note 11).

restrictions have influenced the United States' score on the EDI with respect to the scope of citizen suit provisions.

In South Korea, class action lawsuits are generally prohibited, with the sole exception of certain securities-related transactions (Park 2020). There, Securities-Related Class Action Act specifies both the transactions and eligible plaintiffs (Park 2020). This reflects a narrower approach to standing. However, South Korea's legal system includes a Constitutional Court, established under Chapter 6 of the Constitution alongside the ordinary courts under Chapter 5.[18] This court hears appeals beyond the scope of conventional judicial authority, including: (1) constitutional review of statutes, (2) impeachment trials, (3) dissolution of political parties, (4) disputes over authority among state agencies, and (5) constitutional complaints against unlawful state action (Article 111(1)). Inspired by continental European models, notably Germany and France, the Constitutional Court was designed to check government power while operating independently of the general judiciary (Rodrigo 2010).

Japan's standing requirements differ markedly from those of both the United States and South Korea. Article 9 ACLA limits standing to individuals who can demonstrate a specific legal interest harmed by an administrative disposition.[19] Under this framework, organizations typically lack individual rights or legal interests sufficient to qualify as plaintiffs. This restriction severely narrows the strategic options of environmental movements, since organizations are typically better positioned than individuals to shoulder the evidentiary and financial burdens of proving causation. The supportive role of the Kiko Network in Japan's CCL must be understood against this backdrop.

Japanese courts have occasionally interpreted standing more flexibly (Uga 2006, 163–178). One early example is *Sakamoto v. Japan* (1962), a case concerning regulation of public bathhouse locations.[20] The plaintiff, a competing bathhouse owner, claimed economic harm from the approval of a nearby competitor's license. The Kyoto District Court dismissed the case for lack of legal interest, but the Supreme Court reversed the decision, reasoning that the Public Bathhouse Law's aim of preventing excessive competition created a legally protected interest. It concluded that individual economic harm in this context constituted a legitimate legal interest required to admit individual standing (Upham 1987, 240).

18 Constitution of the Republic of Korea, effective on July 17, 1948, https://elaw.klri.re.kr/eng_service/lawView.do?hseq=1&lang=.

19 See Secs. 4.2.3 and 4.2.4 for the role of ACLA in the *Kobe* administrative and *Yokosuka* cases.

20 Saiko Saibansyo [Sup. Ct.], January 19, 1962, 16 Minshu 1–57.

A more recent example is *Citizen Group v. Japan* (2005), known as the *Odakyu Elevated Railroad* case.[21] Local residents sought cancellation and compensation for a project to build an elevated railway, arguing that it would increase noise and vibration and worsen their living environment. They also claimed the rejection of an underground alternative was unjustified. The Supreme Court held that standing under Article 9 ACLA applies to individuals whose legally protected rights or interests are infringed – or are at risk of infringement – and that the relevant regulation must protect individual rather than merely public interests. Applying this reasoning, standing was granted only to residents of areas specifically designated under the Tokyo Metropolitan Government Ordinance on Environmental Impact Assessment as likely to suffer significant environmental impact from the project.[22]

These cases illustrate a pattern in Japanese judicial reasoning: courts emphasize whether a statute specifically protects individual legal interests, rather than whether actual harm has occurred – a notable contrast with the US approach, exemplified by *Massachusetts* (Upham 1987, 240). This interpretive framework, established in the *Odakyu* case, was later invoked in both the *Kobe* administrative case and the *Yokosuka* case, where attorneys submitted local hazard maps to demonstrate plaintiffs' residence in flood- and storm urge–prone zones, along with plaintiffs' ages to underscore their heightened vulnerability to heat-related illnesses.[23]

5.2.2 *Available Resources*

While regulative standing conditions affect access to justice in formal legal processes, the availability of resources determines whether access is feasible in practice. Litigation entails filing fees, administrative expenses, and (in most cases) the professional costs of attorneys and other legal professionals – burdens that often deter ordinary citizens from pursuing environmental cases without external support.

International conventions directly address this concern. Article 9(1) of the Aarhus Convention provides:

> In circumstances where a Party provides for such a review by a court of law, it shall ensure that such a person also has access to an expeditious procedure established by law that is free of charge or inexpensive for

21 *Citizen Group* (Chapter 4, supra note 39).

22 Per Article 13(1) of the Tokyo Metropolitan Government Ordinance on Environmental Impact Assessment (Ordinance No. 96 of 1980).

23 See Secs. 4.2.3 and 4.2.4.

> reconsideration by a public authority or review by an independent and impartial body other than a court of law.

Similarly, the Guideline 20 of the Bali Guidelines emphasize affordability and assistance mechanisms:

> States should ensure that the access of members of the public concerned to review procedures relating to the environment is not prohibitively expensive and should consider the establishment of appropriate assistance mechanisms to remove or reduce financial and other barriers to access to justice.

Building on these principles, the EDI provides specific indicators to evaluate whether legal systems provide affordable access to justice. Table 8 summarizes the legal and practice indicators used in EDI's Guideline 20 assessment.

The EDI includes these indicators in part because it was designed to promote citizen participation in environmental matters, particularly in developing countries. The results for the United States and Japan are shown in Table 9.

Japan outscored the United States on the first two legal indicators, while both countries earned the same points on the remaining ones. Japan's higher score likely reflects the existence of its official legal aid system, established under the Comprehensive Legal Support Act.[24] This system provides financial support to parties unable to pay full legal fees,[25] and its presence was a major factor in Japan's strong EDI showing (Okubo 2017, 42).

In practice, however, the legal aid system is primarily designed to assist parties facing urgent legal issues – such as financial disputes or wrongful accusations – rather than environmental claims, which are not generally regarded as urgent. Statistics confirm that environmental cases receive little to no support under this framework (Figure 4).

Since Figure 4 omits environmental litigation as a category and focuses mainly on individual legal disputes, the EDI results may present a misleading picture.

In reality, plaintiffs in environmental cases are often low-income individuals who face significant obstacles in covering the costs of litigation. This is partly because marginalized communities tend to be disproportionately affected by

---

24 Comprehensive Legal Support Act, Act No. 74 of June 2, 2004, https://www.japaneselawtranslation.go.jp/en/laws/view/3233/en.

25 Japan Legal Support Center, https://www.houterasu.or.jp/en/consultation_service/index.html (in Japanese).

TABLE 8 Guidance notes for EDI Indicator 20

Legal Indicators	Guidance Note
1. To what extent are there legal mechanisms in place to ensure that access to review procedures relating to the environment for members of the public concerned is not prohibitively expensive?	The law (i) requires access to review procedures relating to the environment to **not** be prohibitively expensive, **and** (ii) has legal mechanisms in place to ensure that **all** such review procedures will not be prohibitively expensive **in practice** = 3 The law (i) requires access to review procedures relating to the environment **to not** be prohibitively expensive **and** (ii) has legal mechanisms in place to ensure that **a majority** of review procedure will not be prohibitively expensive **in practice** = 2 The law (i) requires access to review procedures to **not** be prohibitively expensive, **and/or** (ii) has legal mechanisms in place to ensure that **a minority of** review procedures will not be prohibitively expensive **in practice** = 1 The law contains (i) no requirement; **and** (ii) very few or no legal mechanisms to ensure that access to review procedures is not prohibitively expensive = 0
2. To what extent does the law provide assistance mechanisms to reduce financial barriers to access to justice?	The law provides assistance mechanisms to remove **all or most** financial barriers for accessing such problems = 3 The law provides assistance mechanisms **to significantly reduce** financial barriers for accessing such procedures = 2 The law provides some **minimal** assistance mechanisms to reduce financial barriers for accessing such procedures = 1 The law **does not** provide any assistance mechanisms to reduce financial barriers for accessing such procedures = 0
3. To what extent does the law provide assistance mechanisms to reduce gender-related nonfinancial barriers to access to justice?	The law provides assistance to remove **all or most** gender-related barriers for accessing such procedures = 3 The law provides assistance mechanisms to **significantly reduce** gender-related barriers for accessing such procedures = 2 The law provides some **minimal** assistance mechanisms to reduce gender-related barriers for accessing such procedures = 1 The law **does not** provide any assistance mechanisms to reduce gender-related barriers for accessing such procedures = 0

Legal Indicators	Guidance Note
4. To what extent does the law provide assistance mechanisms to reduce other nonfinancial and nongender barriers to access to justice?	The law provides assistance mechanisms to remove all or most nonfinancial and nongender barriers for accessing such procedures = 3 The law provides assistance mechanisms to significantly reduce nonfinancial and nongender barriers for accessing such procedures = 2 The law provides some minimal assistance mechanisms to reduce nonfinancial and nongender barriers for accessing such procedures = 1 The law does not provide any assistance mechanisms to reduce nonfinancial and nongender barriers for accessing such procedures = 0
Practice Indicators	**Scoring Guide**
1. In the last 5 years, has a public interest case relating to environmental or natural resources been filed that was supported by governmental legal aid?	YES LIMITED (only partially supported by legal aid or the legal aid was not from the governmental but a nongovernmental or private source) NO (or no information is accessible to the public to respond to this indicator)

SOURCE: REPRODUCED FROM EDI TECHNICAL NOTE, PP. 42–44

TABLE 9 Scores for EDI Indicator 20: United States and Japan

Countries	L1	L2	L3	L4	P1
United States	0.5	1	0	0	1
Japan	1.5	3	2	0	1

SOURCE: REPRODUCED FROM EDI FULL RESULT DATA

environmental degradation and pollution. Many such individuals live in areas with poor environmental conditions and limited capacity to shield themselves from harm, while their immediate concern remains maintaining health, livelihoods, and day-to-day stability.

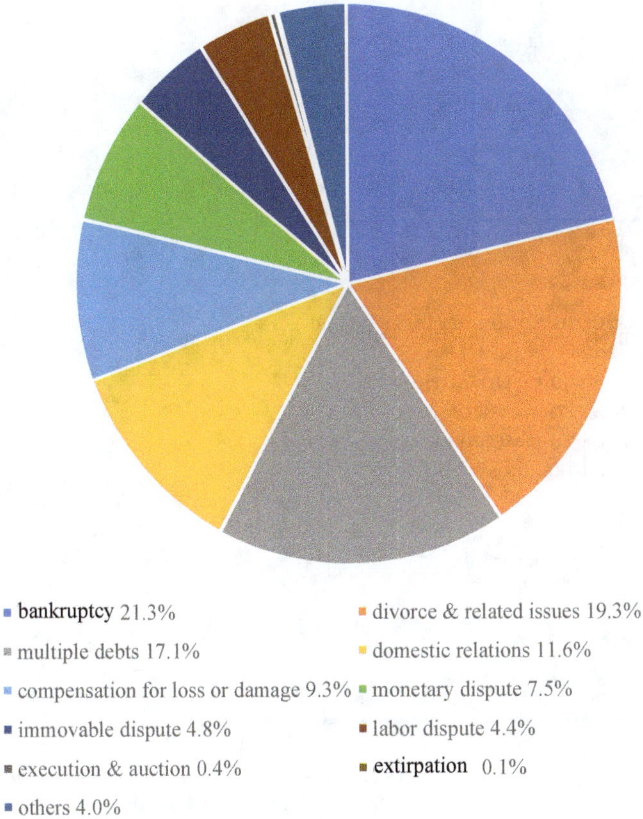

FIGURE 4 Percentages of case categories employing legal aid, 2019
SOURCE: TRANSLATED AND MODIFIED FROM WHITE PAPER ON ATTORNEYS (2020B, 252)

In Japan, as we have seen, the problem is compounded by a lack legal standing for environmental groups. Victims of environmental harm must therefore pursue lawsuits individually, despite the high costs, lengthy procedures, and uncertain outcomes (Hirano 2005, 96–97). Residents of rural areas, where polluting industries often provide vital economic support, are sometimes reluctant to bring cases for fear of jeopardizing local livelihoods (Miyamoto 2012, 6).

These obstacles highlight the need for systematic reform. Despite its challenges, litigation remains one of the most effective means for citizens to raise environmental concerns to both society and government (Awaji 2012, 23–25; Otsuka 2020a, 25–26). In this context, ensuring meaningful access to the courts – particularly through financial support mechanism – is essential to preventing further environmental harm.

Another crucial resource for effective environmental litigation is the availability of qualified legal professionals. In Japan, the number of attorneys

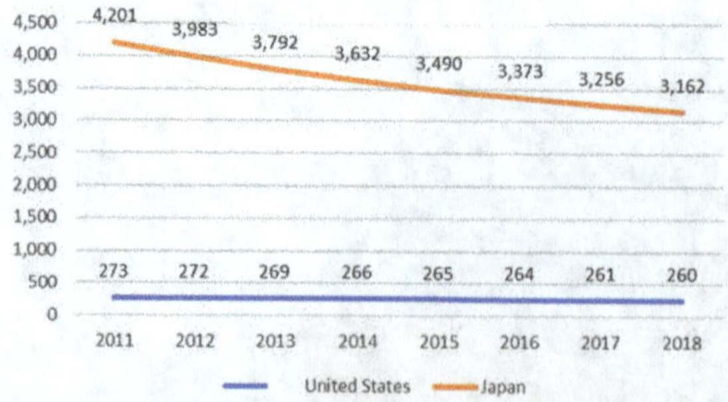

FIGURE 5 Number of citizens per attorney in the US and Japan, 2011–2018
SOURCE: CREATED BY THE AUTHOR BASED ON DATA IN WHITE PAPER ON ATTORNEYS (2018, 63). DUE TO LIMITED AVAILABLE DATA, SOUTH KOREA IS NOT INCLUDED.

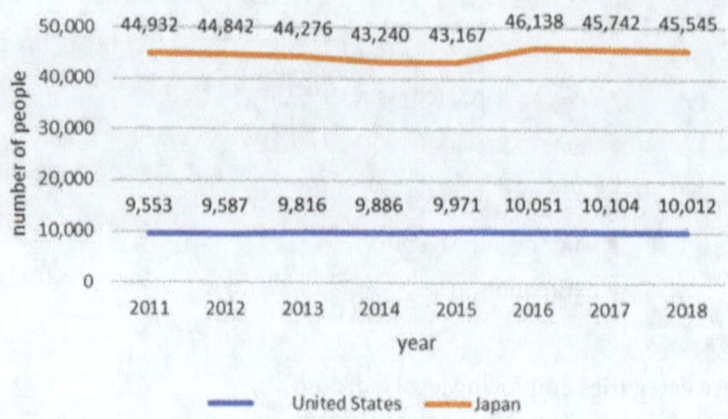

FIGURE 6 Number of citizens per judge in the US and Japan, 2011–2018
SOURCE: CREATED BY THE AUTHOR BASED ON DATA IN WHITE PAPER ON ATTORNEYS (2018, 63). DUE TO LIMITED AVAILABLE DATA, SOUTH KOREA IS NOT INCLUDED – BUT SEE INTERNATIONAL BAR ASSOCIATION (2024, 27).

specializing in environmental cases is limited, and information on both procedures and litigation costs remains scarce. This uncertainty itself acts as a barrier, discouraging citizens from pursuing legal action.

Figures 5 and 6 present the attorney–citizen and judge–citizen ratios in the United States and Japan between 2011 and 2018.

As the figures show, there is a significant disparity among the two countries. Access to attorneys is considerably more widespread in the US, with one attorney per 260 citizens in 2018. By contrast, Japan had one attorney per 3,162 citizens – roughly twelve times fewer. The ratio differences for citizens per judge is

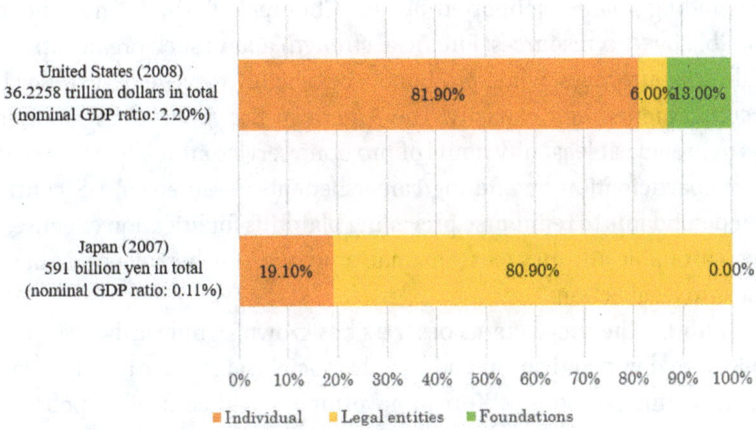

FIGURE 7 Percentage share of donations to US (2008) and Japanese (2007) NPOs
SOURCE: CREATED BY THE AUTHOR BASED ON DATA FROM THE JAPANESE CABINET OFFICE, NPO HOMEPAGE, WHICH INCLUDES DATA BOTH FROM UNITED STATES AND JAPAN, HTTPS://WWW.NPO-HOMEPAGE.GO.JP/KIFU/KIFU-SHIROU/KIFU-HIKAKU (IN JAPANESE)

similarly stark. In 2011, there were 9,553 citizens per judge in the US but 44,932 citizens per judge in Japan.

The social position of nonprofit organizations (NPOs) further shapes legal opportunities. In the United States, NPOs have established considerable credibility and status, attracting substantial financial donations and even being viewed as desirable places of employment (Salmon and Tanner 2024). The financial foundation of US NPOs also surpasses that of their Japanese counterparts, as shown in Figure 7.

The orange belt in Figure 7 represents the share of donations to NPOs made by individuals, the yellow donations by legal entities, and the green donations by foundations.[26] In 2008, total donations in the United States reached 36.23 trillion yen (approximately 3.54 trillion US dollars).[27] That year, donations amounted to 2.2 percent of US nominal GDP – twenty times Japan's 2007 ratio of 0.11 percent.

This financial capacity, combined with the established social standing of US environmental organizations, enables them to pursue legal action through citizen suits and other administrative procedures. Several climate change

26 Kidder and Miyazawa (1993, 607) refer to the existence of thousands of voluntary donors who support social movements in the United States.

27 Calculated by the author based on the exchange mean rate in 2008.

cases – including *Juliana*, supported by Our Children's Trust,[28] – have been made possible by NPO resources. Financial strength allows such organizations to hire full-time attorneys, while pro bono work, highly respected in US legal culture, supplements their capacity. The American Bar Association requires attorneys to provide at least fifty hours of pro bono service annually, a rule that incentivizes participation by offering career benefits.[29] Moreover, US courts may order defendants to reimburse prevailing plaintiffs for litigation expenses, including reasonable attorney fees (Salzman 2019, 393), further lowering financial barriers to legal action.

In South Korea, the social status of NPOs has grown significantly since the 1990s, following democratization and broader social transformation (Rodrigo 2010). Prior to this period, the Korean government had controlled political activities and suppressed civic activism. Democratization created an environment more conducive to NPO activity, and today, NPOs often confront government and business interests directly, enjoying considerable media visibility and public support.

By contrast, NPOs in Japan have yet to establish comparable recognition or trust. University students rarely view NPOs as viable employers, and donations remain limited. In 2007, total donations amounted to 591 billion yen – the lowest among the three countries – and represented just 0.11 percent of GDP (Figure 7).[30] Unlike in the US, Japanese attorneys are also not subject to any formal pro bono requirements. Since the antipollution era, most have participated in environmental litigation voluntarily basis or for minimal compensation.[31] These attorneys, while representing only a small fraction of all registered lawyers in Japan, have shaped the country's environmental litigation history.

The attorneys leading Japan's five climate cases reflect this pattern. For instance, the *Kobe* legal team meets monthly online in the evenings, after completing their regular caseloads.[32] Such efforts remain largely invisible to the public, limiting awareness of the potential role of legal professionals in CCL. Consequently, most attorneys prioritize more secure legal practices with

28 On Our Children's Trust, see supra note 15.

29 According to the Association's Model Rule 6.1, "Every lawyer has a professional responsibility to provide legal services to those unable to pay. A lawyer should aspire to render at least (50) hours of pro bono publico legal services per year." See http://www.americanbar.org/groups/probono_public_service/policy/aba_model_rule_6_1.

30 According to the Charities Aid Foundation's 2021 World Giving Index report, Japan ranked 107th out of the 125 "Most Charitable Countries". See https://worldpopulationreview.com/country-rankings/most-charitable-countries.

31 For a list of such cases, see https://www.jelf-justice.org/jelf/wp-content/themes/jelf-justice/backnumber/newsletter/contents/kougaisoshou.html.

32 As observed by the author.

guaranteed incomes. Further complicating matters, Japan adheres to the loser-pays rule[33] – under which plaintiffs must cover defendants' costs if they lose – which further discourages litigation, especially where prospects for success are uncertain.

5.3 Existing Law

5.3.1 *Statutes*

A 2020 policy report by the Grantham Research Institute on Climate Change and the Environment found that every country has at least one climate-related regulation (Setzer and Byrnes 2020, 9).[34] However, as the report notes, the relationship between climate legislation and litigation remains ambiguous. Two contrasting examples illustrate this point. In the United States, over a thousand cases have been filed despite relatively few statutes. Over half of the 1,200 US cases rely on just four legislative domains: the National Environmental Policy Act, the CAA, certain state-level impact assessment laws, and wildlife protection statutes. Conversely, Brazil has twenty-eight climate-related laws – including a national Climate Act that provides a comprehensive legal framework[35] – but only six climate cases, two of which directly invoked climate legislation. Brazil thus exemplifies a country with extensive legislation but limited litigation.

The Grantham Institute report highlights the complementary roles of legislation and litigation. In countries with few climate laws, litigants may push for new statutes. Where frameworks exist, litigation can be used to enforce or improve them.

In the United States, climate cases have spanned a wide spectrum – from tort liability claims against fossil fuel companies (*New York v. BP*) to corporate liability suits over failure to disclose climate risks affecting stock prices (*Exxon Mobil Corp.*).[36] Although thirteen climate-related laws and four policies are in force,[37] most litigation still rests on the four core statutes noted above.[38]

---

33 Per Article 61 (Principle of Burden of Court Costs) of the Code of Civil Procedure, the defeated party bears the court costs. Code of Civil Procedure (Chapter 4, supra note 49).

34 See also the Climate Change Laws of the World (CCLW) website: https://climate-laws.org.

35 Law No. 12, 187, passed in 2009.

36 City of New York v. BP p.l.c., 325 F. Supp. 3d 466 (S.D.N.Y. 2018), https://climatecasechart.com/case/city-new-york-v-bp-plc; In re Exxon Mobil Corp. Derivative Litigation, No. 3:19-cv-01067-K (N.D. Tex. 2019), https://climatecasechart.com/case/von-colditz-v-exxon-mobil-corp.

37 Per the CCLW dataset (supra note 34).

38 The Sabin Center database categorizes US climate litigation into eight types: federal statutory claims, constitutional claims, state law claims, common law claims, public trust

The federal system adds another layer of complexity. Multiple venues allow overlapping jurisdiction, often producing disputes about where to file (Sher 2020). Some state courts have dismissed cases, reasoning that climate change falls under federal jurisdiction because of its transboundary nature. A California state district court noted that a "patchwork of fifty different [state court] answers to the same fundamental global issue would be unworkable. … [T]he transboundary problem of global warming raises exactly the sort of federal interests that necessitate a uniform solution."[39] Others have remanded claims to state courts, pointing to savings clauses in the CAA and Clean Water Act that do not bar state-level causes of action.[40]

South Korea has enacted thirty-one climate-related laws, and twelve cases are listed in the Sabin Center database. These laws cover carbon sinks, emissions trading, insurance for climate disasters, renewable energy, and decarbonization measures. While they have been invoked in litigation, nine of the twelve cases relied on human rights-based claims.[41] Of the remaining three, one seeks to halt a loan to a South Korean company for an overseas fossil gas extraction project due to alleged deficiencies in its EIA (*Kang et al. v. KSURE and KEXIM*); another challenges the National Pension Service for failing to address climate-related risks in its investment strategy, alleging breach of fiduciary duty (*Kim Min et al. v. Kim Tae-Hyun et al.*); and a third seeks disclosure of records from the Service's Fund Management Committee concerning its coal divestment policy (*SFOC et al. v. Minister of Health and Welfare*). All three remain pending.

By contrast, CCL in Japan has drawn on only a handful of statutes. All five cases seek injunctions against CFPPs. The *Sendai*, *Kobe* civil, and *Youth* suits relied solely on Articles 13 and 25 of the Constitution[42] – the basis of *jinkakuken* (personal rights). The *Kobe* and *Yokosuka* administrative cases invoked the EIA Act, the EBA (which specifically addresses EIA for power plants), and the ACLA.

Judicial infrastructure also diverges significantly. Serving a population of around 124 million, Japan maintains one Supreme Court, eight appellate

---

claims, securities and financial regulation claims, trade agreement claims, and adaptation claims.

39 California v. BP plc (/OAK SF I), Nos. C 17-06011 WHA & C 17-06012 WHA, 2018 WL 1064293, at *5 (N.D. Cal. Feb. 27, 2018).

40 A typical precedent is Boulder, 405 F. Supp. 3d at 968–973.

41 For a compilation of South Korean CCL cases, see https://climatecasechart.com/non-us-jurisdiction/south-korea. For legislation, see https://climate-laws.org/geographies/south-korea.

42 For the text of Articles 13 and 25 of the Japanese Constitution, see Chapter 2, supra note 3.

courts, and 203 district courts.[43] The United States, with a population of about 340 million, has 108 federal courts plus numerous state courts.[44] This difference in court-to-citizen ratios may partly explain the stark gap in CCL caseloads (5 in Japan vs. c. 1,200 in the US).

5.3.2 *Case Law*

Case law, or jurisprudence, shows how statutes are interpreted in practice, shaping expectations for future litigation. In this way, judicial interpretation broadens the scope of legal application over time.

In the United States, case law is foundational within the common law system. The landmark 2007 decision in *Massachusetts* was later cited in *Juliana* (2016), where the District Court for Oregon adopted a modified standard for redressability in assessing standing.[45] Plaintiffs in *Juliana* also invoked the public trust doctrine, long applied in environmental cases to argue that governments must safeguard certain natural and cultural resources for public use (Nanda and Ris 1975, 296–298).[46]

In South Korea, the Constitutional Court ruled in August 2024 that the Climate Change Act violated citizens' constitutional right to a healthy environment (Article 35). It ordered the National Assembly to amend the law by February 2026. The judgment consolidated four cases, including one brought by nineteen young people in 2020 and another naming a fetus as a plaintiff (*Woodpecker et al. v. South Korea*).[47] The court held that the state has an constitutional duty to mitigate climate change and that national measures must: (1) reflect Korea's proportional responsibility, based on scientific evidence and international standards; (2) avoid imposing excessive burdens on future generations; and (3) ensure continuous GHG reduction through a clear legal framework. It found the existing law deficient, especially for lacking targets for 2031–2049, and stressed the need to consider impacts on fundamental rights and the limited avenues available to future generations.

Japan also has case law in pollution and environmental litigation, which plaintiffs in the climate cases have drawn upon, as we have seen. One example

43 See https://www.courts.go.jp/about/sosiki/kakyusaibansyo/index.html. It should be noted that some of the larger prefectures have several branches within these jurisdictions.

44 Population figures are World Bank estimates for 2024, see https://data.worldbank.org/indicator/SP.POP.TOTL.

45 The precedent came from *Larson* (supra note 13).

46 For more on the public trust doctrine, see https://www.law.cornell.edu/wex/public_trust_doctrine.

47 Woodpecker et al. v. South Korea, https://climatecasechart.com/non-us-case/woodpecker-et-al-v-south-korea.

is the doctrine of shared responsibility under joint tort, developed in the *Yokkaichi* asthma case (1972), which established that:

> When a victim of a joint tort proves the interconnected nature of the tortfeasors' actions and the causal relationship between the joint tort and the resulting damage, the court presumes causation for each tortfeasor. Under such circumstances, each tortfeasor is liable unless they can prove the absence of causation between their conduct and the damage.[48]

While this doctrine clarified causation, it left unresolved the question of apportioning liability among tortfeasors. This point was clarified in the first *Nishi-Yodogawa* case (1978), which involved air pollution–related health damage, where the court held that liability should be distributed in proportion to each tortfeasor's contribution.[49] Relying on this principle, plaintiffs in the *Kobe* civil case argued that Kobe Steel was evading responsibility for its emissions of PM2.5 and CO_2.

A further issue concerned whether plaintiffs could demand full compensation from a single tortfeasor. If permitted, the defendant could be held responsible for damages caused in part by others, potentially creating inequitous penalties. Legal scholars have long debated this problem. The *Kobe* plaintiffs advanced a theory of proportionate liability, under which each contributor should bear responsibility based on its share of emissions. On this basis, they demanded that Kobe Steel operate its CFPP in a manner that enables compliance with emission-reduction obligations. This is equivalent to a partial emission-reduction obligation calculated from the company's share of all emissions. While limiting the operation of CFPP in this way would be economically unfeasible, the attorneys presented this argument strategically to demonstrate the theoretical logic of proportional responsibility and to press the company toward ceasing operations altogether.[50]

5.4 Judicial Receptiveness

5.4.1 *General Cases*

Judicial receptiveness refers to the degree to which courts admit, even partially, claims brought by social activists (Vanhala 2020, 1). In this context, the

48 *Yokkaichi asthma* case (Chapter 3, supra note 8).
49 *Nishi-Yodogawa* case (Chapter 4, supra note 15).
50 Observed at a meeting held following the hearing on February 16, 2021.

court's substantive authority over the branches of government becomes significant, as activists often seek systemic reforms to address underlying social issues. Where the judiciary holds strong institutional power, activists can pursue strategies such as public interest litigation or citizen suits to demand institutional reform. Thus, the relationship between the judiciary, legislative, and executive branches – the *trias politica* – is central in this regard.

The United States is often viewed as a jurisdiction with a strong tradition of judicial activism, though its character has varied over time. Several institutional features contribute to this reputation. First, US Supreme Court justices hold lifetime appointments, which strengthen their independence and capacity to influence other branches of government. While not all US judges enjoy this level of job security, this protection is particularly important for Supreme Court justices, who issue final decisions that constitute binding precedent within American case law. Second, most US judges, particularly at higher levels, have prior experience in legal practice and policymaking roles within government institutions (Tanaka [1991] 2008, 966–69). This background provides them with a concrete understanding of sociolegal realities, enabling them to interpret laws with a balanced perspective that integrates legal theory and real-world context. Third, as a common law system, the United States places case law at the center of legal development. Public interest litigation – including citizen suits – has long been a recognized strategy for advancing not just the interpretation of statutes but broader institutional reform. This longstanding tradition has also been evident in CCL, as was seen in the *Juliana* case.

In contrast, Japan is widely regarded as a jurisdiction characterized by judicial passivism (Sec. 1.2.3). Rooted in the civil law tradition, the judiciary is generally expected to implement the will of the legislature rather than reshape it. In practice, courts also tend to defer to the discretion of the executive branch, as strongly evidenced in judicial decision-making. Historically, courts have often invoked the doctrine of judicial self-restraint to avoid even minimal risks of encroaching on administrative authority.

A distinctive feature of the Japanese judiciary lies in its system for judge assignment and evaluation. Unlike in the United States, judges in Japan are appointed soon after completing legal training and placed into specific judicial departments. They face reappointment every ten years, based on recommendations from the Supreme Court.[51] Additionally, they are routinely transferred

51 Article 81 of the Japanese Constitution provides the Supreme Court with authority to determine the constitutionality of any law, order, regulation, or official act. However, this authority is rarely exercised in practice. The Constitution of Japan (Chapter 2, supra note 3).

to other locations by the Supreme Court every two to three years. These conditions generate subtle but significant pressure arising from the Supreme Court's evaluations of a judge's achievements throughout their career. Consequently, many judges hesitate to issue rulings that might conflict with the Court's implicit preferences – preferences that frequently align, visibly or not, with government policy. This institutional conservatism has long drawn scholarly critique.[52]

5.4.2 *Antipollution and Environmental Cases*

The US government's limited regulatory response to climate change – particularly under the first Trump administration (2017–2021) – prompted a wave of citizen litigation. Plaintiffs sought not only to advance climate legislation (Peel and Osofsky 2015, 29) but also to reinforce constitutional checks and balances. The *Massachusetts* case (2007) arose during the Bush administration, which had consistently resisted international climate commitments. Under President Trump, further rollbacks of pro-climate initiatives spurred a marked rise in CCL since 2020 (Adler 2019, 5).

In Japan, courts have occasionally departed from their general passivism in the environmental sphere. As we have noted, several landmark rulings of the 1960s and 1970s sided with victims of industrial pollution, contributing to the convening of the "Pollution Parliament" in 1970, which enacted sweeping environmental laws.[53] Simultaneously, environmental movements gained momentum nationwide, not only in heavily polluted regions. During this era, legal opportunities proved most effective when judicial intervention coincided with movement-led social mobilization to exert pressure on the legislature to implement environmental protections (Awaji 2012, 25). It is also significant that many plaintiffs in antipollution cases were gravely ill and required urgent relief. Judges, acutely aware of these circumstances, may have felt compelled by a sense of duty to uphold human rights and ensure access to justice.

It is still too early to assess the policy impact of Japanese CCL, as only four rulings have been issued to date – in the *Sendai*, *Kobe* civil, *Kobe* administrative, and *Yokosuka* cases – and all claims were dismissed. The courts have yet to recognize a legally protected interest, let alone human rights, in relation to climate change. More broadly, Japanese courts have generally taken a highly

---

52 Article 76(3) of the Constitution states: "All judges shall be independent in the exercise of their conscience and shall be bound only by this Constitution and the laws." However, as Urabe (2016, 354–356) claims, the reality is often very far from this ideal.

53 See Sec. 3.2.2 for a discussion of this era of antipollution lawsuits. On the "Big Four" cases, see Chapter 3, supra note 5. See also Kidder and Miyazawa (1993, 611).

conservative approach, granting wide administrative discretion in national climate policy. However, the Osaka High Court's ruling in the *Kobe* administrative case left open the possibility that a right to be free from climate-related harm could form the basis for standing in the future, depending on evolving domestic and international norms. Japanese CCL, therefore, remains in its early stages.

As discussed in the previous chapter (esp. Sec. 4.4), the climate cases typically involve less immediate and severe harm than the earlier antipollution disputes. Courts may therefore be less responsive to plaintiffs' appeals for urgent protection or aid. Nonetheless, Prime Minister Suga's 2020 policy speech announcing Japan's commitment to net-zero GHG emissions by 2050 marked a turning point.[54] Since then, decarbonization efforts have accelerated,[55] and CFPPs now face growing political and operational challenges. These broader social changes may in turn influence CCL outcomes.

Civil and administrative procedures, however, operate under different temporal frameworks. Civil courts must consider all matters presented up to the close of proceedings, whereas administrative courts assess conditions as they existed at the time of the challenged administrative act.[56] In the *Kobe* administrative case, the Osaka District Court explicitly considered the sociolegal context surrounding the final notification under the CFPP's EIA process. This reasoning leaves open the possibility that the *Kobe* civil case – when adjudicated – may reach a conclusion more favorable to the plaintiffs.[57]

5.5 Discussion

The LOS framework raises a central question: How do the three indicators – standing, existing laws, and judicial receptiveness – interact in the context of

54 Suga's speech (Chapter 1, supra note 25).

55 For example, see the various METI press releases under the theme of "Technology for Carbon Neutral" at https://www.meti.go.jp/english/policy/energy_environment/global_warming/technology.html.

56 There is no provision specifying the reference time, but both academic societies and legal practice have treated the relevant point as the time when the questioned disposition was made, which deserves acknowledgment (Fujita [1980] 2004, 446–447).

57 In a previous study on climate change cases in the Global South, each judge's affirmative recognition of plaintiffs' rights concerning climate impacts was highly evaluated (Setzer and Byrnes 2019). The authors concluded that such individual judicial efforts cumulatively encouraged many governments to adopt stronger climate measures. This illustrates how judges can exert political influence on governments.

Japanese CCL? Although prior studies applying the LOS framework in other fields have noted interconnections among the indicators, their dynamics in Japanese CCL warrant closer scrutiny. This section first considers the procedural sequence, then evaluates their relative weight.

5.5.1 *Procedural Relationship among the LOS Indicators*

The foregoing analysis suggests a general procedural relationship among the indicators as they operate within Japanese CCL. First, climate activists seeking institutional reforms to strengthen mitigation typically approach the legislative and executive branches, the most direct and straightforward route. Because most legislation in Japan originates as cabinet-submitted bills, the executive wields substantial influence over lawmaking.[58] Open channels between civil society and the government – including the cabinet – are therefore essential for ensuring public voices are heard. This constitutes a sphere of political opportunity rather than legal opportunity.

Yet both the legislative and executive branches often hesitate to pursue stronger climate regulation, largely due to persistent pressure from business interests.[59] Public awareness of the climate emergency has also proved insufficient to compel decisive action. The UNDP's "People's Climate Vote" (UNDP and University of Oxford 2021) – the world's largest climate opinion survey – ranked Japan third among thirty-seven countries in recognizing the climate crisis, but only seventeenth in believing citizens should take comprehensive action (Table 10). Although some studies, such as one by the Carbon Tracker Initiative (2019),[60] indicate that renewables are becoming cheaper than fossil fuels, many in Japan still perceive large-scale adoption of renewable energy as a driver of higher electricity costs (Yu 2021).

Table 10 suggests that while many Japanese people acknowledge the urgency of climate change, far fewer support immediate, decisive action to address it. This ambivalence allows the government to avoid strong regulation

58 According to a March 2019 *Nikkei* article, statistics suggest that cabinet-submitted bills are far more likely to pass than those introduced by members of congress (Nikkei 2019).

59 Top executives from the business community frequently sit on advisory councils on climate policy legislation, while participation by ordinary citizens and NGOs is extremely rare. This suggests that the business community's perspectives strongly shape the content of climate-related laws and policies. For example, see the list of members of the 11th Subcommittee on the Next-Generation Energy Supply and Demand Structure Aiming for Carbon Neutrality by 2050 at https://www.enecho.meti.go.jp/committee/council/basic_policy_subcommittee/carbon_neutral/011 (in Japanese).

60 Available via https://carbontracker.org.

TABLE 10 Public recognition and support for climate action by country

Ranking	Public belief in the climate emergency	Proportion of respondents who say we should do everything necessary, urgently
1	United Kingdom (81%)	Italy (78%)
2	Italy (81%)	United Kingdom (77%)
3	Japan (79%)	Australia (76%)
4	France (77%)	Spain (75%)
5	Germany (77%)	Canada (75%)
6	South Africa (76%)	France (73%)
7	Canada (75%)	Germany (73%)
...	...	...
17		Japan (62%)

Notes: The "act urgently" group (right) is a subset of the "believe in climate change" group (left).
SOURCE: CREATED BY THE AUTHOR BASED ON FIGS. 3 AND 6 IN UNDP AND UNIVERSITY OF OXFORD (2021, 16, 19)

and discourages activists from mobilizing a broad civil movement. As a result, political opportunities for climate action often appear limited.

In this setting, activists may turn to legal opportunities. Even a small group of plaintiffs can initiate litigation if they meet the requirements for court access – including standing and necessary resources – the first LOS indicator. Existing statutory and case law then shape their arguments – the second indicator. Finally, judicial receptiveness, the third indicator, determines how these claims are processed and resolved. When courts respond favorably, their rulings may pressure the legislature and executive to strengthen climate policy, which in turn can generate further legislation and legal mobilization.

5.5.2 *Weight Distribution among the LOS Indicators*

Although the three LOS indicators function sequentially, examining their relative weight sheds additional light on their role in Japanese CCL. Scholars broadly agree that access to court (standing, resources) – the first indicator – is decisive in shaping legal opportunity (Vanhala 2012, 526–527). As the gateway to litigation, any restriction on standing narrows the range of potential claims.

Here Japan diverges sharply from the United States. Japan's restrictive standing rules, modeled on an earlier version of the German system, remain among the strictest worldwide. Germany has since reformed its model, introducing an alternative legal avenue granting standing to environmental NGOs

(Schall 2008, 436), Japan has not. Attorneys in Japan's five climate cases attempted to establish standing by linking climate change to air pollution. Yet this strategy backfired in *Sendai*, where the presiding judge used it to exclude climate-related damage claims early in the proceedings. More broadly, rigid standing rules and entrenched judicial practices deter citizens and attorneys from pursuing novel arguments. They also prolong preliminary reviews, subsequently delaying substantive examination of arguments and ultimately weakening plaintiffs' and attorneys' motivation to litigate. By contrast, US courts apply more flexible standards that gradually expanded standing through judicial interpretation.

Available resources – particularly financial capacity – play a decisive role in sustaining litigation. While access to qualified lawyers is valuable, in Japan individuals may file lawsuits without legal representation, making this less of a limiting factor. By contrast, insufficient funds often compel litigants to abandon proceedings regardless of their merits.[61] Environmental activists are frequently ordinary citizens or marginalized individuals already burdened with medical expenses, further reducing their ability to finance lawsuits. For this reason, plaintiffs often seek support from organizations and volunteer lawyers. In the five climate cases, most plaintiffs did not suffer direct environmental harm yet still lack the means to sustain long trials. The Kiko Network therefore covers litigation costs and manages financial affairs, while many attorneys participate on a voluntary basis, accepting only nominal fees.

Although resource-related challenges also exist in the United States (Boutcher and McCammon 2019, 309–312), they are generally less severe, as reflected in the large number of climate cases filed there. Numerous non-profit public interest law organizations, such as Earthjustice, provide stable support.[62] In the 2020 fiscal year, Earthjustice paid $4,021,630 in attorney salaries from net assets of $223,636,169.[63] No comparable organization exists in Japan.

The second indicator – existing law (statutes and judicial precedents established by case law) – provides the framework for arguments in court. Here Japan presents a distinctive case. Unlike many constitutions that set out detailed human rights protections – for instance, South Africa's constitutional right to water (Setzer and Benjamin 2020, 97) – Japan's provisions are sparse

61 In the Civil Litigation Surveys conducted in 2001 and 2016, the high cost of litigation expenses was recognized as the second-largest barrier to filing lawsuits. See Sec. 6.2.

62 On which see https://earthjustice.org.

63 According to the organization's audit report at https://earthjustice.org/sites/default/files/files/earthjusticeauditedfinancialsfy20.pdf.

and vague. Although Japan has ratified many international human rights treaties, its courts rarely rely on them, since such treaties appear to rank below the Constitution in legal practice.[64] Even so, constitutional ambiguity leaves space for creative interpretation. Japanese courts have gradually recognized new human rights concepts in environmental and antipollution litigation, including *jinkakuken* (personal rights) and derivative rights to a clean environment, sunlight, and quiet (Sec. 3.2.3). The *Kobe* climate cases extend this line of reasoning by asserting a right to a stable climate system (4.2.2). In several instances, such interpretive strategies have succeeded in securing judicial remedies. Thus, while existing law is not the primary barrier to initiating litigation, it can become a meaningful resource once proceedings begin.

The third indicator – judicial receptiveness – also warrants attention. As noted earlier, Japanese judges wield considerably less influence over policy than their US counterparts. Nevertheless, litigation can achieve indirect effects by raising public awareness and shaping legal discourse. Many plaintiffs pursue litigation not only to win but also to catalyze broader legal and social change.[65] This dynamic mirrors the United States, where climate lawsuits often fail on the merits yet still contribute to climate advocacy (McCormick et al. 2018, 831). Globally, the rise in CCL underscores its function as part of wider social movements (Setzer and Byrnes 2020, 4). Within this context, judicial receptiveness in Japan may carry less weight than the other two indicators.

The interrelationship among the three indicators is illustrated in Figure 8. In sum, access to court – including standing and financial resources – emerges as the most decisive factor in shaping legal opportunity. Since Japanese CCL is still in its early stages, the trajectory of future cases may depend largely on how this first indicator develops.

64 This hierarchy may be at least partly recognized within the text of the Constitution itself. While Article 7 appears to place "treaty" on an even footing with "the constitution, laws, cabinet orders and treaties," Article 98(1) states that the Constitution "shall be the supreme law of the nation and no law, ordinance, imperial rescript or other act of government, or part thereof, contrary to the provisions hereof, shall have legal force or validity." However, Article 98(2) provides that "treaties concluded by Japan and established laws of nations shall be faithfully observed." The Constitution of Japan (Chapter 2, supra note 3).

65 Of Kidder and Miyazawa's (1993) four types of plaintiff objectives, three relate to social change or raising awareness. See Sec 6.4.

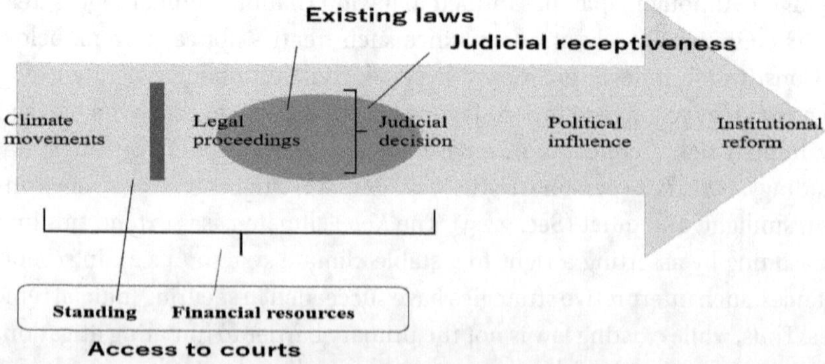

FIGURE 8 Interrelation among the three LOS indicators as applied to Japanese CCL
SOURCE: CREATED BY THE AUTHOR

5.6 Summary

This chapter examined institutional obstacles hindering the development of Japanese CCL through the lens of the adapted LOS framework. Focusing on access to courts (including standing and resources), existing law, and judicial receptiveness, it identified key features of the Japanese context and contrasted them with those in both the United States and South Korea. Findings indicate that access to courts, particularly standing, is the most decisive factor shaping the trajectory of Japanese CCL.

CHAPTER 6

Cognitive Obstacles

6.1 Overview

Chapter 5 identified institutional obstacles to Japanese CCL using the LOS framework, concluding that the most significant barrier lies in access to the courts – particularly strict standing rules and the limited financial resources of many plaintiffs. This chapter turns to cognitive obstacles that may hinder the development of CCL in Japan. Because plaintiffs initiate legal action, their perceptions of legal obstacles are critical in shaping whether they choose to litigate. In this sense, examining plaintiffs' perceptions provides an alternative lens on legal opportunity structures.

This chapter therefore investigates the perceptions of plaintiffs involved in the first four Japanese climate cases, drawing on survey and interview data collected by the author between 2019 and 2024.[1] These individuals likely confronted various cognitive barriers before initiating their lawsuits, while their motivations and expectations played a central role in overcoming them. Both dimensions are key to understanding cognitive obstacles to legal action.

Section 6.2 summarizes findings from previous studies on plaintiff motivations and expectations. Section 6.3 introduces the methods used in the data collection. Section 6.4 presents the first-stage surveys and interviews and Section 6.5 the second survey conducted four years later, in each case presenting and analyzing the results. Section 6.6 then discusses these findings further, identifying shifts in respondents' perceptions and recognition of cognitive barriers between the two survey periods, before addressing continuing barriers to potential litigants. Section 6.7 summarizes the chapter.

6.2 Previous Studies

Several Japanese studies have examined plaintiffs' motivations and expectations regarding barriers to litigation. A key source is the Civil Litigation Survey,

1 It is true that obstacles could be more precisely clarified by those who ultimately refrained from initiating litigation because of such obstacles. However, such individuals cannot practically be surveyed, as their number is indeterminate. As noted earlier, the surveys were conducted prior to the filing of the *Youth* case and therefore do not include that case.

DOI:10.1163/9789004757035_008

TABLE 11 Three highest-ranking motivations and deterrents to litigate according to the 2001 and 2021 Civil Litigation Surveys

	2001	2021
Motivation to bring lawsuit		
Due process and fair solutions	91.1%	87.3%
Protect own rights	86.7%	71.1%
Protect own economic interests	84.8%	67.7%
Disincentive to bring lawsuit		
Lengthiness of proceedings	72.0%	81.8%
Expensiveness of costs	67.2%	74.0%
Desire to avoid conflict	36.6%	35.6%

SOURCE: CREATED BY THE AUTHOR BASED ON DATA FROM SHIHO SEIDO KAIKAKU SHINGIKAI (2001); SUGAWARA AND KAKIUCHI (2023)

a nationwide survey on parties' reasons for initiating lawsuits (2001, 2006, 2011, 2016, 2021).[2] The first survey was conducted in 2001 by the Judicial System Reform Council of the Ministry of Justice. Since then, the Society for the Study of the Civil Procedural System has repeated the survey every five years, targeting parties to cases in selected district courts.[3]

The survey format has remained largely consistent. For example, the 2021 version asked plaintiffs to rate, on a five-point scale, their reasons for filing a lawsuit, using nineteen multiple-choice answers.[4] Motivations included protecting individual freedom, privacy, and health; obtaining a fair resolution; punishing the defendant; resolving a public dispute; securing dialogue with the opposing party; and promoting public interest. The survey also asked respondents to assess factors discouraging litigation across thirteen items, including cost, the length of the proceedings, fear of conflict with the opposing party, concern over social reactions, and lack of familiarity with legal procedures.

The most frequently cited motivations and deterrents to litigate in the 2001 and 2021 surveys are summarized in Table 11.

2 The results of the surveys can be found in the following sources: for 2001, see Shiho Seido Kaikaku Shingikai (2001); for 2006, 2011, and 2016, see Minji Sosyou Seido Kenkyu-kai (2007, 2012, 2018); for 2021, see Sugawara and Kakiuchi (2023). Only the 2011 survey report has been translated into English: see Society for the Study of the Civil Procedural System (2014).

3 For example, the initial 2006 survey selected sixteen district courts and included 592 informants (Sato, Sugawara, and Yamamoto 2006, 2).

4 Sugawara and Kakiuchi (2023, 748).

As the table shows, patterns remained consistent over a ten-year timeframe, with the desire to observe due process and obtain fair resolutions (91%/87%), protect rights (87%/71%), and safeguard economic interests (85%/68%) being the three key drivers behind plaintiffs' motivations to litigate in 2001 and 2021. In both years, the length of proceedings (72%/82%), high costs (67%/74%), and desire to avoid conflict (37%/36%) ranked highest among disincentives to file lawsuits.

Secondary analyses was conducted of the 2001 and 2006 surveys.[5] Using factor analysis, these studies identified two dominant motivational factors affecting litigation. The 2001 survey revealed that plaintiffs sought fair outcomes in terms of both due process and economic interest (Fujimoto 2006, 26). The 2006 survey highlighted the importance of plaintiffs' desire for neutral third-party judgment and their pursuit of psychological satisfaction (Takahashi 2010, 8). Other studies examined the relationship between plaintiffs' expectations and personal characteristics, such as Kinoshita (2006).

Notably, gaps between expectations and reality – particularly with respect to time and cost – were found to be strong deterrents to litigation in the 2001 survey (Fujita 2006). Uncertainty over outcomes discouraged litigants more than the actual duration or expenses they ultimately experienced. Consequently, Fujita (2006) recommended expanding public access to legal information. Similar results emerged from the secondary analysis of the 2006 survey, which also emphasized "hesitation to hire attorneys" as an additional hurdle (Fujita 2010). More recent qualitative analyses (Sugawara et al. 2021) identified ensuring patterns, including the high barrier to legal access faced by young people (Hashiba 2023, 59) and a continuing reluctance among individuals in general to initiate litigation (Hori 2023, 127).

Another important study by Kidder and Miyazawa (1993) investigated plaintiffs' motivations and expectations in two Japanese air pollution cases: the *Amagasaki* case (1988) and the *Nishi-Yodogawa* case (1978).[6] The authors found that, paradoxically, the small number of environmental lawsuits in Japan gave them disproportionate political and social influence – an effect plaintiffs themselves sought to leverage. From this perspective, even protracted litigation played a strategic role by sustaining pressure on public institutions. Kidder and Miyazawa identified four categories of plaintiff objectives in these

5 For analysis of the 2001 survey, see Sato, Sugawara, and Yamamoto (2006); for the 2006 survey, see Sugawara, Yamamoto, and Sato (2010).

6 On these two cases, see Sec. 4.2.2. For citations, see *Amagasaki* (Chapter 4, supra note 17); *Nishi-Yodogawa* (Chapter 4, supra note 15).

cases: obtaining compensation damages, securing legal victory, achieving nationwide justice, and advancing global environmental awareness.

6.3 Methodology

To contribute a multi-case study from the emerging field of CCL, this research examines plaintiffs' perceptions of the legal proceedings through surveys and interviews conducted as part of the author's PhD research. The data was collected in two broad stages: In the first stage (Sec. 6.4), a pilot survey was conducted with plaintiffs and auditors in the *Kobe* civil case in October 2019, followed by surveys with the same in the *Sendai* and *Kobe* administrative cases (both Nov. 2019) and the *Yokosuka* case (Dec. 2019). Semi-structured interviews with *Kobe* litigants took place across November and December 2019, while the same were administered to those involved in *Sendai* and *Yokosuka* in March 2020. Throughout this first stage, respondents were plaintiffs and auditors (Table 12).

In the second stage of data collection (Sec. 6.5), the target respondents expanded to include supporters of the litigants. Surveys were carried out with respondents in the *Sendai* and *Yokosuka* cases in April 2024, followed by those involved in the two *Kobe* cases from April to November 2024 (Table 21). As of that time, both the *Sendai* and *Kobe* administrative case had concluded. As mentioned, neither stage included the *Youth* case due to the timing of data collection.

6.4 First-Stage Surveys and Interviews

In the *Kobe* and *Yokosuka* cases, respondents included courtroom auditors, individuals who regularly observe hearings. Although not formal plaintiffs, auditors arguably share similar concerns and interests. Many made efforts to participate actively by attending proceedings, and in the *Kobe* cases most had previously submitted petitions during mediation or arbitration. Their perspectives therefore provide valuable insights into perceptions of legal obstacles. Details of the surveys in the first stage are presented in Table 12 and the demographic characteristics of respondents in Table 13.

After an in-person pilot survey with participants in the *Kobe* civil case in October 2019, questionnaires were administered to *Kobe* administrative and *Sendai* participants in the November, with the *Yokosuka* survey following in December. In the two *Kobe* and *Yokosuka* cases, questionnaires were conducted

TABLE 12 Details of the first-stage surveys

Cases	*Kobe* civil (pilot)	*Kobe* (administrative)	*Sendai*	*Yokosuka*
Survey date	Oct. 15, 2019	Nov. 22, 2019	Nov. 29, 2019	Dec. 23, 2019
Survey format	In-person	In-person	Mail	In-person
Total number of plaintiffs	40	12	124	45
Number of respondents	27 Plaintiffs: 11 Auditors: 16	6 Plaintiffs: 2 Auditors: 4	49 Plaintiffs: 49	60 Plaintiffs: 23 Auditors: 37

SOURCE: CREATED BY THE AUTHOR

TABLE 13 Demographic characteristics of respondents to the first-stage surveys on *Sendai*, *Kobe*, and *Yokosuka*

	Kobe (n = 33)	*Sendai* (n = 49)	*Yokosuka* (n = 60)
Gender			
Male	48% (16)	71% (35)	50% (30)
Female	45% (15)	29% (14)	38% (23)
No answer	7% (2)	0% (0)	12% (7)
Age			
≤30	15% (5)	0% (0)	7% (4)
31–40	6% (2)	2% (1)	3% (2)
41–50	6% (2)	8% (4)	3% (2)
51–60	3% (1)	8% (4)	13% (8)
61–70	30% (10)	33% (16)	23% (14)
70 >	30% (10)	49% (24)	40% (24)
No answer	10% (3)	0% (0)	10% (6)
Children			
Have	64% (21)	84% (41)	62% (37)
Have not	24% (8)	14% (7)	23% (14)
No answer	12% (4)	2% (1)	15% (9)
Residence (proximity from CFPP)			
≤ 5 km	45% (15)	49% (24)	20% (12)
5–10 km	6% (3)	12% (6)	38% (23)

TABLE 13 Demographic characteristics of respondents (*cont.*)

	Kobe (n = 33)	*Sendai* (n = 49)	*Yokosuka* (n = 60)
10 km >	39% (13)	39% (19)	28% (17)
No answer	6% (2)	0% (0)	13% (8)
Vocation			
Retired or social activist	51% (17)	37% (18)	42% (25)
Full-time worker	3% (1)	20% (10)	19% (11)
Part-time worker	6% (2)	0% (0)	0% (0)
Medical worker	0% (0)	10% (5)	5% (3)
Educational/childcare worker	0% (0)	10% (5)	7% (4)
Homemaker	3% (1)	12% (6)	5% (3)
Student	12% (4)	2% (1)	3% (2)
Other	15% (5)	0% (0)	0% (0)
No answer	9% (3)	8% (4)	20% (12)
Educational background			
Compulsory (junior high school)	0% (0)	6% (3)	2% (1)
High school	18% (6)	26% (14)	37% (22)
College/vocational school	12% (4)	10% (5)	17% (10)
University/higher education	61% (20)	55% (27)	32% (19)
Other	0% (0)	0% (0)	2% (1)
No answer	9% (3)	0% (0)	12% (7)
Income (in million yen)			
≤ 2.0	12% (4)	12% (6)	18% (11)
2.1–3.0	12% (4)	20% (10)	27% (16)
3.1–5.0	36% (12)	31% (15)	27% (16)
5.1–8.0	12% (4)	10% (5)	8% (5)
8.1–10.0	12% (4)	10% (5)	3% (2)
10.1–15.0	0% (0)	12% (6)	0% (0)
15.1–20.0	0% (0)	4% (2)	0% (0)
20.1 >	0% (0)	0% (0)	0% (0)
No answer	15% (5)	0% (0)	17% (10)
Appearance at past hearings			
Yes (at least once)	85% (28)	65% (32)	47% (28)
No	0% (0)	29% (14)	40% (24)
No answer	15% (5)	6% (3)	13% (8)

Notes: The figures for *Kobe* comprise both civil and administrative cases (cf. Table 12). Percentages are rounded; ≤ less than or equal to; > greater than.

SOURCE: CREATED BY THE AUTHOR

in person to both plaintiffs and auditors on the date of a court hearing. However, this was not possible with *Sendai* participants. By November, nearly two years had passed since that case had been initially filed (September 2017; see Table 3), and courtroom attendance had noticeably declined. At the ninth hearing in the Sendai District Court, held on November 30, 2019, only about 15 out of the 124 plaintiffs were present.[7] Accordingly, printed surveys were mailed directly to plaintiffs' residences. Only plaintiffs were contacted, as auditors' addresses could not be identified.

6.4.1 *Survey Respondent Demographics*

Table 13 reveals distinct demographic profiles across the three respondent groups (combining the two *Kobe* suits into one). In *Sendai*, 49 out of 124 plaintiffs (39%) responded to the survey, most of whom were male (71%), older than sixty (81%), and parents (84%). Educational attainment was relatively high (55% university graduates, some with advanced degrees), and income levels skewed higher than in the other cases, with 37 percent reporting annual incomes above five million yen. Leadership was concentrated in two university professors, and nearly a third of respondents had no prior courtroom experience. Nearly half of respondents (49%) lived within 5 kilometers of a CFPP.

For the *Kobe* cases combined, thirteen out of fifty-two plaintiffs (25%) responded, though this number of was supplemented with twenty auditor respondents. In contrast to *Sendai*, the response group displayed near gender parity and greater generational diversity, with 61 percent over sixty years old. Educational attainment was the highest among the three cases (61% university graduates), possibly reflecting the concentration of universities in Kobe and its surrounding region. A high proportion of respondents (85%) had attended at least one hearing, indicating active engagement, while 45 percent reported living within five kilometers of a CFPP. A majority (61%) reported annual incomes up to five million yen, while just over half (51%) were retirees or activists, suggesting the *Kobe* cases were strongly rooted in grassroots civic action.

The *Yokosuka* respondent group was the largest, with just over half of all plaintiffs participating, supplemented by thirty-seven auditors. It was the second-oldest (63% over sixty) and most economically modest, with 72 percent reporting annual incomes up to five million yen. Educational attainment was also lower (37% high school graduates), and leadership came from a retired teacher and local activist rather than university professors.[8] Only 47

7 Directly observed by the author. As previous research notes, participation tends to diminish over time as momentum and commitment wane (Kidder and Miyazawa 1993, 619).

8 This teacher recruited friends, colleagues, and acquaintances to join the case. Interviews with the author, March 3–6, 2020.

percent had attended at a hearing previously, suggesting a less legally experienced group but one shaped by strong community ties. A lower percentage (20%) reported living within five kilometers of a coal plant; however, this share increased for those living within ten kilometers or less (57%, compared to 55% in *Kobe* and 61% in *Sendai*).

Taken together, the three respondent group profiles reveal that Japanese CCL is largely driven by older (70 or older), middle-income (2–5 million yen annual income) individuals – often retirees or social activists – who possess the time and resources to sustain lengthy lawsuits. The suggests the difficulty of engaging in long-term litigation during one's working life and the necessity of a certain level of financial stability to do so. The data shows that *Sendai* was propelled by a highly educated, professionally connected cohort led by university professors; *Kobe* combined a university-influenced group with broader grassroots participation; and Yokosuka reflected a retiree-led citizen movement with modest means but strong local ties. These contrasts highlight how social composition shapes litigation strategies and engagement, while the common reliance on older, economically stable participants underscores the challenges of mobilizing younger generations in CCL.

6.4.2 *Survey Questions*

Respondents were asked to rate a series of statements about their experience of litigation across the following areas:

- Motivations to litigate: Their reasons for becoming plaintiffs or auditing the case (Q1)
- Expectations: What they thought might be the outcomes of the case (Q2)
- Air pollution versus climate change: Whether they recognized differences between the two types of lawsuit (Q3)
- Protracted proceedings: Their perception of the effects of a lengthy trial (Q4) (asked to plaintiffs only)

For Q1, Q2, and Q4, respondents were asked to rate each statement on a five-point scale, from 1 (not at all relevant) to 5 (very relevant). Responses of 4 (considerably relevant) and 5 were treated as affirmative (and are thus the basis of the figures below), and in the case of Q1 led to a further question (Q1-1). For Q3, respondents selected one of three options that best reflected their recognition of the differences between air pollution and CCL. Nine further questions were asked to collect the demographic data presented in Table 13.[9]

9 For full details of the first-stage survey questionnaire, see Appendix 1.

After the *Kobe* pilot survey, some questions were revised: notably, Q2 and Q3 were not included in either *Kobe* surveys. Most questions were adapted from the Civil Litigation Survey mentioned in the previous section, with several additional items developed by the author to address climate change–specific issues. For example, Q3 was designed to compare plaintiffs' perceptions in past antipollution cases with those in CCL and subsequently included in the other three surveys.

6.4.3 *Survey Results*

On what their motivations were to litigate (Q1), respondents were asked to rate nine reasons:[10] to protect self and others from air pollution (statement 1), to protect future generations from air pollution (S2), to protect self and others from global warming (S3), to protect future generations from global warming (S4), to raise public awareness (S5), to support or work with civil society (S6), to achieve a solution to the issue (S7), to win the case in court (S8), and to prove litigation the most effective strategy to solve the problem (S9).

Figure 9 presents the number of respondents who rated items 4 (considerably relevant) or 5 (very relevant). Statements 1 to 4 investigated whether respondents were primarily concerned with air pollution or global warming, and whether they were motivated by protecting current or future generations.[11] High affirmative rates were recorded across all four statements. However, protecting future generations from air pollution (S2) and protecting the current generation from climate change (S3) drew slightly fewer responses. Support for civil society cooperation (S6) also scored highly, while raising public debate (S5) was rated as less motivating. Confidence in judicial victory (S8) was relatively low. Although many respondents considered litigation a legitimate means to pursue fundamental solutions (S7), fewer regarded it as the most effective strategy overall (S9).

---

10 As has been noted in the text, in both the first-stage and second-stage surveys, not all questions were asked of both plaintiffs and auditors. However, readers should also note that the wording, and in some cases the number, of statements differed slightly between plaintiff and auditor questionnaires. The examples in the text generally refer to the plaintiff statements, but most results depicted in figures encompass both groups unless otherwise specified. See Appendixes 1 and 2 for the full questionnaires in each survey.

11 Although both terms are used interchangeably throughout this analysis (and in the appendixes), the original questionnaires adopted the term "global warming" rather than for "climate change" because plaintiffs and attorneys in all four cases preferred the former term. In Japan, "global warming" has historically been more widely used and may be more readily understood by the general public. The author ran a search on Google Trends, revealing that "global warming" consistently appears more frequently than "climate change" as of 2020.

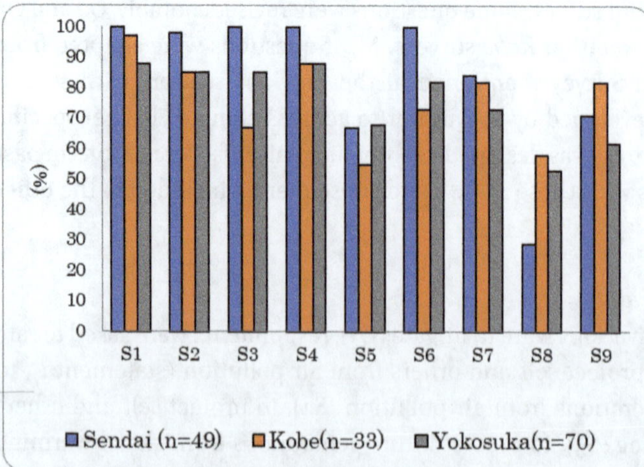

FIGURE 9 Motivations to litigate (Stage 1 Survey Q1)
SOURCE: CREATED BY THE AUTHOR

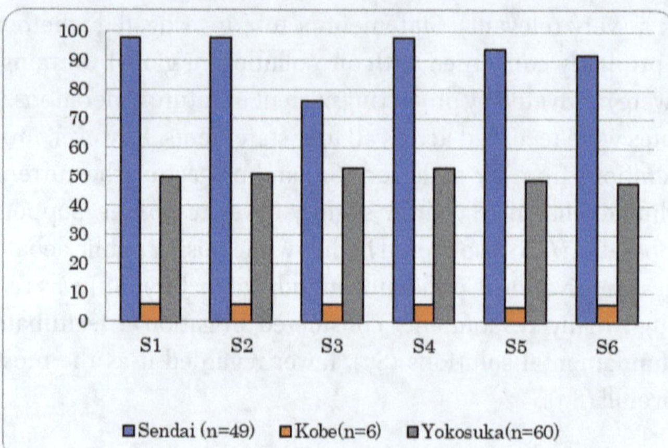

FIGURE 10 Expectations about case outcomes (Stage 1 Survey Q2)
SOURCE: CREATED BY THE AUTHOR

On their expectations about case outcomes (Q2), respondents were presented with six statements: improvement in current (S1) and future (S2) air quality, mitigation of current (S3) and future (S4) adverse effects of global warming, pressure government and municipal authorities (S5), and broader social impact (S6) (Figure 10).

It should be noted that responses from the two *Kobe* cases are excluded here, as this question was not included in the pilot survey. As in the motivations question, four items addressed concerns about air pollution and climate change, and about protecting current or future generations. Respondents expressed strong concern about air quality (S1, S2), particularly in the *Sendai* case, but showed less concern about present (as of 2019) effects of global warming (S3). By contrast, *Yokosuka* respondents indicated greater concern about climate change than air pollution, as reflected in a comparison of their responses to S1–S2 and S3–S4. Expectations of pressure on government and municipal policy (S5) and litigation's broader social impact (S6) also received high marks, suggesting that plaintiffs viewed litigation as a tool for achieving both legal and societal objectives.

The third question – asking respondents if they recognize differences between air pollution litigation and CCL – gave three response options: Yes, No, and I don't know (Figure 11).

As Figure 11 shows, while the most frequently selected responses differed between the *Sendai* and *Yokosuka* cases, nearly one-fourth of respondents in both groups regarded the two types of litigation as essentially the same. A considerable number of respondents also selected "I don't know." Again, this question was not asked in the *Kobe* pilot.

The question on the perceived effect of lengthy proceedings (Q4) was directed only at plaintiffs (not auditors). Respondents were given eight statements, the first five of which were on the perceived benefits of a lengthy trial and the final three on the disadvantages. The positive statements suggested

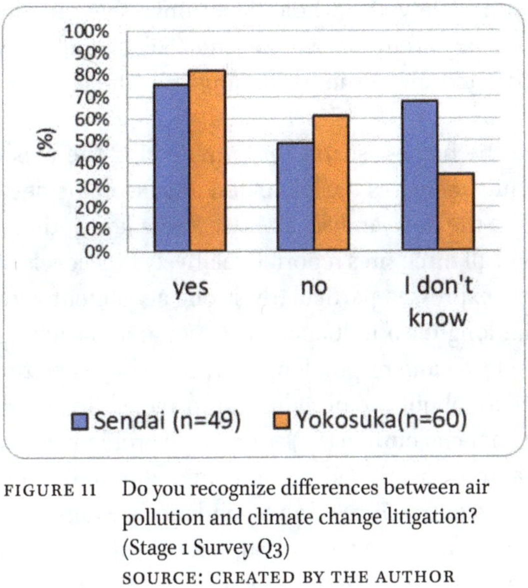

FIGURE 11 Do you recognize differences between air pollution and climate change litigation? (Stage 1 Survey Q3)
SOURCE: CREATED BY THE AUTHOR

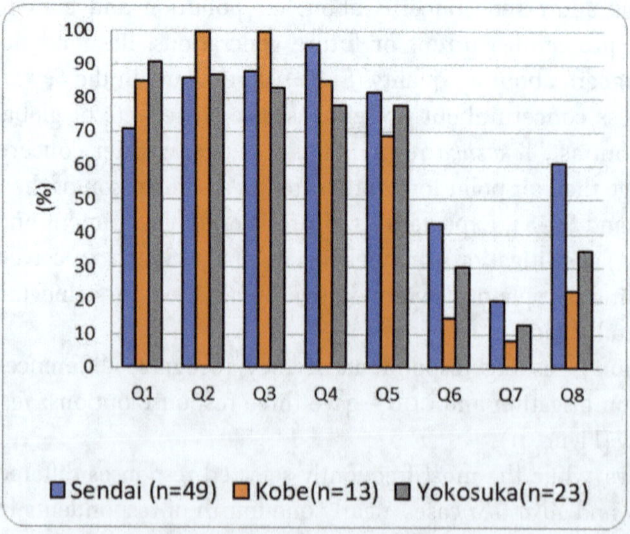

FIGURE 12 Perceived effect of protracted proceedings (Stage 1 Survey Q4)
SOURCE: CREATED BY THE AUTHOR

that a protracted trial would motivate positive action and thereby increase the possibility of a desirable outcome (S1), advance solidarity with local people under a common objective (S2), do the same but with individuals outside the local area (S3), have a long-term impact on national and municipal policy (S4), and have a long-term impact on society as a whole (S5). Conversely, lengthy proceedings would mentally and physically exhaust litigants (S6), create heavy financial burdens on them (S7), and mean the social impact of the case will diminish over time (S8) (Figure 12).

Yokosuka respondents gave the highest scores for S1, reflecting the belief that active engagement over time increases the likelihood of a favorable decision. In contrast, respondents in the *Kobe* and *Sendai* cases were less optimistic. Regarding solidarity (S2, S3), all three sites reported relatively high levels of agreement. *Sendai* respondents expressed particularly strong agreement with S5, which concerned potential long-term influence on national and municipal policies. On the negative side, *Sendai* respondents – whose case lasted the longest – showed greater concern about the burdens of protracted litigation. Even so, few respondents saw financial burden (S7) as a serious problem, likely due to the support from the Kiko Network and the pro bono efforts of attorneys noted earlier. Finally, 35 percent of *Yokosuka* respondents – whose case was the most recent at the time of the survey – worried that the social impact of litigation might diminish over time (S8). Indeed, while the *Yokosuka* case initially drew significant media interest, including from abroad, the onset of the COVID-19 pandemic quickly diverted attention. This is reflected in the absence of media coverage when the Supreme Court issued its decision in the case in October 2024.

6.4.4 *Survey Analysis*

When the survey results are considered alongside the regional demographic profiles summarized in Table 13, several observations emerge.[12] First, there are notable differences in plaintiffs' primary concerns. *Sendai* respondents expressed almost the same expectations for improvements in local air pollution conditions (Q2-S1/S2) and addressing climate change (Q2-S3/S4), whereas *Yokosuka* respondents showed slightly more support for both climate change statements than for the local air pollution statements. This divergence likely reflects differences in residential proximity to CFPPs: *Sendai* plaintiffs tend to live closer (i.e., under 5 km) to a CFPP and are thus more directly affected by air pollution, while distance has little bearing on CO_2 exposure. By contrast, more *Yokosuka* plaintiffs live farther away, and their responses emphasize climate change impacts more strongly.

Kobe respondents, meanwhile, reported lower motivation to support civil groups (Q1-S6) but expressed strong agreement that a lengthy trial would bolster group solidarity (Q4-S2/S3), suggesting participation was shaped more by community identity. This contrasts with *Sendai* and *Yokosuka*, where plaintiffs appeared to rely more heavily on external support from organized civil groups (Q1-S6). One explanation may lie in the occupational data: 51 percent of *Kobe* respondents are retirees or social activists and only 3 percent are in full-time employment, compared to 37 percent and 20 percent in *Sendai* and 42 percent and 19 percent in *Yokosuka*. Their participation may thus reflect direct personal ties among local residents rather than coordination through NGOs and other organizations.

Second, differences appear in plaintiffs' expectations of litigation. *Yokosuka* respondents expressed greater confidence than *Sendai* respondents in distinguishing between – or rejecting a distinction between – air pollution and CCL (Q3).

Despite these differences, the three groups share several important commonalities. Plaintiffs in all sites expressed strong motivation to protect both themselves and future generations from air pollution and global warming (Q1) and expectations that litigation might achieve such a situation (Q2). All

12 Notwithstanding differences in sample sizes according to the site.

three groups reported low confidence in achieving favorable judicial outcomes (Q1-S8) and recognized that the length of proceedings can foster collaboration and solidarity, with both local people and those further away (Q4-S2/S3). Across sites, respondents also reported relatively low levels of exhaustion or financial strain from participating in the litigation (Q4-S6/S7).

6.4.5 *Interview Details*

Such broad trends based on questionnaire data may not fully reflect individual views. In fact, one area of ambiguity is the perception of timeliness. As previous Civil Litigation Surveys have shown, prolonged proceedings are often viewed negatively. Yet plaintiffs may reframe protracted litigation in a more positive light to sustain momentum and justify continued participation. As such, the interview phase in late 2019 and March 2020 was designed to probe this kind of cognitive framing in greater depth, situating responses within each participant's background and experience.

Details of the interview process are summarized in Table 14 and the demographic characteristics of interviewees in Table 15. The questionnaire included a note inviting participants for interviews, and all interviews described below were conducted with individuals who responded to this invitation. Interviews began in Kobe in November 2019 with eleven individuals involved in the two *Kobe* cases. Due to the COVID-19 pandemic, thirty-five respondents from the *Sendai* and *Yokosuka* cases were interviewed via telephone or Skype in March 2020. All interview responses were coded, using categories informed by both the survey questionnaire findings and the prior Civil Litigation Survey research discussed earlier.

TABLE 14 Details of the interviews

Cases	*Kobe* civil (pilot)	*Kobe* (administrative)	*Sendai*	*Yokosuka*
Number of interviewees	Plaintiffs: 7 Auditors: 4 Across both *Kobe* cases		Plaintiffs: 14 Auditors: 12	Plaintiffs: 9
Interview period	Nov.–Dec. 2019		March 2020	March 2020
Interview format	In-person		Telephone & Skype	Telephone & Skype

SOURCE: CREATED BY THE AUTHOR

TABLE 15 Demographic characteristics of interviewees from the *Sendai*, *Kobe*, and *Yokosuka* cases

	Sendai plaintiffs (n = 9)	*Kobe* plaintiffs (n = 7)	*Kobe* auditors (n = 4)	*Yokosuka* plaintiffs (n = 14)	*Yokosuka* auditors (n = 12)
Gender					
Male	78% (7)	57% (4)	75% (3)	76% (11)	58% (7)
Female	22% (2)	43% (3)	25% (1)	24% (3)	17% (2)
No answer	0% (0)	0% (0)	0% (0)	0% (0)	25% (3)
Age					
≤ 20	0% (0)	14% (1)	0% (0)	0% (0)	0% (0)
21–30	0% (0)	0% (0)	0% (0)	0% (0)	0% (0)
31–40	0% (0)	0% (0)	0% (0)	0% (0)	0% (0)
41–50	11% (1)	0% (0)	50% (2)	0% (0)	0% (0)
51–60	22% (2)	14% (1)	0% (0)	0% (0)	8% (1)
61–70	44% (4)	14% (1)	0% (0)	29% (4)	17% (2)
70 >	11% (1)	29% (2)	50% (2)	71% (10)	75% (9)
No answer	11% (1)	29% (2)	0% (0)	0% (0)	0% (0)
Children					
Have	100% (9)	100% (7)	75% (3)	86% (12)	67% (8)
Have not	0% (0)	0% (0)	0% (0)	7% (1)	17% (2)
No answer	0% (0)	0% (0)	25% (1)	7% (1)	17% (2)
Residence (proximity from CFPP)					
≤ 25 km	89% (8)	86% (6)	50% (2)	86% (12)	17% (2)
5–10 km	11% (1)	14% (1)	50% (2)	7% (1)	58% (7)
10 km >	0% (0)	0% (0)	0% (0)	0% (0)	17% (2)
No answer	0% (0)	0% (0)	0% (0)	7% (1)	8% (1)

Notes: The *Kobe* figures are from both cases; percentages are rounded; ≤ less than or equal to; > greater than.
SOURCE: CREATED BY THE AUTHOR

As Table 15 shows, male participants outnumbered female participants. Very few were in their thirties, forties, or fifties; most were in their sixties or older. Plaintiffs tended to live close to CFPPs – especially in *Sendai* – while auditors were more geographically dispersed. Most interviewees had children, and some also had grandchildren.

The interviews aimed to dig deeper into the perceptions of obstacles to legal proceedings by asking respondents:

- Motivations to litigate: How they reached their decision to become a plaintiff in the case (asked to plaintiffs only) (Q1)
- Hesitations to litigate: Whether they hesitated to become a plaintiff, or to auditors, why they didn't become a plaintiff (Q2)
- Expectations: What they thought might be the outcomes of the case (Q3)
- Protracted proceedings: What effect they thought a lengthy trial would have (Q4)

The interview questions were designed to clarify respondents' perceptions related to the main survey questions: interview Q1 relates to survey Q1 (motivations to litigate), interview Q3 to survey Q2 (expectations about case outcomes), and interview Q4 to survey Q4 (effect of lengthy proceedings). Some items related to survey Q3 (distinction between air pollution and CCL) were also prepared, but only a few interviewees addressed them, and their answers are therefore omitted. One additional item on inhibiting factors (interview Q2) was included to capture cognitive obstacles to initiating legal action. Because of the semi-structured format, not every interviewee answered every question.

6.4.6 *Interview Results and Analysis*

The interviews revealed several regional features. In *Sendai*, interviewees frequently emphasized the direct harms of air pollution from the CFPP. For instance, one explained, "We've been exposed to foul-smelling air, and there's nowhere to escape" (*Sendai* plaintiff no. 8). Another added, "I seriously worry about my grandchildren who live close to the plant – they have bronchitis" (*Sendai* plaintiff no. 2). At the time of the interviews, Sendai was the only site where the CFPP is already operational, making its circumstances particularly comparable to earlier air pollution cases.

In *Kobe*, respondents expressed strong resentment toward emissions from local industries: "Environmental pollution is unjust – some companies prioritize profit over public welfare without justification" (*Kobe* auditor no. 1). Kobe also has a long history of air pollution cases, including the *Amagasaki* and *Nishi-Yodogawa* cases, and some plaintiffs in the *Kobe* case had previously been involved in the latter.

Interviewees in *Yokosuka*, by contrast, were more critical of national climate and energy policy. As one put it: "Japan is clearly out of step with global decarbonization efforts" (*Yokosuka* plaintiff no. 1). Another asked: "Why coal now? I don't understand" (*Yokosuka* auditor no. 3).

Beyond the four main questions, the interviews also highlighted regional differences in leadership and solidarity. In *Sendai*, the 124 plaintiffs had already been engaged in litigation for nearly two years at the time of the interviews. Many reported drawing psychologically supported by group leaders and fellow plaintiffs. In *Yokosuka*, which had forty-five plaintiffs, some interviewees explained that they joined out of solidarity with longtime friends or former colleagues. By contrast, none of the *Kobe* interviewees mentioned their group leaders by name – suggesting that plaintiffs may have acted more on individual initiative, a finding suggested by the earlier survey too.

Table 16 presents the results for interview Q1 on motivations to litigate.

TABLE 16 Motivations to litigate (interview Q1)

Code		Keywords	*Sendai* plaintiffs (n = 9)	*Kobe* plaintiffs (n = 7)	*Kobe* auditors (n = 4)	*Yokosuka* plaintiffs (n = 14)	*Yokosuka* auditors (n = 12)
1	justice, fairness, due process	moral issue; injustice; corporate social responsibility; civil surveillance	100% (9)	71% (5)	25% (1)	36% (5)	75% (9)
2	solidarity	cooperation; network nationwide; sympathy	67% (6)	14% (1)	50% (2)	14% (2)	8% (1)
3	air pollution	bronchitis; smell; air quality	56% (5)	29% (2)	75% (3)	36% (5)	42% (5)
4	climate change	heavy rain; hot summer; sea temperature rise; CO_2 emissions	56% (5)	57% (4)	50% (2)	71% (10)	58% (7)
5	future generation	Greta Thunberg; inherit safe environment; responsibility of current generation	11% (1)	0% (0)	25% (1)	7% (1)	25% (2)
6	international tendency	decarbonization; contradiction of of Japanese policy with the global trends	11% (1)	14% (1)	25% (1)	14% (2)	25% (3)

SOURCE: CREATED BY THE AUTHOR

As the table illustrates, interviewees frequently referred to concepts of justice, fairness, and due process (code 1). All *Sendai* plaintiffs used terms from this category. One *Yokosuka* plaintiff noted, "Legal proceedings will be fair and effective in stopping this construction plan." Many also expressed concern about air pollution (code 3). Site-specific patterns emerged with respect to solidarity (code 2) and climate change awareness (code 4): *Sendai* interviewees emphasized community solidarity, while *Yokosuka* interviewees more often highlighted climate-related concerns. Overall, plaintiffs' motivations were grounded in a strong sense of justice and fairness.

Responses to the question about inhibiting factors (Q2) are summarized in Table 17.

Only a few interviewees reported hesitation to litigate, and some explicitly stated they felt none (code 3). One remarked, "My sense of justice prevailed over my fear. Many neighbors have ties to Kobe Steel, so suing them affects my daily life" (*Kobe* plaintiff no. 3). Financial concerns were also raised, though generally downplayed thanks to external support: "Thanks to Kiko Network's support, we are spared the economic burden" (*Yokosuka* plaintiff no. 6); "Kiko Network pays a large part of the legal costs, and we truly appreciate it" (*Yokosuka* plaintiff no. 8). Other interviewees – especially younger plaintiffs – worried about career repercussions: "Some friends ask if I'll still be able to get a job after being involved in this case" (*Kobe* plaintiff no. 1); "I was definitely concerned about how this might affect my future career in Japan" (*Sendai* plaintiff no. 1).

Taken together, these findings suggest that hesitation stemmed mainly from limited personal resources (especially time and knowledge) and fears of negative social or professional consequences.

Responses to Q3 (expectations) are summarized in Table 18.

Interviewees frequently emphasized the potential social impact of litigation (code 1). As one *Yokosuka* plaintiff explained, "Legal proceedings have enormous influence on society" (*Yokosuka* plaintiff no. 6). A *Kobe* interviewee added, "The existence of such cases forces companies to consider the risk of being sued" (*Kobe* plaintiff no. 3). Many hoped for victory in court (code 5), even though this contrasts with the survey findings. However, low expectations of success (code 6) were also common. Some interviewees expressed both views at once: "Of course we want a judicial victory, but it won't be easy. Still, the lawsuit itself is meaningful even if we lose" (*Sendai* plaintiff no. 1); "We want to win, but we also want to raise awareness – even if we lose at the district court" (*Sendai* plaintiff no. 2). *Yokosuka* interviewees again placed stronger emphasis on the adverse impacts of climate change (code 4) than those elsewhere.

Overall, these responses suggest that interviewees were primarily concerned with the broader social and political effects of litigation, even when judicial appears uncertain.

TABLE 17 Hesitations to litigate (plaintiffs) / reasons for not becoming plaintiffs (auditors) (interview Q2)

Code		Keywords	*Sendai* plaintiffs (n = 9)	*Kobe* plaintiffs (n = 7)	*Kobe* auditors (n = 4)	*Yokosuka* plaintiffs (n = 14)	*Yokosuka* auditors (n = 12)
1	limited time available	busy with job; busy with other movements	33% (3)	0% (0)	0% (0)	0% (0)	24% (2)
2	lack of knowledge about legal process	unfamiliarity; beyond one's capacity	11% (1)	0% (0)	0% (0)	26% (4)	8% (1)
3	no hesitation	strong interests; moral obligation	33% (3)	26% (2)	0% (0)	36% (5)	0% (0)
4	negative effect on one's career	job application; job promotion	22% (2)	14% (1)	50% (2)	0% (0)	0% (0)
5	(asked to auditors) lack of enthusiasm	interested but do not want to be involved	0% (0)	0% (0)	25% (1)	0% (0)	25% (3)
6	(asked to auditors) missed the chance to become a plaintiff	know the cases after recruiting plaintiffs	0% (0)	0% (0)	25% (1)	0% (0)	17% (2)

SOURCE: CREATED BY THE AUTHOR

Finally, responses to Q4 (lengthiness of proceedings) are summarized in Table 19.

Very few interviewees commented on the issue of lengthy proceedings, even when prompted. Some identified the potential of protracted litigation to create sustained public impact (code 2). As one noted, "Through a lengthy process, we can raise awareness of this issue" (*Sendai* plaintiff no. 3). Another said, "I hope more people take notice through our long fight" (*Yokosuka* plaintiff no. 5).

TABLE 18 Expectations about case outcomes (interview Q3)

Code		Keywords	*Sendai* plaintiffs (n = 9)	*Kobe* plaintiffs (n = 7)	*Kobe* auditors (n = 4)	*Yokosuka* plaintiffs (n = 14)	*Yokosuka* auditors (n = 12)
1	social impact	amplify social impact; distribute information; raise social awareness; increase corporate responsibility	78% (7)	57% (4)	25% (1)	50% (7)	75% (9)
2	political impact	policy change; alignment with international standards; political influence of judicial decision	22% (2)	43% (3)	25% (1)	57% (8)	33% (4)
3	air pollution	arrest deterioration of air quality	11% (1)	14% (1)	0% (0)	7% (1)	8% (1)
4	climate change	difficult but important arguments in court; court as the last resort to protect future climate	11% (1)	14% (1)	25% (1)	64% (9)	50% (6)
5	desire to win	stop CFPPs; obtaining a favorable judgment	45% (4)	26% (2)	50% (2)	43% (6)	33% (4)
6	low expectation of victory	unlikelihood of success; unprecedented types of legal cases	56% (5)	0% (0)	25% (1)	21% (3)	75% (9)

SOURCE: CREATED BY THE AUTHOR

In contrast, others cited a sense of urgency: "I want the court to move faster, given how urgent this issue is" (*Yokosuka* plaintiff no. 3); "The construction is moving forward – it may be too late by the time the court decides" (*Yokosuka* plaintiff no. 1).

TABLE 19 Perceived effect of lengthy proceedings (interview Q4)

Code		Keywords	*Sendai* plaintiffs (n = 9)	*Kobe* plaintiffs (n = 7)	*Kobe* auditors (n = 4)	*Yokosuka* plaintiffs (n = 14)	*Yokosuka* auditors (n = 12)
1	networking	cooperation; network creation	0% (0)	0% (0)	0% (0)	7% (1)	0% (0)
2	continuous impact on society and policy	raise social awareness; information distribution; political influence	11% (1)	14% (1)	50% (2)	21% (3)	8% (1)
3	urgency	unable to stop construction of CFPPs; urgency of climate crisis; gives advantage to defendants	0% (0)	26% (2)	25% (1)	29% (4)	8% (1)
4	deliberation at court	full argument is needed; complication of issues	0% (0)	0% (0)	50% (2)	7% (1)	0% (0)
5	exhaustion	I might die before the decision; occupied with legal proceedings	0% (0)	14% (1)	0% (0)	7% (1)	0% (0)

SOURCE: CREATED BY THE AUTHOR

These results suggest that many plaintiffs view prolonged litigation as one strategy within a broader social movement. This inference aligns with the perceptions of plaintiffs in pollution lawsuits revealed by the literature (Kidder and Miyazawa 1993). On the other hand, some plaintiffs recognized that litigation is not an appropriate method to address the urgent demands of environmental issues like climate change, where the window for effective action is rapidly closing. In this regard, the fundamental insight of this study – the dual nature of CCL: both an extension of past pollution lawsuits and a distinct, novel phenomenon – was also evident in plaintiffs' perceptions of the litigation's long-term nature.

6.5 Second-Stage Questionnaire Survey

6.5.1 *Survey Details*

In the second stage of data collection, another questionnaire survey was submitted to litigants from all four cases, this time also including supporters – defined as individuals who share the plaintiff's aims and participate in related activities, including auditors. Supporters were added in the second-stage survey for two main reasons: first, the *Sendai* case had already concluded, making the category of "courtroom observers" (how auditors were defined in the first stage) obsolete; second, during the survey period there were no scheduled court dates, leaving no natural opportunities for plaintiff gatherings in Sendai or Yokosuka, though meetings with supporters still took place as part of broader social movements. In Kobe, where such gatherings could not be captured, the questionnaire was distributed via Google Form to both plaintiffs and supporters, with a specific response deadline.

Fifteen *Kobe* plaintiffs and supporters responded by November, followed by thirty-three from *Sendai* and thirty-three from *Yokosuka* in April 2024. Details of the surveys are presented in Table 20 and the demographic characteristics of participants in Table 21.

As the table shows, income and education data were not collected in this round. Male respondents outnumbered females at all sites, though the gap was smaller in *Sendai* and *Yokosuka*. No respondents were under twenty years old. More than 70 percent of respondents in both *Kobe* and *Yokosuka* were seventy or older, consistent with the first-stage surveys. Most respondents at all sites had children. Retirees and social activists accounted for nearly half of respondents overall.

TABLE 20 Details of the second-stage surveys

Cases	*Sendai*	*Yokosuka*	*Kobe* (both cases)
Survey date(s)	Apr. 22, 2024	Apr. 27, 2024	Apr. to Nov. 2024
Survey format	In-person	In-person & Online	Online
Total number of plaintiffs	40	45	40 (civil) 12 (administrative)
Number of respondents	Plaintiffs: 19 Supporters: 14	Plaintiffs: 19 (16 Collective & 3 Online) Supporters: 14 (12 Collective & 2 Online)	Plaintiffs: 5 Supporters: 10

SOURCE: CREATED BY THE AUTHOR

TABLE 21 Demographic characteristics of respondents to the second-stage surveys on *Sendai*, *Kobe*, and *Yokosuka*

	Sendai (n = 33)	*Kobe* (n = 15)	*Yokosuka* (n = 33)
Gender			
Male	48% (16)	80% (12)	57% (19)
Female	36% (12)	20% (3)	40% (13)
No answer	15% (5)	0% (0)	3% (1)
Age			
≤ 20	0% (0)	0% (0)	0% (0)
21–30	0% (0)	7% (1)	3% (1)
31–40	3% (1)	0% (0)	3% (1)
41–50	3% (1)	0% (0)	3% (1)
51–60	0% (0)	14% (2)	15% (5)
61–70	27% (9)	7% (1)	9% (3)
70 >	52% (17)	73% (11)	70% (23)
No answer	15% (5)	0% (0)	0% (0)
Children			
Have	67% (22)	66% (5)	82% (27)
Have not	18% (6)	33% (10)	18% (6)
No answer	15% (5)	0% (0)	0% (0)
Vocation			
Retired or social activist	56% (19)	73% (11)	45% (15)
Full-time worker	15% (5)	7% (1)	21% (7)
Part-time worker	0% (0)	7% (1)	9% (3)
Researcher	3% (1)	7% (1)	0% (0)
Fisher	0% (0)	21% (3)	6% (2)
Homemaker	3% (1)	0% (0)	3% (1)
Other	3% (1)	0% (0)	0% (0)
No answer	21% (7)	7% (1)	15% (5)

Notes: The figures for *Kobe* comprise both civil and administrative cases. Percentages are rounded; ≤ less than or equal to; > greater than.

SOURCE: CREATED BY THE AUTHOR

The questionnaire aimed to assess how plaintiffs' and supporters' perceptions of the court system evolved through their actual litigation experience – specifically, how their initial motivations and expectations shifted over time. Respondents were asked about:

- Motivations to abolish coal plants: Their reasons for seeking injunctions against CFPPs (Q1)
- Reasons for choosing a lawsuit: Why they chose litigation to achieve this aim (Q2)
- Trial experience: Their perceptions of the judicial process (Q3) (asked to plaintiffs only)
- Case outcomes: Their perceptions of the result of the trial (Q4)
- Result satisfaction levels: Whether they are satisfied with the outcome of the case (Q5)
- Overall perception of the judiciary: Their general impressions of the court system and legal code having experienced the case (Q6)

Given the substantial changes in both domestic and international contexts surrounding CCL during the four and a half years between the two surveys, this questionnaire excluded questions on the distinction between air pollution and CCL, as well as perceptions of the lengthiness of litigation.

As in the first-stage survey, the Civil Litigation Survey served as a reference, and Q2, Q3, Q5, and Q6 were based closely on that model. However, the rating method differed from the first survey: For Q1–Q4 and Q6, respondents were asked rate the statements from 1 (relevant) to 2 (not relevant). The figures are based on the affirmative scores of 1. For Q5, they were asked to select only one of five options that best matched their perception. An optional question (Q7) invited them to freely describe their experiences in more detail. No pilot survey was conducted; the same core questionnaire was used across all three sites, with only minor regional modifications. As in the first survey, further questions were included to collect the demographic characteristics of respondents (summarized in Table 21).[13]

In *Sendai*, where roughly three years had passed since the lawsuit's conclusion, a collective survey was conducted at a study meeting hosted by a campaign group that had previously served as the plaintiffs' support organization.[14] In *Kobe* case, responses were asked to fill in the online form during the period shown in Table 20. In *Yokosuka*, an in-person group survey was also conducted during a study meeting organized by the plaintiffs' support organization.[15]

13 For full details of the second-stage survey questionnaire, see Appendix 2.

14 Professor Koichi Hasegawa (Shokei University, at the time of survey), leader of the plaintiff group in *Sendai*, provided valuable feedback on the content of the questionnaire and assistance with coordinating the survey's implementation.

15 Mr. Rikuro Suzuki, the leader of the plaintiffs group, assisted the coordination and implementation of the survey.

6.5.2 *Survey Results*

On their reasons for seeking injunctions against CFPPS (Q1), respondents were asked to rate five options: negative health impacts from air pollutant emissions (S1), concerns about the scale of GHG emissions and their effect on global warming (S2), recognition that coal plants are not a sustainable energy source (S3), solidarity with activist colleagues seeking the abolition of CFPPS (S4), and concerns about wider impacts on the local environment (S5).

As Figure 13 shows, all respondents identified worsening climate change (S2) as a key motivation for opposing CFPPS. Slightly fewer emphasized coal's nonsustainability (S3), suggesting that immediate climate risks carried more weight than longer-term sustainability concerns. While solidarity with colleagues (S4) ranked lower overall, nearly half of plaintiffs across the three cases still cited it as a motivating factor.

Respondents were asked their reasons for pursuing litigation in particular to achieve the abolition of coal plants (Q2). Again, six options were given: protecting the health of them and their families (S1), slowing the acceleration of climate change (S2), ensuring future generations inherit a sustainable world (S3), obtaining a just decision from the courts (S4), resolving the issue in a public forum (S5), and because a more suitable alternative to litigation, such as effective participation in the policymaking process, was lacking in Japan (S6).

This question examined perceptions of litigation as a strategy. As Figure 14 shows, more than 90 percent of respondents in all cases endorsed climate change deceleration (S2) as a central reason, with similarly high support for leaving a sustainable society to future generations (S3). More than half of

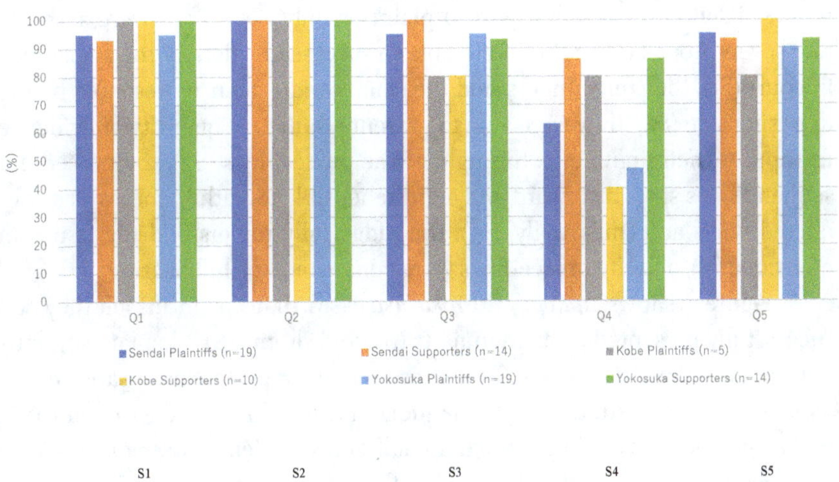

FIGURE 13 Reasons for seeking injunctions on CFPPS (Stage 2 Survey Q1)
SOURCE: CREATED BY THE AUTHOR

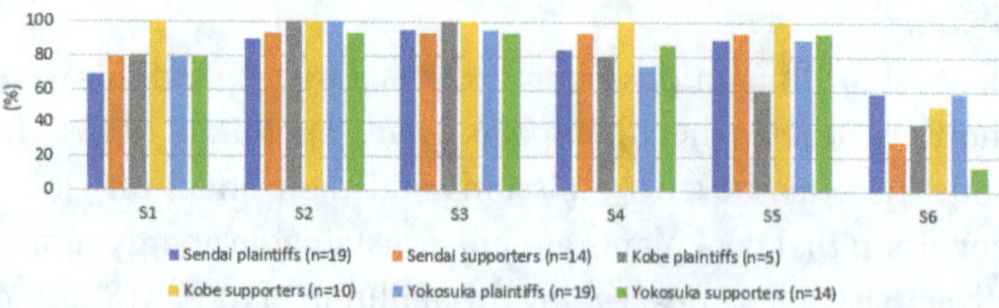

FIGURE 14 Reasons for choosing a lawsuit (Stage 2 Survey Q2)
SOURCE: CREATED BY THE AUTHOR

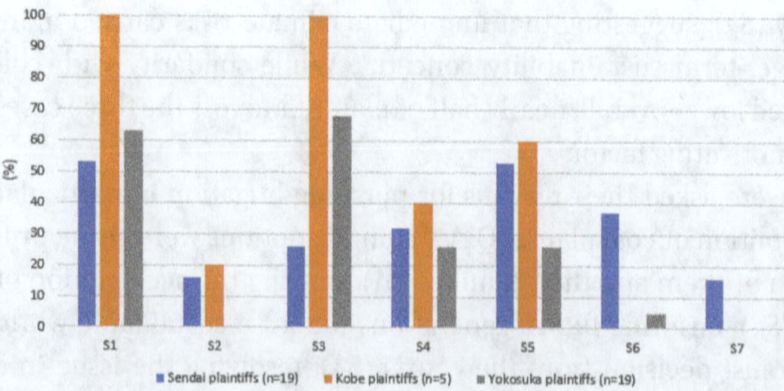

FIGURE 15 Perceptions of the judicial process (Stage 2 Survey Q3)
SOURCE: CREATED BY THE AUTHOR

respondents – including *Sendai* and *Yokosuka* plaintiffs and *Kobe* supporters – also saw litigation as the viable means of addressing climate change due to a lack of alternatives (S6).

The third question focused on respondents' experiences of the litigation process itself and was addressed to plaintiffs only (Q3). They were asked to rate seven propositions: they were able to successfully defend their positions in court (S1), they fully understood the claims and evidence presented by the opposing side (S2), they were able to present a sufficient quantity of evidence to support their arguments throughout the proceedings (S3), the procedural sequence was straightforward and comprehensible (S4), the process was conducted fairly and impartially (S5), the judge fully understood the issues in question (S6), and the proceedings were conducted as a full hearing (S7).

As Figure 15 shows, in *Kobe* and *Yokosuka* cases, many plaintiffs felt they had successfully presented legal arguments (S1) and submitted adequate supporting evidence (S3). In contrast, *Sendai* respondents reported lower satisfaction, likely reflecting frustration after the judge narrowed the case early on to air pollution (Sec. 4.2.1). While more than half of respondents in *Sendai* and *Kobe* considered proceedings fair (S5), fewer than half across all sites found them easy to understand (S4). Many also declined to answer whether the case was conducted as a full hearing (S7).

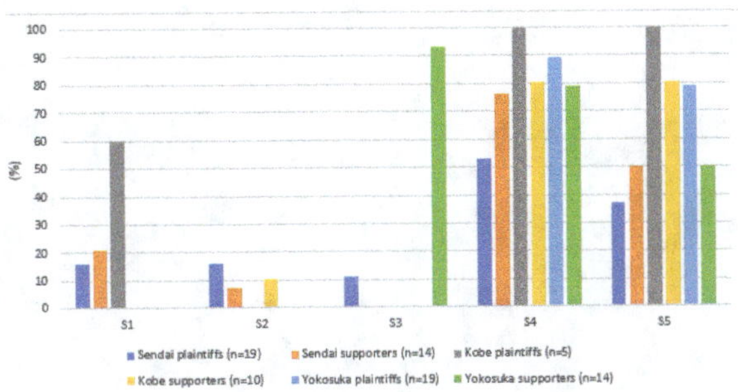

FIGURE 16 Recognition of the case result (Stage 2 Survey Q4)
SOURCE: CREATED BY THE AUTHOR

The fourth question asked both sets of respondents about their perceptions of the result of the case (Q4). This focused on their *recognition* of the outcome, with one statement about satisfaction levels, preceding a further question specifically about those satisfaction levels (Q5). Respondents were asked to rate five statements about the case result: that it aligned with the provisions set forth by the relevant legislation (S1), that it was acceptable (S2), that it was satisfactory (S3), that it may have differed in other countries (S4), and they would again seek litigation on the same or similar issues in the future (S5).

A notable finding, shown in Figure 16, was that many respondents considered it appropriate to bring similar issues to court again in the future (S5), despite expressing dissatisfaction with their actual trial outcomes. On satisfaction (S3), only 10 percent of *Sendai* plaintiffs reported being satisfied; all other respondents expressed dissatisfaction. More than half believed that a more favorable ruling might have been possible in another country (S4). These views reflect a broader awareness – shared by both plaintiffs and their attorneys – of the Japanese judiciary's comparatively conservative stance on climate issues.

The fifth question also centered on case outcomes but shifted focus slightly by asking respondents specifically about their levels of satisfaction with the result (Q5): very dissatisfied (S1), somewhat dissatisfied (S2), neither satisfied nor dissatisfied (S3), somewhat satisfied (S4), and very satisfied (S5).

As Figure 17 illustrates, overall dissatisfaction with trial results was evident, particularly among *Kobe* and *Yokosuka* respondents. In *Yokosuka*, both trial and appellate decisions made little reference to the harms alleged by plaintiffs – such as the effects of warm water discharge on fisheries – or to specific climate damages. The appellate court also gave scant attention to climate science, and judges exited the courtroom immediately after reading the judgment without further explanation – a moment observed by the author.

By contrast, while the *Sendai* trial court ultimately dismissed plaintiffs' claims, it acknowledged their concerns in its written opinion and urged

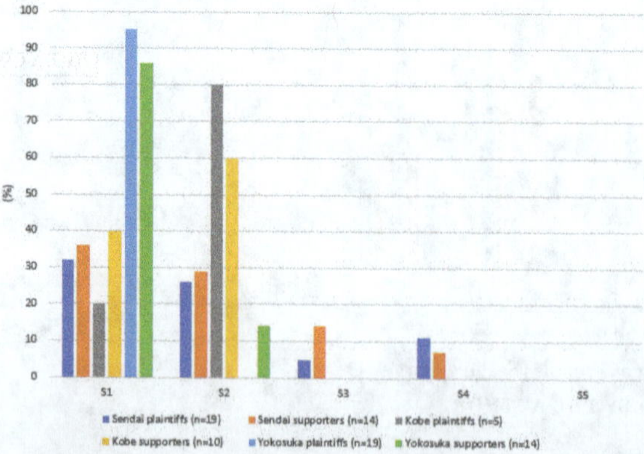

FIGURE 17 Satisfaction with case result (Stage 2 Survey Q5)
SOURCE: CREATED BY THE AUTHOR

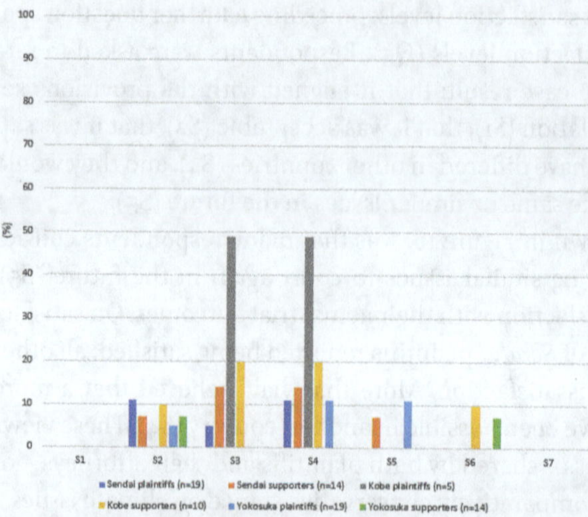

FIGURE 18 General impressions of the Japanese justice and legal system (Stage 2 Survey Q6)
SOURCE: CREATED BY THE AUTHOR

the defendant to meet obligations under the Pollution Control Agreement (Sec. 4.2.1). Similarly, the *Kobe* administrative court of first instance criticized elements of national climate policy in its obiter dicta, showing some sympathy toward plaintiffs. The *Kobe* appellate court adopted a comparable stance. These contrasts in judicial engagement may help explain regional variations in satisfaction.

Finally, the sixth substantive question of the survey investigated respondents' general perceptions of the Japanese court system (Q6). This time, seven statements were proposed, asking respondents to rate whether the civil court system is effective in resolving disputes and social problems (S1) and accessible to the general public (S2), whether civil justice (S3) and Japanese law (S4) are fair, whether legal norms align with contemporary life and social organization (S5), whether the civil justice system is seen as satisfactory to the general public (S6), and whether it effectively realized and protects the rights of citizens (S7).

The results in Figure 18 reveal a high level of dissatisfaction with the Japanese court system and its legal framework. While some respondents acknowledged the fairness of the civil courts and laws (S3, S4), they offered lower ratings for the general public's access to courts (S2) and alignment of legal norms with contemporary life and social organization (S5). Notably, all respondents negatively assessed the courts' performance in dispute resolution (S1) and rights protection (S7). These findings suggest a gap between perceived formal fairness and the system's actual effectiveness in protecting individual rights or meeting public expectations.

In addition to the six statement-based questions (Q1–Q6), survey respondents were invited to share their experiences of litigation in an optional free-text field (Q7). Many provided comments, from which three key themes emerged.

The first theme concerns judicial responsiveness. Several *Kobe* respondents expressed frustration at the judiciary's limited engagement with climate change as a pressing societal problem. One respondent wrote:

> The number of deadlines and time to present evidence was adequate, but I don't know how the process can overcome the judges' lack of recognition of seriousness of the issue in the decision. The court system doesn't seem equipped to handle forward-looking problems like climate change. (*Kobe* plaintiff no. 3)

Another remarked:

> The Japanese courts seem overly bound by traditional textual interpretations. Compared to foreign courts, which treat climate change as a human rights issue, Japan seems far behind. (*Kobe* plaintiff no. 5)

Such comments echo the shared recognition the author observed among *Kobe*'s plaintiffs and attorneys at post-hearing gatherings, preparatory online meeting, and so on. They always pay attention to global developments in CCL and perceive Japanese courts as lagging behind international practice.

The second theme concerns skepticism about the litigation route itself. Some respondents questioned whether filing lawsuits is the appropriate method for addressing climate change grievances. A supporter in the *Sendai* case stated: "I understand why we had to go to court, but we should also focus on movements that shape public opinion." Similarly, a *Kobe* supporter observed: "It's very costly and time-consuming for individuals to prove causality." These remarks suggest that while litigation can advance climate goals, it is viewed as an imperfect and potentially burdensome strategy.

Finally, several respondents voiced concerns about judicial dialogue and transparency, particularly in relation to *Yokosuka* case. One plaintiff stated: "I doubt the ethics of a judge who gave no explanation for dismissing our claims – even though the defendants never refuted them" (*Yokosuka* supporter no. 4). Others criticized the abrupt replacement of judge during proceedings and the lack of substantive discussion in court. One respondent wrote: "Can you even call it a trial if the state says nothing?" (*Yokosuka* plaintiff no. 10). Such responses reflect disillusionment with courtroom procedure and suggest that judicial demeanor and transparency play a crucial role in maintaining public trust.

6.5.3 *Survey Analysis*

Taken together, these voluntary comments deepen the picture painted by the statement-based data. They reveal that dissatisfaction with the court system stems not only from unfavorable outcomes but also from a sense that the judiciary is ill-equipped – both procedurally and conceptually – to engage with complex, forward-looking issues such as climate change. The remarks also show that participants viewed litigation as a double-edged sword: while it offers a formal avenue to demand accountability, it is costly, slow, and often leaves plaintiffs feeling unheard.

This combination of statement ratings and narrative comments underscores a broader tension between the formal availability of legal remedies and their substantive capacity to deliver justice in the climate context. The findings suggest that while plaintiffs and supporters remain committed to pursuing legal action where necessary, they simultaneously recognize the limits of litigation as a tool for systemic change. This ambivalence has implications not only for CCL strategy but also for the design of civil procedure and judicial education in Japan. Without reforms to improve judicial engagement, transparency, and accessibility, courts risk alienating citizens and diminishing public trust – especially on issues where the stakes are intergenerational and global in scope.

The next section will discuss the findings of the surveys and interviews across the whole data collection period between 2019 and 2024. It will highlight observable shifts in perception and recognition between the two stages of research, illustrating how obstacles have evolved, how plaintiffs have overcome them, and what barriers remain for potential litigants.

6.6 Discussion

6.6.1 *Observed Shifts in Litigants' Attitudes Between the Two Surveys*

A comparison of the two surveys conducted four and a half years apart reveals several notable developments in plaintiffs' perception of CCL. First, recognition of CFPPs as drivers of climate change appears to have grown and solidified. In the first-stage surveys, although a majority of *Sendai* and *Yokosuka* respondents acknowledged the differences between air pollution and CCL, this was by no means universal, with significant numbers saying they were different or that they didn't know (Figure 11). This uncertainty might suggest that respondents did not fully understand the contributions CFPPs make to either. Yet, in the second-stage survey, where questions about the effects of plant pollution on climate change were more clearly foregrounded, nearly all respondents affirmed it in their reasons to litigate to abolish coal plants (Figures 13 and 14). This suggests that public awareness has deepened in parallel with the growing domestic and international momentum toward coal-free policies.

Second, the survey data indicate a nuanced but enduring confidence in litigation as a strategy and in the judicial process itself. This is particularly striking given the widespread dissatisfaction in the second-stage survey with actual case outcomes (Figure 17). Many respondents stated that, despite being dissatisfied by the case result, they would still consider litigation appropriate to similar future situations (Figure 16-S5).

This finding invites two possible interpretations. One is that plaintiffs are hopeful for future shifts in how Japanese courts approach CCL. This view is supported by the relatively high number of respondents who believed that a more favorable ruling might have been reached in another country (Figure 16-S4), as well as by observation of the Osaka High Court in the *Kobe* administrative case that evolving domestic and international contexts could lead to different results in the future (Sec. 4.2.3). Japan's history of pollution lawsuits provides precedent for such an evolution: judicial reasoning in those cases changed as similar claims accumulated over time. It is plausible that plaintiffs wish for a similar evolution in CCL.

A second interpretation is that plaintiffs see the value of litigation not only in individual legal outcomes but perhaps more so in its capacity to generate broader societal and political effects. The period between the two surveys saw rapid global and domestic developments on coal policy. Internationally, CCL has contributed to decarbonization and helped frame climate change as a human rights issue – even though favorable judgments remain relatively rare, as previously noted. As Setzer and Higham (2024) point out, the significance of CCL increasingly lies in its transformative potential outside the courtroom. Similarly, in Japan's historical pollution cases, litigation played a catalytic role in shaping policy, even when judicial decisions themselves were not the direct cause of reform.

6.6.2 *Plaintiffs' Recognition of Barriers*

The surveys shed light on how plaintiffs overcame common barriers to litigation. As Japan's Civil Litigation Survey indicates, uncertainty about favorable outcomes is typically more discouraging to potential litigants than trial length or costs. Nevertheless, plaintiffs in the four climate cases managed to pursue their claims through every stage of the legal process and obtained final judgments.

Survey results revealed that most respondents did not regard exhaustion, financial burdens, or the length of proceedings as significant barriers (Figure 12) – factors that often deter the general public from engaging in litigation.[16] Solidarity among plaintiffs appears to have been a key source of emotional resilience, echoing findings from earlier air pollution cases (Kidder and Miyazawa 1993, 614–616; Hirano 2005, 74–88). In the second-stage survey, approximately half or more of the plaintiffs said that peer involvement influenced their decision to join the case (Figure 13-S4). Several interviewees described being inspired by citizen group meetings:

> When an acquaintance invited me to a citizen group meeting, I saw the leaders and members working hard. I wanted to support them, and that's why I became a plaintiff. (*Sendai* plaintiff no. 1)
>
> My family opposed my decision, but I persuaded them. The leaders and group members supported me a lot. (*Sendai* plaintiff no. 4)
>
> The leader and I have known each other for decades. If he fights, I'll help him. (*Yokosuka* plaintiff no. 5)

As noted earlier, many of those dissatisfied with the court experience nevertheless indicated that they would consider going to court again under similar

16 Minji Sosyou Seido Kenkyu-kai (2018, 84–86).

circumstances (Figure 16-S5). This suggests that plaintiffs valued litigation not only as a path to judgment but also as a means of influencing national politics and society (Miyamoto [2014] 2017; Peel and Osofsky 2015). Japanese legal history offers examples of this phenomenon. In one case, plaintiffs seeking a smoke-free environment sued the Japanese National Railways (JNR) to enforce a duty to provide nonsmoking cars. Although they lost the case, JNR voluntarily introduced nonsmoking cars soon after.[17] Such "external effects" of litigation may have shaped respondents' positive views of pursuing future cases.

Moral conviction and a strong sense of justice also played a prominent role (Table 16). Many plaintiffs framed their participation in terms of justice and intergenerational responsibility:

> We absolutely must change Japan's coal policy. I'm in my seventies, and all I can do now is leave a safe and clean environment to future generations. (*Yokosuka* plaintiff no. 11)
>
> I know our claims are unlikely to be accepted, but we can still send a message to society – just like Greta Thunberg did. (*Yokosuka* plaintiff no. 10)

Support from attorneys was another critical factor of support. As one *Kobe* civil plaintiff noted:

> I sincerely appreciate our attorneys. Thanks to them, we can keep fighting. (*Kobe* plaintiff no. 2)

Financial assistance further enabled participation. All four cases were supported by the Kiko Network, which obtained funding through donations and grants. Attorneys worked for minimal fees, and most interviewees reported paying less than 10,000 yen (approximately US $75) toward case expenses. By contrast, the standard filing fee for a nonproperty-based claim is 1.6 million yen (over US $10,000) – a sum that would have made litigation impossible without external support.[18]

---

17 Tokyo Chiho Saibansho [Tokyo Dist. Ct.], March 27, 1987, 1226 Hanrei Jiho [Hanji] 33. On US tobacco litigation, see Sec. 7.3.2.

18 The Japanese costs can be found in Article 4 of the Act on the Costs of Civil Proceedings, Act No. 40 of April 6, 1971, https://www.japaneselawtranslation.go.jp/ja/laws/view/3678. There are other costs in addition to filing fees. For example, plaintiffs in the *Kobe* civil case paid 404,000 yen to seal their complaint. *Kobe* civil case complaint (Chapter 4, supra note 26).

Finally, trial length was generally not perceived as a deterrent. Indeed, some *Kobe* plaintiffs had prior experience with protracted environmental litigation, such as the *Nishi-Yodogawa* and *National Highway No. 43* cases, which ended with settlements that included both compensation and pollution control measures. These earlier experiences likely informed plaintiffs' expectations, reinforcing the idea that while litigation is slow and demanding, it can produce outcomes beyond what government action alone might achieve. As one *Sendai* plaintiff reflected: "Environmental litigation in Japan is very demanding. But we must face reality and learn from those who fought long battles and eventually won" (*Sendai* plaintiff no. 9).

Taken together, these factors – solidarity, moral commitment, legal and financial support, perseverance in the face of lengthy proceedings, and a recognition of litigation's broader social impact – help explain why plaintiffs persisted despite uncertain prospects of legal victory and considerable personal costs.

6.6.3 *Continuing Cognitive Obstacles to Potential Litigants*

As discussed in the previous section, plaintiffs in these cases recognized and overcame significant hurdles through solidarity, external support, and moral conviction. This astounding perseverance, however, is likely the exception rather than the norm, and many barriers remain in place for potential litigants. This section examines three main cognitive obstacles citizens face that may prevent broader public participation in CCL.

The first obstacle is continued limited public awareness of the urgency of the climate crisis. Many Japanese citizens either underestimate the severity of climate crisis or treat it as a secondary issue. Online reactions to the Osaka District Court's decision in the *Kobe* administrative case illustrate this gap in understanding, with many criticizing the plaintiffs for failing to grasp Japan's supposed dependence on CFPPs.[19] Comments included: "The plaintiffs should stop using electricity themselves!" "Do they care about Japan's future prosperity? We need coal!"

Even after the government's dramatic policy shift toward decarbonization in October 2020, public awareness of the urgent need for decarbonization has lagged behind. Many remain skeptical about the reliability and affordability of renewable energy, which undermines broad support for decarbonization. Moreover, although climate-related disasters are becoming more frequent,

19 See https://news.yahoo.co.jp/articles/8a32765531ac0976d83229e76fd5c2d7297762d4 (in Japanese).

Japan's long history of natural disasters – earthquakes, tsunamis, volcanic eruptions – may lead people to view recent events as unrelated to anthropogenic climate change. In short, many citizens may not fully connect present environmental damages to their human causes.

Legal uncertainty is another key deterrent. Each of the four cases examined here represents a novel category of litigation in Japan. In the *Kobe* administrative case, for example, the Osaka District Court held that Japan's strict standing rules did not allow individuals to claim a legal right to a stable climate system, as such interests were not considered sufficiently concrete.[20] Standing was granted only for PM2.5 pollution, effectively sidestepping substantive consideration of climate change claims and leaving plaintiffs and the public with little guidance for future litigation.

Concerns over trial length also weigh heavily. Even among committed *Yokosuka* plaintiffs – who had already chosen to overcome this hurdle – some worried that the prolonged proceedings would blunt the impact of their claims (Figure 12). Two elderly plaintiffs expressed fear that they might not live to see the verdict (Table 19 – code 5). For the average citizen, such uncertainty may deter engagement given the significant investment of time, energy, and emotional resources required.

Together, these barriers help explain the relatively small number of climate lawsuits in Japan. Paradoxically, the rarity of such cases may magnify their social significance but also reinforce judicial caution, making courts less likely to issue transformative rulings.

6.7 Summary

This chapter examined the cognitive obstacles that hinder the development of CCL in Japan. Drawing on questionnaire surveys and interviews, it explored respondents' motivations and hesitations to litigate, expectations of case outcomes, recognition of the differences between air pollution and climate change cases, trial experiences, views of the lengthiness of proceedings, and overall impressions of the Japanese judiciary. This study represents the first comprehensive investigation of Japanese CCL from this perspective.

The findings suggest that the main barriers include limited public recognition of the urgency of climate action, legal uncertainty regarding outcomes,

20 For the written decision, see https://www.courts.go.jp/app/files/hanrei_jp/203/090203_hanrei.pdf (in Japanese).

and concerns over the cost and duration of lawsuits. Overcoming these obstacles will be crucial to expanding public participation in CCL and increasing its potential to drive systemic change. As such, the next chapter turns to possible countermeasures that can be taken to improve future prospects, looking at how these obstacles may evolve and be overcome, and drawing on the trajectory of tobacco litigation in the United States as a comparative case.

CHAPTER 7

Countermeasures: Possible Improvements and Future Prospects

7.1 Overview

The previous two chapters examined institutional and cognitive obstacles to CCL in Japan. This chapter builds on those findings to consider how such barriers might evolve, be reduced, or overcome. Japanese CCL remains at an early stage, with five observed cases, despite an unfavorable legal opportunity structure. Yet, given the urgency of the climate crisis and the rapid rise of CCL worldwide, it seems unlikely that Japan will remain an outlier. As domestic CCL develops, new challenges to the litigation process will emerge, and some cases can be expected to exert wider influence on policy and society.

To explore potential trajectories for Japanese CCL, this chapter traces the possible evolution and overcoming of institutional and cognitive obstacles (Sec. 7.2), before comparing the prospective development of domestic CCL with the historical evolution of tobacco litigation in the United States (Sec. 7.3). Although climate change and tobacco litigation may appear unrelated, both involve complex, long-term disputes over public health and welfare, as well as questions of corporate and governmental responsibility. As the wealth of scholarly literature on the subject suggests, there are sound reasons to study and compare the legal development of such broad societal phenomena (Baird 2004; Olszynski, Mascher, and Doelle 2017; Normann 2019). Comparative analysis can shed light on possible future stages of Japanese CCL. The chapter closes with a brief summary (Sec. 7.4).

7.2 Obstacles to CCL

7.2.1 *Possible Evolution of Institutional Obstacles*

Chapter 5 used the LOS framework to analyze key institutional obstacles hampering CCL in Japan, using three indicators: access to the courts, existing law, and judicial receptiveness.

Access to the courts remains highly constrained, particularly by strict standing rules and limited available resources. Japan's standing requirements have frequently been criticized for their narrowness compared to other developed countries. As noted earlier, the standing framework was heavily influenced by German administrative procedure (Okubo 2013, 254–255). German courts historically excluded *actio popularis* – public interest suits brought by citizens to protect collective welfare (Garner et al. 2014) – and many Western jurisdictions still take a similar view, reserving courts for the resolution of individual harm and leaving public welfare to the political and policymaking branches.[1]

This strict approach has inadvertently excluded much environmental litigation, since such cases often involve diffuse public interests not easily framed as discrete individual rights (Okubo 2016, 450; Otsuka 2020b, 96). To fill this gap in legal representation, Germany introduced a system for environmental group actions in 2006 (Okubo 2013, 228).[2]

---

1 In this regard, Germany recognizes constitutional litigation that allows citizens to bring claims not directly related to their individual rights. However, the German Constitution still imposes certain requirements to ensure such claims fall within the scope of judicial authority. Under its Article 93 (Jurisdiction of the Federal Constitutional Court):

"(1) The Federal Constitutional Court shall rule:

1. on the interpretation of this Basic Law in disputes concerning the extent of the rights and obligations of a supreme federal institution or other concerned institutions that have been vested with rights of their own by this Basic Law or by the rules of procedure of a supreme federal institution;
2. in the event of disagreements or doubts concerning the formal or substantive compatibility of federal law or Land law with this Basic Law or the compatibility of Land law with other federal laws on application of the Federal Government, of a Land government, or of one-fourth of the Members of the Bundestag; 2a. in case of disagreement as to whether a law meets the requirements of paragraph (2) of Article 72, on request from the Bundesrat or the government or the parliament of a Land;
3. in case of disagreement on the rights and obligations of the Federation and the Länder, particularly in the implementation of federal legislation by the Länder and in the exercise of federal supervision;
4. on other disputes involving the public law between the Federation and the Länder, between Länder or within a Land, unless recourse to another court exists;
   - 4a. on constitutional complaints that may be filed by anyone claiming that one of their basic rights or one of their rights under paragraph (4) of Article 20 or under Articles 33, 38, 101, 103, or 104 has been violated by public authority;
   - 4b. on constitutional complaints by municipalities or associations of municipalities alleging violation of their right of self-government under Article 28 by a (federal) law; in case of violation by a Land law, however, only where a complaint cannot be lodged with the Land constitutional court;
   - 4c. on constitutional complaints filed by associations concerning their nonrecognition as political parties for an election to the Bundestag;
5. in the other cases provided for in this Basic Law."

German Constitution (Chapter 2, supra note 6).

2 The German Law on Supplementary Provisions Governing Actions in Environmental Matters under Directive 2003/35/EC (Umwelt-Rechtsbehelfsgesetz) of December 7, 2006 (BGBl. 2006 I, 2816).

Japan, by contrast, has been reluctant to introduce comparable reforms. The Ministry of Justice has expressed concern that relaxing standing requirements could unleash a flood of litigation and overburden the courts (Takahashi 2013, 45–46). As discussed in Chapter 4, this fear appears overstated, given Japan's historically low litigation rates and limited legal resources.

Increasingly, however, a stable climate system is being recognized domestically and internationally as a public good rather than a purely individual legal interest.[3] This emerging consensus helps explain why so many climate cases worldwide are brought by environmental organizations, which assume responsibility for representing the public interest (Peel and Osofsky 2015, 43–45).

One partial exception to Japan's strict standing rules is the consumer organization collective litigation system, introduced in 2007.[4] Under this framework, a qualified consumer organization certified by the prime minister may initiate litigation on behalf of consumers. The system was created to address three concerns: (1) the informational and power imbalance between consumers and businesses; (2) the high cost of individual litigation to recover typically small damages; and (3) the need for consistent remedies (Ito 2007, 165). Similar considerations apply to climate change. Nagashima (2014, 164–167) argues that the development of Japanese CCL may likewise require new collective action mechanisms, such as environmental public interest litigation.

Access to available legal resources in Japan may also improve. As part of a series of reforms to the judicial system in 2002, the Ministry of Justice took action to expand the number of legal professionals. This included overhauling the bar examination and professional training systems, resulting in a marked increase in the number of practicing attorneys. As Figure 19 shows, the number of attorneys registered with the Japan Federation of Bar Associations grew steadily over fifty years from around 5,800 in 1950 to circa 17,000 in 2000, before rising sharply after the period of reforms, reaching just over 42,000 by 2020.[5]

---

3 For example, plaintiffs in the *Juliana* case attempted to base their public trust claim on this notion. See Sec. 5.3.2 and Chapter 1, supra note 5.

4 See the website of the Consumers Affairs Agency at https://www.caa.go.jp/en/policy/consumer_system. Collective action is provided for under the Act on Special Measures Concerning Civil Court Proceedings for the Collective Redress for Property Damage Incurred by Consumers, Act No. 96 of December 11, 2013, https://www.japaneselawtranslation.go.jp/en/laws/view/2727/en.

5 The number of candidates passing the bar examination may also indicate growth in the pool of potential legal professionals. However, not all successful candidates go on to practice law. Therefore, the number of attorneys registered as members of the Japan Federation of Bar Associations may serve as a more accurate measure of available legal professionals.

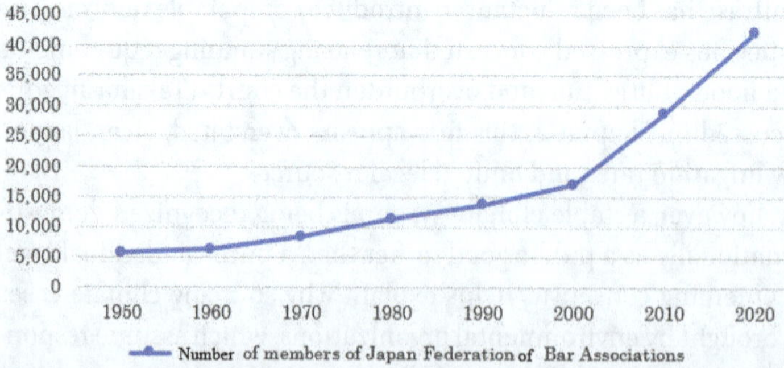

FIGURE 19 Number of attorneys in Japan, as defined by membership of the Japan Federation of Bar Associations, 1950–2020
SOURCE: TRANSLATED AND MODIFIED FROM WHITE PAPER ON ATTORNEYS (2020A, 44)

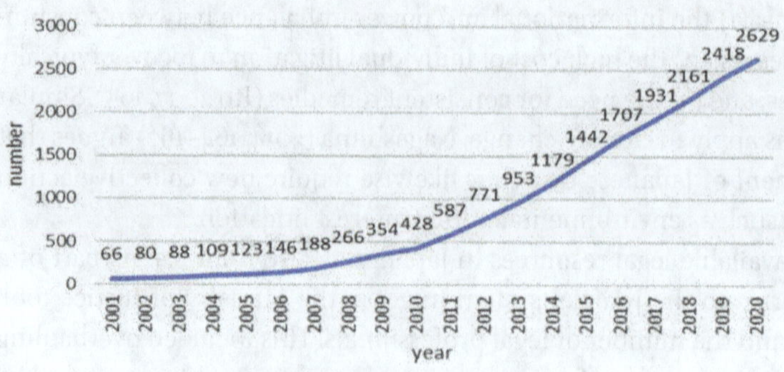

FIGURE 20 Number of in-house attorneys, 2001–2020
SOURCE: TRANSLATED AND MODIFIED FROM JAPAN IN-HOUSE LAWYERS ASSOCIATION, HTTPS://JILA.JP/MATERIAL/STATISTICS (IN JAPANESE)

New professional fields emerged, notably in-house lawyers (corporate counsel) and school lawyers. In-house lawyers provide legal services to companies and organizations,[6] while school lawyers address issues such as bullying and disputes with parents under a cooperative framework involving the Ministry of Education, Culture, Sports, Science, and Technology (MEXT), education boards, and bar associations.[7] The number of in-house lawyers has grown

6 Article 50 of the Basic Regulations on the Duties of Attorneys (Bengoshi Shokumu Kihon Kitei), https://www.nichibenren.or.jp/library/ja/jfba_info/rules/data/rinzisoukai_syokumu.pdf (in Japanese).

7 For the definition of a school lawyer in the Japanese context, see https://kodomoroppo-school.jp/dictionary/%E3%82%B9%E3%82%AF%E3%83%BC%E3%83%AB%E3%83%AD%E3%82%A4%E3%83%A4%E3%83%BC.

rapidly – from 428 in 2010 to 2,629 in 2020 (Figure 20) – providing businesses with greater access to legal expertise and lowering barriers to legal action. Similarly, MEXT announced in 2019 the deployment of approximately 300 school lawyers to respond to school-related legal issues.[8]

These developments have enhanced public awareness of legal rights and structures and may indirectly promote legal mobilization. Nonetheless, regional disparities in access to attorneys remain a significant challenge. According to the 2024 White Paper on Attorneys, Tokyo had 9,231 attorneys, whereas the largely rural Tottori Prefecture had only 73. This mismatch in access to legal representation in urban and rural communities is particularly relevant for environmental justice: many power plants and industrial facilities are located in rural areas, meaning that those most exposed to environmental risks often have the least access to legal support.

The financial burdens of litigation may also evolve in the coming years. One potential area of development is reforming the current loser-pays rule, requiring the losing party to bear court costs.[9] While these costs are regulated under the Act on the Costs of Civil Proceedings, they exclude attorney fees – often the most expensive and least predictable element of litigation.[10] As noted earlier, plaintiffs in the four climate cases relied on attorneys who volunteered their time or charged minimal fees. By contrast, US citizen suits allow courts to order defendants to pay prevailing plaintiffs' legal expenses, including attorney fees (Salzman 2019, 393), a mechanism that significantly reduces financial risk and could serve as a model for Japan.

The second LOS indicator – existing law and the availability of legal bases on which to ground claims – may also shift in light of Japan's statutory commitment to achieve carbon neutrality by 2050 under the revised APGWC. This commitment could provide plaintiffs with a legal basis to challenge the consistency of government regulations or policies, similar to the *Urgenda* case in the Netherlands. In the *Kobe* cases, attorneys submitted an official summary of the Dutch Supreme Court's *Urgenda* decision to argue that climate change constitutes a human rights violation. Although they acknowledged differences between the Dutch and Japanese legal systems, they emphasized the universal relevance of the principle that climate change threatens fundamental human rights.

---

8 MEXT Minister's press conference, September 24, 2019, https://www.mext.go.jp/b_menu/daijin/detail/1421558.htm (in Japanese).

9 Code of Civil Procedure (Chapter 4, supra note 49). In 2000, the Japan Federation of Bar Associations requested that the Judicial System Reform Council not recommend to the government that it implements the unilateral loser-pays rule; see https://www.nichibenren.or.jp/document/opinion/year/2000/2000_22.html (in Japanese).

10 Act on the Costs of Civil Proceedings (Chapter 6, supra note 18).

The third LOS indicator – judicial receptiveness – may likewise evolve. One possibility is to expand the scope of cases eligible for adjudication by lay judges (*saiban-in*), a system introduced in May 2009 and currently limited to certain serious criminal cases.[11] Extending lay participation to civil cases of significant public interest could encourage professional judges to take greater account of prevailing social values in their decisions, including those related to climate change (Kawabata 2000, 30). Moreover, as climate science continues to refine causal links between anthropogenic emissions and extreme weather events,[12] judges may become more willing to engage substantively with climate claims.

7.2.2 *Overcoming Cognitive Obstacles*

Chapter 6 identified four main persistent cognitive obstacles faced by potential litigants: (1) low awareness of the urgency of the climate crisis, (2) uncertainty regarding legal outcomes, and (3) concerns about the costs and time required by proceedings. Public reluctance to prioritize climate measures may partly stem from Japan's geographic experience with frequent natural hazards, such as earthquakes and volcanic eruptions, which normalize risk and obscure the distinct urgency of climate change. While many people are aware of climate change, they remain reluctant to make sacrifices to prioritize countermeasures. Their experience of adapting to natural hazards may inhibit full recognition of the immediacy and urgency of the crisis. As climate science advances and extreme weather events become more visible, public recognition of climate risks may increase, potentially leading to greater willingness to litigate, or to support those that do.

---

11 According to Article 2 (Cases Subject to Saiban-in Trials and the Organization of Panels) in Chapter I (General Provisions) of the Act on Criminal Trials with the Participation of Saiban-in:

"(1) Except when a ruling under the following Article or Article 3–2 is rendered, district courts handle the following cases through a panel with the participation of saiban-in after the panel and the participation of saiban-in is organized in accordance with the provisions of this Act, notwithstanding the provisions of Article 26 of the Court Act:

(i) cases involving offences punishable with the death penalty, life imprisonment, or life imprisonment without work; and

(ii) cases listed in Article 26, paragraph (2), item (ii) of the Court Act that involve offences that have caused a victim to die by intentional criminal acts (excluding those falling under the preceding item)."

Act on Criminal Trials with the Participation of Saiban-in, Act No. 63 of May 28, 2004, https://www.japaneselawtranslation.go.jp/en/laws/view/3474/en.

12 Known as climate or event attribution science, which has been widely employed in climate change cases worldwide. For more details, see https://climateattribution.org.

The proliferation of social networks also facilitates rapid, transnational dissemination of climate-related information. Unlike the era of Japan's major air pollution lawsuits, today's activists operate within global communication networks. For example, a *Kobe* plaintiff active in FFF used both national and international FF channels to share updates on the case, amplifying its visibility and mobilizing broader support.

Informational barriers could also be mitigated by improving public access to practical legal knowledge – such as typical litigation timelines, filing costs, and attorney fees. In Japan, attorney fees are unregulated: lawyers set their own rates, leaving potential litigants to negotiate such costs on their own.[13] By contrast, some countries regulate litigation costs. Germany's Rechtsanwaltsvergütungsgesetz (Act on the Renumeration of Lawyers), for example, sets standardized fee schedules, enhancing price transparency and reducing competitive pressure on lawyers' incomes (Fukui 2011, 63). Expanding legal education, historically underemphasized in Japan, could further demystify legal processes and modes of reasoning and encourage public engagement with litigation (Otomo and Nihei 2014).

The length of litigation may also be shortened. The Act on the Expediting of Trials, enacted in 2003,[14] stipulates in Article 2 that first-instance trials should conclude within two years. Combined with the steady increase in the number of legal professionals, this could lead to more efficient proceedings in future CCL.

7.3 Prospects for the Future: through Comparison with US Tobacco Litigation

7.3.1 *Background*

One of the key obstacles in Japan discussed above is the low awareness of climate issues. While this can be a reason for fewer cases coming to court, the relationship goes in both directions: with an increase in cases comes greater public recognition of the issue. In many jurisdictions, litigation has historically served as a mechanism to raise awareness of previously invisible or narrowly perceived social problems. In the United States, scholars have repeatedly documented this phenomenon (McGovern 1986; Sanders 1992; Schmit 1994). Mark

13 For the rule on attorneys' fees, see https://www.nichibenren.or.jp/library/ja/jfba_info/rules/pdf/kaiki/kaiki_no_68_160704.pdf (in Japanese).

14 Act on the Expediting of Trials, Act No. 107 of July 2003, https://www.japaneselawtranslation.go.jp/en/laws/view/3779.

Galanter (1998; 2000, 24) describes the pattern of litigation in the following terms:

> US tort cases are brought to shift part of the costs of harmful products to manufacturers and users. Typically, a few tentative claims are filed initially. A small number of successful cases then provide models and incentives for other attorneys and litigants. As a result, similar cases flood the courts, sometimes leading to corporate bankruptcy. This litigious pressure prompts defendants and stakeholders to offer compensation and initiate reforms. Eventually, the wave of litigation subsides.

The process that Galanter describes here, which we will return to in the next section on the development of US tobacco litigation, may be mapped visually, as in Figure 21.

A recent example in Japan can be seen in the surge of asbestos-related litigation, which progressed through phases 1 and 2 and culminated in a landmark Supreme Court ruling on May 17, 2021, ordering the government and private companies to pay substantial compensation.[15] Following the decision, the government proposed a compensation scheme offering up to 13 million yen per qualifying plaintiff still engaged in litigation. A parallel system was introduced to compensate victims who had not filed claims. This proposal was accepted by the plaintiffs' attorneys, effectively marking the transition to phase 3. As a result, the number of asbestos cases is expected to decrease, corresponding to phase 4.[16]

This phased pattern of litigation provides a useful lens through which to consider the possible trajectory of CCL in Japan. A particularly instructive comparison may be drawn with US tobacco litigation, where key cases transformed both regulatory landscapes and public discourse. For example, in *Massachusetts* (2007), the US Supreme Court recognized CO_2 as a pollutant under the CAA. This decision marked a significant development while remaining consistent with earlier jurisprudence. Prior to this ruling, the Court had questioned whether the EPA possessed the statutory authority to regulate CO_2 emissions under the CAA. During that review, an EPA memorandum cited *FDA v. Brown & Williamson*, where the Food and Drug Administration (FDA) was

15 Supreme Court Decision on Construction Asbestos Litigation, Saiko Saibansho [Sup. Ct.], May 17, 2021, no. 75, 5 Saiko Saibansho Minji Hanreisyu [Minshu] 1359.

16 The Act on Asbestos Health Damage Relief was revised in 2022, to extend the deadline for claiming special survivor benefits and expanded the scope of eligibility. Act No. 4 of February 10, 2006, https://www.japaneselawtranslation.go.jp/en/laws/view/3797/en.

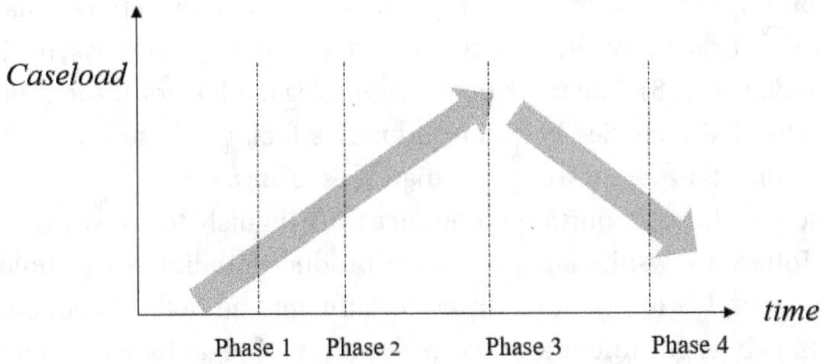

FIGURE 21 Galanter's four phases of litigation of a certain social problem (e.g., tobacco litigation, climate litigation, etc.). As a small number of cases win in court (phase 1), they serve as models, and more cases are subsequently filed (phase 2). This caseload grows and reaches a peak point (phase 3), whereupon defendants begin to settle out of court, propose compensation, or initiate reforms. Consequently, the number of cases fall (phase 4). As Galanter's choice of wording might suggest, the pattern of litigation depicted here resembles a "wave"; however, the author retains "phase" to distinguish it from the historical waves of litigation discussed in the next sections.
SOURCE: CREATED BY THE AUTHOR BASED ON THE CONCEPTUALIZATION OF GALANTER (2000)

similarly required to defend its regulatory mandate over tobacco.[17] In *FDA v. Brown*, the Court eventually held that the FDA lacked authority to regulate tobacco products because they were not traditionally treated as unsafe drugs and because Congress had continued to endorse their legal sale. The fact that the reasoning in *FDA v. Brown* was subsequently overcome was cited in support of the EPA's authority to regulate GHGs, thereby reinforcing the regulatory mandate over CO_2.

Beyond parallels in legal reasoning, similarities between tobacco control and climate action have also appeared in social movements. In 2014, several Canadian environmental organizations – including Greenpeace Canada and the World Wildlife Fund (WWF) Canada – sent letters to thirty-two energy companies demanding disclosure of their climate-related lobbying and communication practices. These letters explicitly invoked the precedent of

17 Memorandum from Robert E. Fabricant (EPA General Counsel) to Marianne L. Horinko (Acting EPA Administrator), August 28, 2003, https://yosemite.epa.gov/oa/EAB_Web_Docket.nsf/Filings%20By%20Appeal%20Number/BC82F18BAC5D89FF85257417006 6B7BD/%24File/UARG%20Attchmnt%20G ...43.pdf; Food and Drug Administration v. Brown & Williamson Tobacco Corp, 529 U.S. 120 (2000).

tobacco litigation, warning that energy companies faced a similar reputational and legal risk to that faced by the tobacco industry in the 1980s (Olszynski, Mascher, and Doelle 2017, 8). The two organizations' legal advisors at the time also noted structural similarities between industries facing tobacco liability and those reliant on coal-fired power (Canadian Press 2014).

Despite these parallels, important differences distinguish tobacco litigation and CCL. Tobacco lawsuits largely rely on product liability law to hold corporations accountable for manufacturing harmful and addictive products. By contrast, CCL is brought under a much wider array of legal bases, including administrative, constitutional, and human rights law.[18] Moreover, while tobacco litigation typically targets private corporations, nearly 75 percent of CCL cases worldwide are filed against governments or municipalities (Setzer and Byrnes 2020, 9).

Social movement dynamics also differ. Antitobacco campaigns have been primarily led by victims, their families and communities, and local governments seeking to protect health, whereas climate movements are more heterogeneous, often driven by coalitions of environmental NGOs, scientists, youth activists, and older or retired citizens. This broader social base reflects the global and intergenerational character of climate change.[19]

As Table 22 illustrates, one key similarity is the shift in social norms regarding both tobacco use and GHG emissions. Initially, both were accepted – and even promoted – by many governments, including those of the US and Japan. The tobacco industry, for example, received strong government support due to its economic importance (Isayama 1983, 91–92; Cairney, Studlar, and Mamudu 2012). Over time, scientific findings on health risks (in tobacco) and environmental harm (in climate change) reshaped public attitudes, leading to regulation, litigation, and reduced social acceptance.

---

18 Beyond the two Japanese administrative lawsuits discussed in this book, which contest the improper exercise of regulatory authority, the Dutch *Urgenda* case (Chapter 1, supra note 6) pursued state liability in tort. Other notable suits alleging constitutional violations include *Neubauer* (Chapter 1, supra note 8) and *Do-Hyun Kim* (2024, supra note 7), both alleging breaches of the state's duty to consider environmental protection. Recently, litigation targeting "climate wash" – a form of greenwashing in which entities misrepresent their progress toward climate goals (Vélez-Echeverri, Higham, and Setzer 2024) – has increased. Examples include *FossielVrij* (2023, supra note 12).

19 For example, Association of Swiss Senior Women for Climate Protection v. Federal Department of the Environment Transport, Energy and Communications (DETEC) and Others, [2016], https://climatecasechart.com/non-us-case/union-of-swiss-senior-women-for-climate-protection-v-swiss-federal-parliament..

TABLE 22 Comparison of sociolegal aspects between tobacco litigation and CCL worldwide

Issue	Tobacco litigation	CCL	Comparison
Social norm	*Past:* Legal, socially accepted, and government-supported *Present:* Widely regulated after recognition of health risks	*Past:* Legal, socially accepted, and government-supported *Present:* Increasingly regulated as public awareness of climate risk grows	Common points Common points
Causal proof in proceedings	*Past:* Difficult *Present:* Well established	*Past:* Difficult *Present:* Improving	Common points Difference
Scope	Confined (affects smokers and nearby individuals)	Widespread (global affects, intergenerational)	Difference
Degree of damages	Relatively clear (e.g., bronchial disease)	Diverse, diffuse, often indirect (e.g., floods, sea-level rises)	Difference
Avoidability	Yes (individuals can refrain from smoking)	No (climate impacts are unavoidable)	Difference

SOURCE: CREATED BY THE AUTHOR

Another commonality is the progressive development of causal proof. In early tobacco cases, plaintiffs struggled to demonstrate that smoking caused their specific illnesses. Over time, medical research produced robust epidemiological evidence linking smoking to disease (Rabin 1992, 855). CCL is undergoing a similar trajectory: event attribution science now strengthens plaintiffs' ability to link extreme weather events – such as floods, heatwaves, and typhoons – to anthropogenic GHG emissions.[20]

Nonetheless, important differences remain. Tobacco-related harm, such as lung cancer and bronchitis, is relatively direct, observable, and individualized, while climate impacts like flooding and heatwaves are systemic, geographically

20 For example, IPCC reports utilize event attribution science (supra note 228), and these have been cited in claims of many climate cases, including *Urgenda* (supra note 6), *Juliana* (supra note 4), four Japanese cases (in each complaint), and *Do-Hyun Kim* (supra note 7).

diffuse, and temporally distributed. Establishing causation in climate cases therefore requires multiple inferential steps and substantial supporting evidence. In all four Japanese cases (excluding *Youth*), defendants denied a causal link between their emissions and the harm alleged by plaintiffs. Foreseeability remains a contested point, with defendants arguing that they could not reasonably have anticipated such outcomes (Olszynski, Mascher, and Doelle 2017, 32).[21]

Moreover, tobacco harm is considered avoidable – individuals can stop smoking or limit exposure – whereas climate change impacts cannot be personally avoided by affected citizens. Finally, whereas tobacco litigation has a clear target (tobacco manufacturers), CCL involves a broader array of defendants: CFPP operators, carbon majors, pipeline companies, local governments, and national governments. These differences *may* lead CCL along a distinct trajectory from tobacco litigation.

The next sections proceed as follows: in Section 7.3.2, the trajectory of US tobacco litigation is described in terms of its three waves. In Section 7.3.3, the development of US CCL is outlined and compared to those periods, and Section 7.3.4 offers a brief comparison of US tobacco and CCL cases. Section 7.3.5 reviews Japanese tobacco cases, before comparing the trajectory of Japanese climate cases with US tobacco litigation to identify the current developmental stage of Japanese CCL.

7.3.2 *US Tobacco Litigation*

In the early twentieth century, tobacco was considered among the most important crops in the United States and a cornerstone of the US economy, supporting millions of farmers, entire rural communities, and generating substantial export earnings (Normann 2019, 106–107). This economic importance – albeit amid fluctuations in tobacco product prices – solidified the industry's social and political status, allowing it to exercise significant influence and resist regulatory efforts, even as evidence of health risks accumulated.

Tobacco also enjoyed broad social acceptance. Popular media in the 1950s and 1960s routinely depicted smoking as glamorous or sophisticated, reinforcing cultural normalization. As a result, consumption rose sharply, followed by a parallel increase in tobacco-related illnesses (Figure 22). As recently as 2013, the United States remained one of the world's leading tobacco producers (Table 23).

---

21 For example, in *Urgenda*, one argument was to identify when the Dutch government acknowledged the real and imminent danger of climate-related harm to people's rights. See National Cancer Institute and WHO (2017, chap. 10).

TABLE 23 Top tobacco-growing countries in the world, 2013

Ranking	Country	Production in 2013 (metric tons)
1	China	3,148,547
2	Brazil	850,673
3	India	830,000
4	United States	345,837
5	Indonesia	260,200
6	Zimbabwe	150,000
7	Malawi	132,849
8	Argentina	115,334
9	Pakistan	108,307
10	Turkey	90,000

SOURCE: REPRODUCED WITH SLIGHT MODIFICATIONS FROM NATIONAL CANCER INSTITUTE AND WHO (2017, 353, TAB. 10.1)

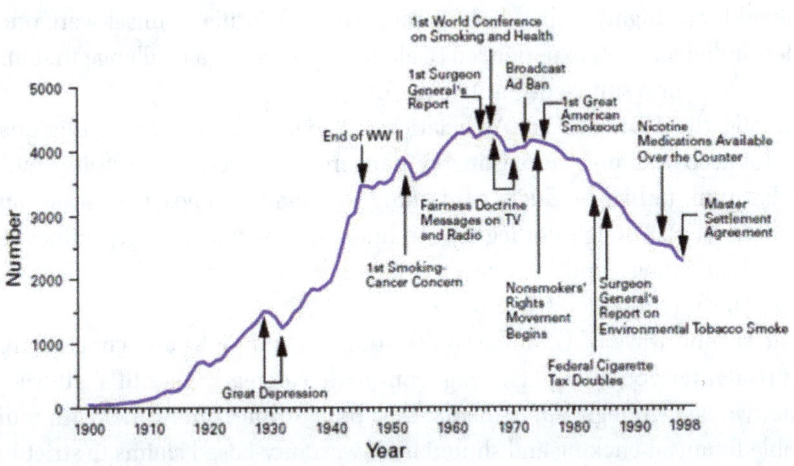

FIGURE 22 Annual adult per capita cigarette consumption, major smoking, and health events in the United States, 1990–1998
SOURCE: REPRODUCED FROM CDC (1999, FIG. 1)

The trajectory of US tobacco litigation is commonly divided into three waves (Galanter 2000, 25; Olszynski, Mascher, and Doelle 2017; Goguen 2022; Law Library n.d.):

- First wave (1954–1973)
- Second wave (1983–1992)
- Third wave (early 1990s–present)

The first wave began shortly after a 1952 article in *Reader's Digest* (Norr 1952) publicly linked smoking to lung cancer. In 1954, *Lowe v. Reynolds* became the first major case,[22] and by 1973, roughly 100–150 similar cases had been filed (Rabin 1992, 857).

Plaintiffs relied primarily on product liability theories, arguing that tobacco companies should be held legally responsible for the health harms caused by their products, and citing tort liability and implied warranty. Under tort liability, plaintiffs needed to prove that companies knowingly marketed a dangerous product without adequate warnings, constituting a breach of their duty of care (argument of negligence). Under the Uniform Commercial Code, an implied warranty holds that a merchant's goods must be fit for their ordinary purpose unless otherwise specified (Garner et al. 2014, 1822). Plaintiffs argued that tobacco products failed this standard because they were inherently harmful.

Despite growing scientific evidence, plaintiffs faced significant hurdles, particularly in proving causation between smoking and specific illnesses. Courts were reluctant to impose strict liability solely on the basis of implied warranty, and legal precedent generally favored the industry.

A further obstacle was the imbalance of legal resources. Tobacco companies retained large, highly skilled legal teams, while plaintiffs' counsel were often underfunded and less experienced (Galanter 2000, 25) – a challenge that mirrors the current resource disparities in CCL.

In 1965, the American Bar Association issued guidance asserting that qualified tobacco was not "unreasonably dangerous" merely because its smoke was harmful, unlike products containing marijuana (Laposata, Barnes, and Glantz 2012, 2). Though not legally binding, this position strongly influenced subsequent rulings, and by 1973, most first-wave cases had failed, effectively ending this initial period (Galanter 2000, 26–27).

The second wave of US tobacco litigation began in 1983 and concluded in 1992 (Galanter 2000, 27). Learning from earlier defeats, plaintiffs' attorneys made two key strategic adjustments: they built stronger networks with more reliable financial backing and shifted from warranty-based claims to strict liability claims. After the 1966 Cigarette Labeling and Advertising Act mandated health warnings on cigarette packaging, previous legal arguments based on failure to warn became obsolete.[23] Plaintiffs therefore focused on negligence, while defendants relied heavily on the doctrine of assumed risk. To rebut this defense, plaintiffs argued that nicotine addiction undermined consumer

22 Lowe v. R.J. Reynolds, 75 A.D.2d 967.

23 Federal Cigarette Labeling and Advertising Act of 1965 (Public Law 89–92).

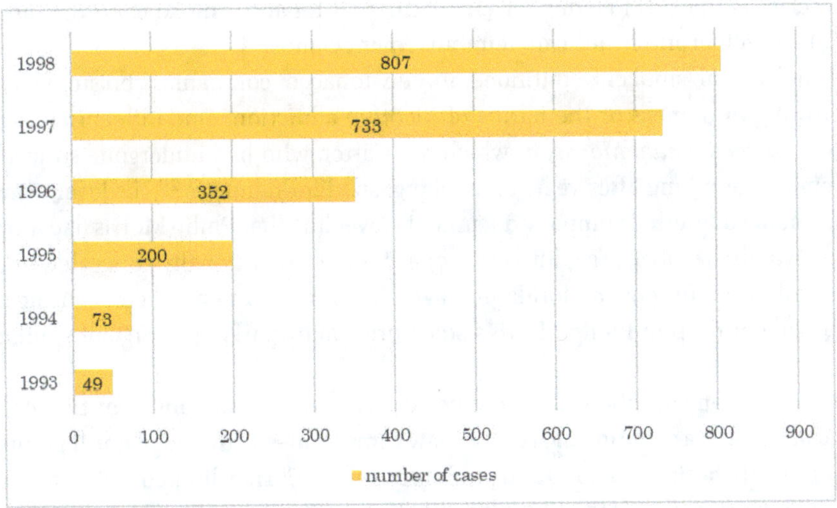

FIGURE 23 Number of lawsuits against the tobacco industry, 1993–1998
SOURCE: TRANSLATED AND MODIFIED FROM GALANTER AND TANASE (1998, 38)

choice. Nevertheless, juries frequently attributed responsibility for addiction to smokers themselves (Galanter 2000, 28; Tanase 2000, 12–13).

This period began with the landmark case of *Cipollone v. Liggett*.[24] In 1983, Mr. and Ms. Cipollone, both heavy and long-term smokers suffering from tobacco-related illnesses, filed a tort action against multiple tobacco companies alleging negligence, fraud, and conspiracy. After Ms. Cipollone's death in 1984, a jury awarded $400,000 in damages – the first such award to a smoker – but this decision was overturned on appeal. Although the case eventually reached the US Supreme Court in 1992, it was remanded and abandoned five months later when plaintiffs' attorneys withdrew, mostly due to financial exhaustion. By the end of the second wave, after more than four decades and over 800 cases (Bernstein Research 1994), no case had resulted in compensation being paid to plaintiffs. Tobacco companies reportedly spent $75 million in legal fees during *Cipollone* alone, while plaintiffs' counsel incurred over $35 million in unreimbursed costs (Galanter 2000, 29).

A third wave of began in the early 1990s, before the second wave had fully ended, and was marked by an explosion in litigation (Figure 23).[25]

Four key features distinguished this third wave (Galanter 2000, 31; Olszynski, Mascher, and Doelle 2017, 11–13): (1) individual product liability claims; (2) rise

24 Cipollone v. Ligget Group Inc., 693 F. Supp. 208 [1988].
25 See https://www.sompo-wf.org/katsudou/sousho/sousho-no_00058.pdf (in Japanese).

of class actions; (3) claims for environmental tobacco smoke exposure; and (4) municipal and healthcare reimbursement claims.

Individual smokers continued to sue tobacco companies, bolstered by growing awareness of the harms of nicotine addiction. One influential case was *Carter v. Philip Morris*, in which Mr. Carter, who had undergone surgical removal of a lung after years of smoking, sued for damages.[26] His legal team introduced internal company documents revealing that Philip Morris had long known about tobacco's addictive properties and intentionally concealed this information. In 1996, a Florida jury awarded $750,000 in damages, causing a 14 percent drop in Philip Morris's stock price and sparking a surge of similar lawsuits.[27]

Public concern about tobacco fueled a rise in class actions.[28] In the 1994 *Castano* case, a coalition of sixty-two law firms formed a unified plaintiff group, each contributing $100,000 and pooling expertise.[29] They limited claims to the addictive nature of nicotine. Although a district court initially certified the class, the Court of Appeals reversed certification due to inconsistencies among state laws.[30] This setback led to a series of so-called "baby *Castano*" suits across roughly ten states. Only Florida's *Engle* case proceeded to trial, where the circuit court upheld the class action and imposed a $2 billion bond on tobacco companies.[31] However, higher courts later decertified the class, resulting in numerous individual *Engle progeny* cases in Florida.

Environmental tobacco smoke litigation also gained momentum because its victims – unlike smokers – could not be blamed for their exposure. In the *Broin* case, more than 60,000 plaintiffs, mostly flight attendants, filed a class action seeking $500 million in punitive damages.[32] Shortly after the trial began, the

---

26 Carter v. Philip Morris, 96 Fla. Jury Verdict Rep. 9–59 [Fla. cir. xt., 1996].

27 For example, Weitek v. Brown & Williamson Tobacco Co., 723 So. 2d 833 [Fla. App. 1998].

28 On class actions, Rule 23 of the Federal Rules of Civil Procedure provides:

"(a) Prerequisites. One or more members of a class may sue or be sued as representative parties on behalf of all members only if:

(1) the class is so numerous that joinder of all members is impracticable;

(2) there are questions of law or fact common to the class;

(3) the claims or defenses of the representative parties are typical of the claims or defenses of the class; and

(4) the representative parties will fairly and adequately protect the interests of the class."

Federal Rules of Civil Procedure, https://www.law.cornell.edu/rules/frcp/rule_23.

29 Castano v. American Tobacco Co. (94–1044.E.D., La.)

30 *Castano*, 84F. 3d 734 [5th Cir., 1996].

31 Engle v. R.J. Reynolds Tobacco Co. (94–08273 CA [20]).

32 Broin v. Philip Morris Co., 641 So.2d 888 [Fla. Dist. Ct. App. 1994].

parties reached a settlement: the defendant paid \$300 million, and plaintiffs agreed to withdraw their tort claims.

The fourth feature of the third wave was the rise of state and healthcare cost-recovery suits. Beginning in 1994, Mississippi, Minnesota, and West Virginia filed lawsuits seeking reimbursement for public medical expenses related to tobacco use. Florida enacted legislation authorizing similar claims. By 1998, 41 states had filed lawsuits, with 182 law firms involved (Kranz 1998, 161).

These efforts culminated in a series of global settlements. The *Castano* group negotiated with Philip Morris and R.J. Reynolds, reaching a proposed \$368.5 billion settlement over twenty-five years. In exchange, the companies would avoid FDA regulation, and plaintiffs agreed to a fifteen-year moratorium on new lawsuits. Separately, the 1998 Tobacco Master Settlement Agreement (MSA) was concluded between forty-six states and four major tobacco companies, including Brown & Williamson and Lorillard.[33] The MSA prohibited youth-targeted advertising and required payments totaling at least \$206 billion over twenty-five years. To return to Figure 21, these settlements correspond with Galanter's phase 3 of litigation.

Today, tobacco litigation continues but with a narrower focus, addressing issues such as misrepresentation of "light" cigarettes (Sweda, Gottlieb, and Banthin 2007) and compliance with FDA regulations (Henry 2020).[34] Case volume has declined sharply from its late-1990s peak (corresponding to phase 4 in Figure 21). The cumulative impact of litigation has been significant: advertising restrictions were tightened, public awareness of tobacco's health hazards grew, and companies adopted stronger measures to prevent harm from smoking. In 2022, the Florida Supreme Court further raised the evidentiary standard for plaintiffs alleging misleading tobacco advertising, resulting in dismissal of a major case.[35]

7.3.3 *US CCL*

Scientific evidence linking GHG emissions to global temperature increases began to emerge in the 1970s. The first international climate change conference

---

33 National Association of Attorneys General, The Master Settlement Agreement, https://www.naag.org/wp-content/uploads/2020/09/2019-01-MSA-and-Exhibits-Final.pdf.

34 A more recent emerging issue concerns the proliferation of illegal e-cigarettes. While a few products have received marketing authorization from the FDA, numerous unauthorized products with high nicotine content and lower prices have spread, prompting a growing number of lawsuits. See https://www.lawfirm.com/product-liability/vape/lawsuit.

35 R.J. Reynolds Tobacco Co. v. Prentice, Case No. SC20–291 (Fla. Mar. 17, 2022).

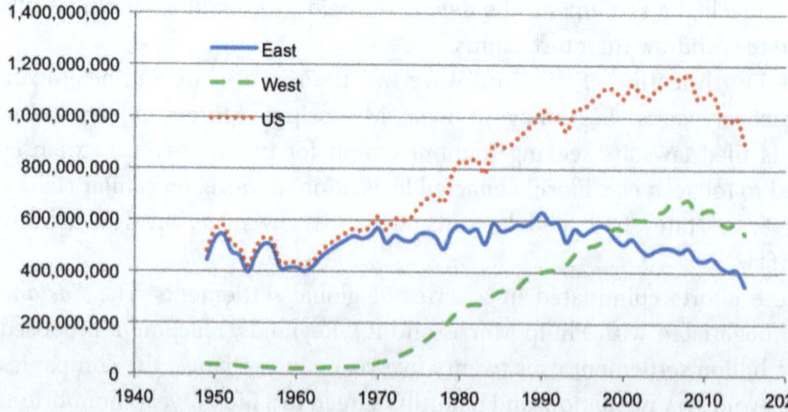

FIGURE 24 Metric tons of annual coal output by region (Eastern US, Western US, and total US), 1949–2015
SOURCE: REPRODUCED FROM KOLSTAD (2017, FIG. 1)

was held in Villach, Austria, in 1985.[36] In 1992, the United Nations Framework Convention on Climate Change (UNFCCC) was adopted. Nevertheless, the US government – like Japan's – was reluctant to impose GHG regulations, viewing them as a threat to economic development (Olszynski, Mascher, and Doelle 2017, 4). As with tobacco, the coal industry enjoyed strong governmental support, and US coal output continued to rise until roughly 2010 (Figure 24).

Consequently, national GHG emissions also grew (Figure 25).

As of July 2021, the Sabin Center database recorded 1,398 US climate change cases. The first case was filed in 1986, questioning a federal agency's decision not to evaluate the impact of its fuel economy standards on global warming.[37] The number subsequently remained relatively low until around 2006 (Figure 26). In 2007, filings rose sharply – nearly sixty new cases – coinciding with the Supreme Court's decision in *Massachusetts* and the release of the IPCC's Fourth Assessment Report (IPCC 2007). Another spike occurred in 2015, the year of the Paris Agreement and the launch of *Juliana*. In 2020, filings fell, likely due to the COVID-19 pandemic (Setzer and Byrnes 2020, 16).

Scholars have categorized the early stage of US CCL as the "first wave" of CCL (Olszynski, Mascher, and Doelle 2017, 15, 19, 23). A representative case is *Kivalina v. ExxonMobil* (2008), in which the Inuit village of Kivalina, Alaska,

36 The International Conference on the Assessment of the Role of Carbon Dioxide and of Other Greenhouse Gases in Climate Variations and Associated Impacts.

37 City of Los Angeles v. National Highway Traffic Safety Administration, 912 F.2d 478, 485 (D.C. Cir. 1990).

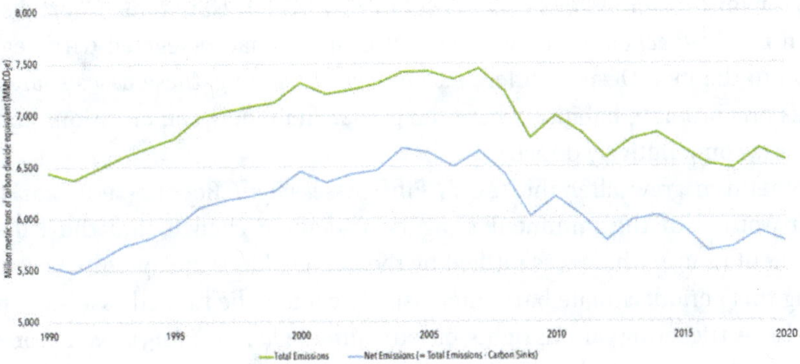

FIGURE 25 US GHG emissions, 1990–2020
SOURCE: ORIGINALLY PUBLISHED IN EPA (2025); HERE REPRODUCED FROM CENTER FOR CLIMATE AND ENERGY SOLUTIONS, HTTPS://WWW.C2ES.ORG/CONTENT/U-S-EMISSIONS

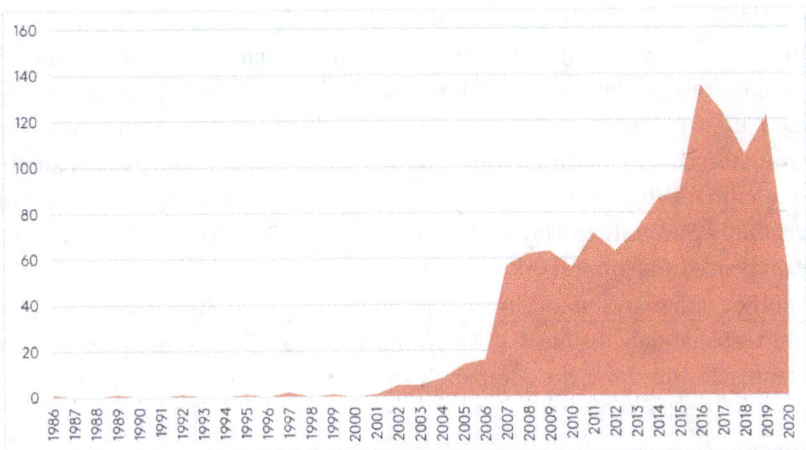

FIGURE 26 Climate cases in the United States, 1986–May 2020
SOURCE: REPRODUCED FROM SETZER AND BYRNES (2020, 7)

sued ExxonMobil for damages after the loss of protective sea ice rendered the village uninhabitable.[38] The district court dismissed the case for lack of justiciability, holding that such issues should be resolved by the political branches.

This case illustrates the broader first-wave strategy of targeting fossil fuel companies. Other notable cases include *Massachusetts* (2007) and *Connecticut v. American Electric Power Co.* (2005), in which seven states sued a major utility

38 Native Village of Kivalina v. ExxonMobil Corporation, 663 E Supp. 2d 863, 870 (N.D. Cal. 2009).

company for GHG emissions under tort law.[39] In 2011, the Supreme Court dismissed the *Connecticut* case, holding that Congress had delegated GHG regulation to the EPA. Despite differences in legal reasoning, these cases shared a focus on corporate liability, where the causal chain between emissions and harm was comparatively direct.

Momentum grew after the IPCC's Fifth Assessment Report (IPCC 2014), which warned of the imminent dangers of climate change, and the Paris Agreement (2015), which was ratified by the United States in September 2016. During this period, climate harm increasingly came to be framed as a human rights issue, triggering various rights-based claims. In *Juliana* (2015), twenty-one young plaintiffs and Earth Guardians alleged that the US government violated constitutional rights to life, liberty, property, and a stable climate system.[40] In *Colorado River Ecosystem* (2017), an environmental group sought legal personhood for the river, asserting its rights to exist, regenerate, and evolve.[41] These cases reflected a growing trend to recognize the rights of present and future generations – and even of nature itself – against climate harm.[42]

From 2017 onward, municipalities and states began suing carbon majors for climate-related damages. Notable cases include *Oakland v. BP* (2017), *San Mateo v. Chevron* (2017), and *New York v. BP* (2018).[43] In the New York case, the city sought recovery for infrastructure costs linked to a 2017 snowstorm attributed to climate change, but the district court dismissed the claim for lack of justiciability. Similarly, in *Mayor/Baltimore v. BP* (2018), the court dismissed the case on procedural grounds.[44]

Another emerging trend concerns climate-related disclosure and corporate transparency. In *Jacob v. Bloom Energy* (2020), a shareholder sought greater disclosure about the company's green energy technology, with the case

---

39 Connecticut v. American Electric Power Company, 206 F. Supp.2d 265 (S.D. N. Y 2005).

40 *Juliana* (Chapter 1, supra note 5). Furthermore, a series of reports between 2014 and 2016 by the Office of the United Nations High Commissioner for Human Rights explored relations between climate change and human rights. See https://www.ohchr.org/EN/Issues/Environment/SREnvironment/Pages/ClimateChange.aspx.

41 Colorado River Ecosystem v. State of Colorado, [2017], https://climatecasechart.com/case/colorado-river-ecosystem-v-state-colorado.

42 For example, in *Future Generations* (2018), the Colombian Supreme Court recognized both the Colombian Amazon and the Atrato River as a "subject of rights." Future Generations v. Ministry of the Environment and Others, [2018], 11001 22 03 000 2018 00319 00, https://climatecasechart.com/non-us-case/future-generation-v-ministry-environment-others.

43 City of Oakland v. BP p.l.c., [2017], https://climatecasechart.com/case/people-state-california-v-bp-plc-oakland; County of San Mateo v. Chevron Corp., [2017], https://climatecasechart.com/case/county-san-mateo-v-chevron-corp; *New York v. BP* (supra note 176).

44 Mayor & City Council of Baltimore v. BP plc, 388 F. Supp. 3d 538 (D. Md. 2019).

concluding in 2021 when Delaware Chancery Court ordered the defendant to allow the required inspection.[45] In *People v. Exxon Mobil* (2024), the plaintiffs alleged that ExxonMobil misled investors about its management of climate regulatory risks. At the time of writing, the case is still pending.[46]

Olszynski, Mascher, and Doelle (2017, 23) group all carbon-major liability cases into the first wave of US CCL, but a chronological perspective suggests greater complexity. Case numbers rose sharply around 2006/2007 (Figure 26), reflecting the initial surge in lawsuits targeting fossil fuel companies. A second phase emerged around 2015 with the rise of rights-based claims and suits against government actors. From 2017 onward, litigation diversified further, with public authorities (in New York, Baltimore, Oakland, San Mateo, etc.) becoming major plaintiffs and disclosure-related claims gaining prominence. Based on these trends, three waves of US CCL can be identified:

- First wave (2006–2014): early corporate liability cases, primarily tort-based.
- Second wave (2015–2016): emergence of rights-based litigation and youth plaintiffs.
- Third wave (2017–present): expanded municipal and state lawsuits, plus disclosure and investor-protection claims.

7.3.4 *US Tobacco and CCL*

Commonalities and differences between US tobacco and climate change cases across the three waves are summarized in Table 24.

Although the two categories of litigation differ in important respects, their trajectories share striking parallels. One key distinction lies in plaintiffs' responsibility for risk: tobacco plaintiffs were often seen as partly responsible for their harm (despite addiction arguments), whereas climate change plaintiffs bear no such responsibility for global warming impacts.[47]

Nevertheless, both litigation trajectories follow a similar pattern: a small number of early cases raised awareness and set precedents, followed by a sharp rise in related lawsuits (Rabin 1992, 120; Peel and Osofsky 2015, 78–81). Over time, the plaintiff base broadened and legal strategies diversified, ultimately

45 Jacob v. Bloom Energy Corp., [2020], https://climatecasechart.com/case/jacob-v-bloom-energy-corp.

46 People v. Exxon Mobil Corp., [2024], https://climatecasechart.com/case/people-v-exxon-mobil-corp-2.

47 Although everyone contributes to climate change by emitting GHGs in daily life, plaintiffs' individual responsibility is minimal compared to that of large emitters. Emphasizing this point risks complicating the argument and adds little analytical value given the vast disparity between individual and corporate emissions. Accordingly, this issue is not addressed further here.

TABLE 24 Comparison between US tobacco and climate change cases

	US tobacco cases	US climate change cases	Similarities/ differences
First wave	1954–1973 Tort claims based on product liability; defendants easily identifiable; harm obvious (lung disease, cancer)	2006–2014 Tort claims targeting major emitters; defendants diffuse, harder to isolate; climate harms less obvious, scientifically complex	Similarities: Pursuit of tort liability; focus on direct harms caused by defendants Differences: Identifiability of defendants; obviousness of harm
Second wave	1983–1992 Caseload rapidly increased; heightened public awareness of tobacco's addictive qualities; focus on fraud claims about addiction	2015–2016 Caseload increased after Paris Agreement and IPCC report; rise in social awareness; human rights–based claims emerged	Similarities: Surge in case volume; heightened public awareness Differences: Bases of claim (rights vs. fraudulent advertising)
Third wave	1990s–present Class actions proliferated; municipalities and states sought medical cost recovery	2017–present Municipal and state cases against carbon majors; growth of information disclosure claims	Similarities: Diversified legal strategies; participation of municipalities and states as plaintiffs Differences: Types of claims made, and actions brought

SOURCE: CREATED BY THE AUTHOR

shaping public discourse and policy responses on tobacco and climate change in the United States.

7.3.5 *US Tobacco and Japanese* CCL

Before comparing US tobacco litigation with Japanese CCL, we should note the limited number of tobacco cases in Japan. Japan has experienced tobacco-related litigation, but on a much more limited scale than the United States. A landmark case was the 1987 *No-Smoking Rights* case, in which four civil plaintiffs, backed by twelve attorneys, sued Japan Rail Company, demanding that over half of all train cars be designated nonsmoking, and arguing that not limiting smoking areas violated passengers' rights.[48] The district court dismissed the claim, but Japan Rail adopted the request before the ruling and later extended it to Shinkansen trains. In 2004, a Chiba workplace case saw a plaintiff sue her employer for mental and physical harm caused by secondhand smoke.[49] The district court partially upheld her claim.

Unlike in the US, where smokers themselves were often plaintiffs, Japanese tobacco cases primarily involved victims of environmental tobacco smoke. This distinction, along with swift regulatory and normative shifts (such as the Japanese Rail response), may be the reason why tobacco litigation has remained limited in Japan (Isayama 1983, 89–91; Mabane 2000, 85–88).

While Japanese tobacco litigation followed a different path from that of the US, placing Japan's four climate change cases (excluding *Youth*) within the timeline of US tobacco litigation offers a useful heuristic for gauging their stage of development. This comparison identifies some key features from each of the three waves of US tobacco litigation that are shared in the comparatively limited timespan of Japanese climate cases (Table 25).

As we have seen, two of Japan's climate lawsuits target METI (*Kobe* administrative and *Yokosuka*; see Table 3), seeking to annul approvals for the construction of coal power plants. In all four cases, however, plaintiffs challenged the plants' substantial GHG emissions in a relatively straightforward manner – closely resembling the first wave of US tobacco litigation.

As of July 2025, Japan's CCL history spans only about eight years, beginning in 2017. Its progress has been slow, constrained by obstacles such as government support for coal plant development, public ambivalence, evidentiary hurdles, and significant disparities in legal resources. Similar barriers – government

---

48 Ken-en-ken Sosho, Tokyo Chiho Saibansho [Tokyo Dist. Ct.], March 27, 1987, 1226 Hanrei Jiho [Hanji] 33. For a discussion of this case, see Isayama (1983, 103–104) and 2000 (65).

49 Tokyo Chiho Saibansho [Tokyo Dist. Ct.], July 12, 2004, 1884 Hanrei Jihou [Hanji] 81.

TABLE 25 Comparison between US tobacco and Japanese climate change cases

US tobacco cases (1954–present)	Japanese CCL cases (2017–present)
First wave (1954–1973): Pursuit of tort liability; focus on direct harms to human health caused by defendants' products	Pursuit of tort liability; METI's breach of obligation; focus on direct contributions to climate change caused by defendants' emissions
Second wave (1983–1992): Caseload rapidly increased; heightened public awareness of tobacco's addictive qualities; focus on fraud claims about addiction	Heightened public awareness of climate harms
Third wave (1990s–present): Diversified legal strategies; growth of class actions; municipalities and states as plaintiffs	Municipalities adopting zero-carbon targets

SOURCE: CREATED BY THE AUTHOR

support for tobacco production, favorable public opinion, challenges in proving causation, and resource imbalances between plaintiffs and defendants – slowed early US tobacco litigation, until advances in medical science exposed tobacco's harms, shifted public opinion, and enabled litigation to catalyze regulatory reform (Galanter's phase 3 in Figure 21).

While current Japanese CCL resembles the first wave of US litigation, it also shares limited features with the second and third waves. For example, public awareness of climate change in Japan is rising, spurred by the government's 2050 carbon-neutrality pledge in 2020 – an evolution comparable to the social awakening in US tobacco litigation's second wave (Sec. 7.3.2). Moreover, municipalities are increasingly adopting zero-carbon targets, echoing the municipal activism that characterized the third wave of US tobacco litigation.[50]

Whether Japanese CCL will follow a similar trajectory to US tobacco litigation in terms of caseload remains uncertain, given differences in legal opportunity structures between the two countries. However, the underlying goal – stimulating institutional and policy reform – remains achievable. Attorneys in these cases, like those in third-wave US tobacco litigation, have advanced novel legal theories, including shared responsibility and event attribution science, that may shape future jurisprudence.

50 Ministry of the Environment, "2050 Zero Carbon Cities in Japan", https://www.env.go.jp/en/earth/cc/2050_zero_carbon_cities_in_japan.html.

Even if Japanese CCL does not achieve major courtroom victories, it may still prompt informal legislative and policy reforms, much like early tobacco cases. In either outcome, current Japanese CCL has the potential to strengthen the country's response to the climate crisis.

7.4 Summary

This chapter explored the possible evolution and ways to overcome obstacles to CCL in Japan. Access to courts could be improved by introducing environmental public interest litigation systems similar to those in Germany. The growing number of attorneys in Japan may help bridge the gap between citizens and legal professionals, while reform of the loser-pays rule could lower financial barriers. Providing clear, accessible information on litigation costs and timelines would further empower prospective plaintiffs.

On legal bases, the revised APGWC could support claims analogous to *Urgenda*, challenging the alignment of national emissions targets with specific regulatory action. Although Japanese courts cannot directly apply foreign rulings, such cases may still be influential. Expanding lay judge participation could also enhance judicial receptiveness by bringing public values into decision-making. Broader legal education may further normalize litigation as a tool for social problem-solving.

Finally, this chapter outlined the historical development of US tobacco litigation, before making various comparisons among tobacco and CCL in both the United States and Japan. In analyzing how Japanese CCL might evolve, it concluded that it currently resembles the first wave of US tobacco cases, with some shared features with the second and third waves. Understanding that trajectory, without disregarding factors unique to the Japanese context, may offer valuable guidance for anticipating future developments and supporting the role of litigation as a driver of climate governance in Japan.

Conclusion

1 Findings and Implications

This study examined obstacles hindering the development of Japanese CCL and revealed five major findings across the preceding chapters.

Chapter 3 highlighted both continuity and divergence between Japan's historical environmental litigation – particularly antipollution cases – and contemporary climate change cases. These climate cases reflect two key characteristics: (1) they extend the tradition of environmental litigation, while (2) introducing unprecedented legal features. Together, these characteristics provided the conceptual foundation for the book and informed the analysis of Japanese CCL in subsequent chapters.

Chapter 4 offered the first comprehensive account of five Japanese climate change cases, which have received little international scholarly attention. It revealed how plaintiffs and attorneys strategically framed their arguments within the context of prior air pollution litigation to persuade judges. Defendants' rebuttals clarified key legal issues, including standing, causation, and justiciability – issues frequently encountered in CCL worldwide. This chapter also showed that a significant portion of argumentation in Japanese climate cases centers on standing and causal proof.

Chapter 5 examined institutional obstacles using the LOS framework, adapted to the Japanese context. Three indicators were analyzed: (1) access to courts, including standing requirements and available financial and professional resources; (2) existing law, including favorable statutes and precedents from past pollution and environmental cases; and (3) judicial receptiveness, particularly courts' historical treatment of environmental claims. This analysis showed how these institutional factors collectively shape the feasibility of CCL in Japan. It found that a combination of limited judicial access, judicial passivity, and extremely constrained legal personnel and financial support for court operations led to low rates of litigation, with access to courts emerging as the most decisive factor in shaping legal opportunity for CCL in Japan.

Chapter 6 addressed cognitive obstacles, drawing on questionnaire surveys and semi-structured interviews conducted between 2019 and 2024 with key actors in four of the five Japanese climate cases. It revealed plaintiffs' motivations and expectations, as well as their awareness of differences between past pollution cases and CCL. The findings suggest that uncertainty of outcomes, financial burdens, and lengthy duration of proceedings were significant cognitive hurdles (though many saw the last of these as an opportunity to raise awareness and push for long-term change). These challenges may be partly mitigated by the legacy of past environmental cases, which contributed to legislative reforms and fostered a public expectation of legal solutions to environmental problems.

Chapter 7 considered potential changes to the obstacles identified in earlier chapters and explored how Japanese CCL might evolve. It first examined the three institutional obstacles identified in the fifth chapter. Access to courts could improve if Japan loosens its strict standing requirements, following models such as Germany's. The growing number of attorneys may also help familiarize the public with legal processes. Expanding the loser-pays rule and improving the dissemination of judicial information could further reduce barriers. Legal frameworks may be strengthened through new legislation on climate mitigation and adaptation and by referencing an increasing number of foreign climate cases, even though such cases cannot be directly applied as precedent. Judicial receptiveness might be enhanced through expanded lay judge participation and improved legal education, encouraging a broader societal engagement with climate issues.

The chapter then compared Japanese CCL with the trajectory of US tobacco litigation. It traced three historical waves of US tobacco cases, beginning in 1954, then outlined the development of US CCL, which displayed similar periodic patterns, albeit over a much shorter timeframe (since 2006). The analysis identified three waves of US CCL analogous to those of tobacco litigation. Finally, Japan's climate change cases were situated within this comparative framework, leading to the conclusion that the current state of Japanese CCL most closely resembles the first wave of US tobacco litigation, in its pursuit of tort liability, focus on obligation breaches, and straightforward allegations of direct harm.

Several implications follow from these observations. First, the study adds new empirical data on East Asian CCL to the global discourse, providing the first detailed academic account of four Japanese climate cases. Given that most CCL scholarship focuses on Western jurisdictions, this contribution fills an important gap. Second, by positioning Japanese CCL within the historical trajectory of environmental litigation, this research connects climate cases to a broader sociolegal tradition in Japan. Finally, by comparing Japanese CCL to US tobacco litigation, the study offers a plausible path for future climate policy development, suggesting that the litigation reviewed here could become a driver of future institutional reform.

2 Contributions

All five Japanese climate change lawsuits are registered in the Sabin Center database, and the author has reported on some of them as a Japanese rapporteur. Although a few studies have examined Japanese cases (Linden 2023; Nishikawa 2023; Otsuka 2023), this book makes three distinctive contributions.

First, it offers a detailed account of the barriers that plaintiffs overcame to initiate these lawsuits and their continuing collective efforts. This analysis is based on a unique set of surveys and interviews conducted by the author, as well as close, sustained observation of the *Kobe* cases through direct participation in plaintiffs' meetings and activities. Such in-depth, firsthand reportage remains rare and valuable for sharing knowledge across geographically dispersed CCL efforts worldwide.

Second, the study situates Japanese CCL within the broader historical trajectory of Japan's antipollution lawsuits (Chapter 3). While climate change cannot be fully addressed through conventional legal theories, this lineage provides a foundation on which new doctrinal developments can be built, opening possibilities for future theoretical innovation.

Third, by comparing the chronological development of CCL with US tobacco litigation, the study highlights structural parallels and suggests a plausible trajectory for future CCL development in Japan. Just as tobacco-related harm prompted regulatory reforms and societal risk absorption through legal and insurance mechanisms, climate change litigation may similarly lead to tighter regulations and risk-distribution frameworks. Over time, GHG emissions may become a strictly controlled practice, analogous to smoking in today's society.

3 Limitations and Future Research

This study has at least three limitations. First, the empirical data in Chapter 5 are limited, partly due to the small number of plaintiffs involved in the four cases and the impossibility of including individuals involved in the *Youth* case, which was filed around the time of the final survey. Additional surveys would strengthen the empirical basis and enhance the persuasiveness of the analysis. Second, the number of observed climate cases in Japan remains small, constraining the generalizability of the findings. Third, the comparative analysis largely focused on the United States (with some space given to South Korea), and expanding the comparison to other jurisdictions would better illuminate Japan's sociolegal particularities.

Beyond these limitations, several promising avenues for future research remain. Although all four cases (*Sendai*, *Kobe* civil, *Kobe* administrative, and *Yokosuka*) were dismissed, one case – *Youth* – is still pending. At the same time, Japan's decarbonization policy landscape has been rapidly evolving since the government's 2020 carbon-neutrality pledge. Continued observation of these lawsuits – and their interaction with ongoing policy reforms – will be essential for understanding the future direction of Japanese CCL.

Subsequently, legislative developments also warrant continuous monitoring. On May 26, 2021, the Revised APGWC was enacted, formally setting Japan's national objective of achieving net-zero emissions by 2050. This statutory goal could provide a legal basis for claims seeking strict regulation of GHG emissions consistent with the 2050 target. Judicial review of specific emission regulations – frequently seen in foreign cases, including the landmark *Urgenda* ruling – may soon become a feature of Japanese CCL.

In parallel, ongoing observation of CCL abroad remains crucial. While foreign court decisions cannot be directly applied in Japan, they can yield valuable general principles and insights. Such lessons can clarify the position of Japanese CCL within a global context and inform litigation strategies for other environmental disputes that implicate climate concerns. For example, claims seeking municipal liability for inadequate urban planning – leading to infrastructure vulnerability during extreme weather events – could be framed as failures to account for necessary climate adaptation measures.[1]

Beyond these academic contributions, this study offers practical implications for addressing current obstacles. Both institutional and cognitive barriers consist of multiple components that demand careful, detailed attention. Loosening standing rules, for instance, could improve court access but may also risk an influx of cases or SLAPP-type claims.[2] Similarly, judicial receptiveness must remain independent from majoritarian pressure to preserve the integrity of the legal system. Each element of the current sociolegal framework has its own purpose, and any reform should proceed with careful consideration of these interdependencies.

---

1 For example, in Australia, inadequate coastal planning has frequently been challenged in court for contributing to damage caused by high tides (Peel and Osofsky 2015, 56–61).

2 SLAPP (strategic lawsuit against public participation) refers to lawsuits brought by individuals and entities to dissuade their critics from continuing to produce negative publicity. See https://www.law.cornell.edu/wex/slapp_suit.

Glossary

Jinkakuken health-related personal rights established in Japanese jurisprudence, partly through Article 13 of the Constitution of Japan. In the absence of explicit environmental rights, *jinkakuken* has often been invoked in antipollution litigation to protect victims' health and the surrounding environment.

Judicial passivism a judicial stance in which courts defer to the legislature and executive, refraining from substantial constitutional review unless a law is clearly unconstitutional.

LOS (legal opportunity structure) an analytical framework used to assess the likelihood that a social movement will engage in legal mobilization. It examines three indicators: access to the courts, the content of existing law, and judicial receptiveness.

Standing the legal requirement that a party has a sufficient connection to a case to participate in it. Also known *as locus standi*, capacity to sue, or proper party status.

Trias politica (separation of powers) the division of governmental authority into three branches – legislative, executive, and judicial – each with distinct powers and responsibilities, preventing one branch from encroaching on another.

Appendix 1: First-Stage Survey Questionnaire

The following is a translation and lightly edited version of the questionnaire administered to plaintiffs and auditors in the *Yokosuka* case in December 2019. Identical questionnaires were conducted in Kobe and Sendai the previous month, except for a few questions tailored to regional features.

Plaintiff Questionnaire

This questionnaire asks about your views related to this case. It takes about 5–10 minutes to complete. All responses are processed statistically for academic research, with complete anonymization and confidential handling.

First, please describe your thoughts when you became a plaintiff.

Q1. Please mark an X for the most relevant statements that reflect your reasons for becoming a plaintiff (give only one score per statement).

1. Not at all relevant	2. Not very relevant	3. Not sure	4. Considerably relevant	5. Very relevant

No.	Statement	1	2	3	4	5
1	To protect myself and those around me from air pollution					
2	To protect future generations from air pollution					
3	To protect myself and those around me from global warming					
4	To protect future generations from global warming					
5	To raise public awareness and encourage discussion					
6	To support and work with civil groups					
7	To achieve a fundamental solution to the problem					
8	Because I believe we could win the case					
9	Because I regard litigation as the most effective way to solve the problem					

Q1-1. If you marked 4 or 5 at Statement 9 above, please mark all relevant statements below:

1. I believed the case would significantly impact the future of CFPPs.
2. I believed the case would significantly influence future policies on air pollution and/or global warming.
3. I believed the case would have a broad impact on society, local communities nationwide, and/or the international community.
4. Based on my past experiences, I believed we could succeed.
5. Other (please specify):

Q2. Please mark an **X** for the most relevant statements reflecting your expectations for this case (give only one score per statement).

No.	Statement	1	2	3	4	5
1	Improvement in current air quality					
2	Improvement in future air quality					
3	Mitigation of current adverse effects of global warming					
4	Mitigation of future adverse effects of global warming					
5	To pressure the government and municipalities, even if the CFPP is not stopped					
6	To have a social impact, even if the CFPP is not stopped					

Q2-1. If you have other expectations not listed above, please specify:

Q3. This is the first case in Japan to pursue a company's liability for contributing to climate change. Do you recognize any differences between air pollution and global warming? Please mark the most relevant statement.

1. Yes (please specify if possible:)
2. No
3. I don't know

Second, please share your thoughts about the length of Japanese litigation.

Q4. Japanese litigation is often longer than in many other countries. This case may also be prolonged. Please mark an X for the most relevant statements about what you think might be the effects of a protracted case (give only one score per statement).

No.	Statement	1	2	3	4	5
1	It will increase the chance of obtaining a favorable judgment by galvanizing plaintiffs to act positively.					
2	It will advance solidarity with local people who share its objective.					
3	It will advance solidarity with people from other regions who share its objective.					
4	It will have a long-term impact on national and municipal policies.					
5	It will have a long-term impact on society.					
6	It will risk mental and physical exhaustion.					
7	It will risk a heavy financial burden.					
8	It will lead to momentum or impact diminishing over time.					

Q4-2. If you have other concerns or expectations not listed above, please specify:

Finally, please tell me about yourself.
(Responses are anonymized and kept strictly confidential.)

F1. Please mark your gender.

1. Male	2. Female

F2. Please mark your age group.

1. Under 20	4. 40s	7. 70s or older
2. 20s	5. 50s	
3. 30s	6. 60s	

F3. Do you have children?

1. Yes	2. No

F4. Please mark your place of residence.

1. Kurihama	5. Kumura	9. Other place in Yokosuka (please specify):
2. Nagase	6. Hairando	
3. Kubiri	7. Shinmeicho	10 Outside Yokosuka (please specify):
4. Funakura	8. Nobi	

F5. Please state your occupation. If you do not have one, please write any other social status appropriate to you.

F6. Please mark your final education.

1. Elementary/junior high school	3. Junior/professional college	5. Other (please specify):
2. High school	4. University and higher	

F7. Please mark your annual household income (in yen).

1. Under 2 million	5. 8–10 million
2. 2–3 million	6. 10–15 million
3. 3–5 million	7. 15–20 million
4. 5–8 million	8. 20 million and over

F8. Today, the second hearing was held at Tokyo District Court. Did you attend the first hearing as well?

1. Yes	2. No

F9. Have you ever been a plaintiff in environmental litigation?

1. Yes (times:_______)	2. No

Thank you for your kind cooperation.

Auditor Questionnaire

This questionnaire asks about your ideas related to this case. It takes about 5–10 minutes to complete. All responses are processed statistically for academic research, with complete anonymization and confidential handling.

First, please describe your thoughts when you decided to audit the case.

Q1. Please mark an **X** for the most relevant statements that reflect your reasons for auditing the case (give only one score per statement).

1. Not at all relevant	2. Not very relevant	3. Not sure	4. Considerably relevant	5. Very relevant

No.	Statement	1	2	3	4	5
1	To protect myself and those around me from air pollution					
2	To protect future generations from air pollution					
3	To protect myself and those around me from global warming					
4	To protect future generations from global warming					

(*cont.*)

No.	Statement	1	2	3	4	5
5	To observe public debate					
6	In hope of achieving a fundamental solution to the problem					
7	In hope that the plaintiffs win the case					
8	I sympathize with the group, but I cannot become a plaintiff					
9	Because I regarded litigation as the most effective way to solve the problem					

Q1-1. If you marked 4 or 5 at Statement 9 above, please mark all relevant statements below:

1. I believed the case would significantly impact the future of CFPPs.
2. I believed the case would significantly influence future policies on air pollution and/or global warming.
3. I believed the case would have a broad impact on society, local communities nationwide, and/or the international community.
4. Based on my past experiences, I believed we could succeed.
5. Other (please specify):

Q2. Please mark an X for the most relevant statements reflecting your expectations for this case (give only one score per statement).

No.	Statement	1	2	3	4	5
1	Improvement in current air quality					
2	Improvement in future air quality					
3	Mitigation of current adverse effects of global warming					
4	Mitigation of future adverse effects of global warming					
5	To pressure the government and municipalities, even if the CFPP is not stopped					
6	To have a social impact, even if the CFPP is not stopped					

Q2-1. If you have other expectations not listed above, please specify:

Q3. This is the first case in Japan to pursue a company's liability for contributing to climate change. Do you recognize any differences between air pollution and global warming? Please mark the most relevant statement.

1. Yes (please specify if possible:)
2. No
3. I don't know

Finally, please tell me about yourself.
(Responses are anonymized and kept strictly confidential.)

F1. Please mark your gender.

1. Male	2. Female

F2. Please mark your age group.

1. Under 20	4. 40s	7. 70s or older
2. 20s	5. 50s	
3. 30s	6. 60s	

F3. Do you have children?

1. Yes	2. No

F4. Please mark your place of residence.

1. Kurihama	5. Kumura	9. Other place in Yokosuka (please specify):
2. Nagase	6. Hairando	
3. Kubiri	7. Shinmeicho	10 Outside Yokosuka (please specify):
4. Funakura	8. Nobi	

F5. Please state your occupation. If you do not have one, please write any other social status appropriate to you.

F6. Please mark your final education.

1. Elementary/junior high school	3. Junior/professional college	5. Other (please specify):
2. High school	4. University and higher	

F7. Please mark your annual household income (in yen).

1. Under 2 million	5. 8–10 million
2. 2–3 million	6. 10–15 million
3. 3–5 million	7. 15–20 million
4. 5–8 million	8. 20 million and over

F8. Today, the second hearing was held at Tokyo District Court. Did you attend the first hearing as well?

1. Yes	2. No

Thank you for your kind cooperation.

Appendix 2: Second-Stage Survey Questionnaire

The following is a translation and lightly edited version of the questionnaire administered to plaintiffs and auditors in the *Sendai* case in April 2024. Identical questionnaires were conducted in Kobe and Sendai the previous month, except for a few questions tailored to regional features.

Plaintiff Questionnaire

This questionnaire asks about your views related to this case. It takes about 10–15 minutes to complete. All responses are processed statistically for academic research, with complete anonymization and confidential handling.

Q1. Please mark an X for the relevant statements reflecting your reasons for seeking the abolition of coal-fired power plants (give only one score per statement). You may write freely for Statement 8.

1. Relevant	2. Not relevant

No.	Statement	1	2
1	Because of negative impacts on my health and my family's health caused by air pollutant emissions, etc.		
2	Because of the large emissions of greenhouse gases, including CO_2, which further exacerbate climate change		
3	Because coal-fired power plants are not a sustainable energy source for the future		
4	Because my colleagues in the movement seek the abolition of coal-fired power plants		
5	Because of concerns about the impact on Gamo mudflats		
6	Because of concerns about the impact on the surrounding environment other than Gamo mudflats		
7	Because of the opposition to operating power plants in areas affected by the Great East Japan Earthquake		
8	Other (please describe freely):		

Q2. Please mark an X for the relevant statements that reflect your reasons for choosing litigation to seek the abolition of coal-fired power plants (give only one score per statement).

No.	Statement	1	2
1	To protect my health and my family's health		
2	To stop the exacerbation of climate change		
3	To pass on a sustainable society to future generations		
4	To obtain a just decision from the court		
5	To resolve the issue in a public forum		
6	Because no better alternative was available and litigation was the only remaining option		

Q3. Please mark an X for the relevant statements that reflect your understanding of the process and progress of this case in relation to your goal of abolishing the coal-fired power plant (give only one score per statement).

No.	Statement	1	2
1	I was able to defend my position in court successfully.		
2	I am fully aware of the claims and evidence presented by the opposing side.		
3	I was able to present sufficient evidence to support my side's arguments during the proceedings.		
4	The sequence of procedures was straightforward and easy to understand.		
5	The procedure was conducted fairly and impartially, regardless of the outcome.		
6	The judge was fully aware of the key issues in the case.		
7	The proceedings were conducted as a full hearing.		

Q4. Please mark an X for the relevant statements that reflect your recognition of the case result (give only one score per statement).

No.	Statement	1	2
1	The result of the case is consistent with the provisions of the relevant legislation.		
2	Ultimately, the outcome of the trial is acceptable to me.		
3	The results of the trial are satisfactory.		
4	The outcome may have been different in other countries.		
5	I would be willing to pursue a similar case in future if a comparable situation arises.		

Q5. Are you satisfied with the outcome of the case? Please mark the most relevant statement.

1. Very dissatisfied
2. Somewhat dissatisfied
3. Neither satisfied nor dissatisfied
4. Somewhat satisfied
5. Very satisfied

Q6. Please mark an **X** for the relevant statements that reflect your general impression of the Japanese court system and legal code after experiencing this case (give only one score per statement).

No.	Statement	1	2
1	The Japanese civil court system effectively fulfills its role in dispute resolution and addressing social problems.		
2	The civil court system in Japan is accessible to the general public.		
3	Japan's civil justice system is fair.		
4	Japanese law is fair.		
5	Japanese legal norms are well aligned with contemporary life and social organization.		
6	The Japanese civil justice system is generally perceived as satisfactory by the public.		
7	The Japanese civil justice system is designed to fully realize (or protect) the rights of the people.		

Q7. Please freely describe your reflections on your experience of taking legal action (optional):

Finally, please tell me about yourself.
(Responses are anonymized and kept strictly confidential.)

F1. Please mark your gender.

1. Male	2. Female	3. Prefer not to answer

F2. Please mark your age group.

1. Under 20	4. 40s	7. 70s or older
2. 20s	5. 50s	
3. 30s	6. 60s	

F3. Do you have children or grandchildren?

1. Yes	2. No

F4. Please state your occupation.

Thank you for your kind cooperation.

Supporter Questionnaire

This questionnaire asks about your views related to this case. It takes about 10–15 minutes to complete. All responses are processed statistically for academic research, with complete anonymization and confidential handling.

Q1. Please mark an X for the relevant statements reflecting your reasons for seeking the abolition of coal-fired power plants (give only one score per statement). You may write freely for Statement 8.

1. Relevant	2. Not relevant

No.	Statement	1	2
1	Because of negative impacts on my health and my family's health caused by air pollutant emissions, etc.		
2	Because of the large emissions of greenhouse gases, including CO_2, which further exacerbate climate change		
3	Because coal-fired power plants are not a sustainable energy source for the future		
4	Because my colleagues in the movement seek the abolition of coal-fired power plants		
5	Because of concerns about the impact on Gamo mudflats		
6	Because of concerns about the impact on the surrounding environment other than Gamo mudflats		
7	Because of the opposition to operating power plants in areas affected by the Great East Japan Earthquake		
8	Other (please describe freely):		

Q2. Please mark an **X** for the relevant statements that reflect your reasons for choosing litigation to seek the abolition of coal-fired power plants (give only one score per statement).

No.	Statement	1	2
1	To protect my health and my family's health		
2	To stop the exacerbation of climate change		
3	To pass on a sustainable society to future generations		
4	To obtain a just decision from the court		
5	To resolve the issue in a public forum		
6	Because no better alternative was available and litigation was the only remaining option		

Q3. Please mark an X for the relevant statements reflecting your recognition of the case result (give only one score per statement).

No.	Statement	1	2
1	The result of the case is consistent with the provisions of the relevant legislation.		
2	Ultimately, the outcome of the trial is acceptable to me.		
3	The results of the trial are satisfactory.		
4	The outcome may have been different in other countries.		
5	It seems reasonable that further resolution of the issue in court would be appropriate in future if a comparable situation arises.		

Q4. Are you satisfied with the outcome of the case? Please mark the most relevant statement.

1. Very dissatisfied
2. Somewhat dissatisfied
3. Neither satisfied nor dissatisfied
4. Somewhat satisfied
5. Very satisfied

Q5. Please mark an **X** for the relevant statements that reflect your general impression of the Japanese court system and legal code after experiencing this case (give only one score per statement).

No.	**Statement**	**1**	**2**
1	The Japanese civil court system effectively fulfills its role in dispute resolution and addressing social problems.		
2	The civil court system in Japan is accessible to the general public.		
3	Japan's civil justice system is fair.		
4	Japanese law is fair.		
5	Japanese legal norms are well aligned with contemporary life and social organization.		
6	The Japanese civil justice system is generally perceived as satisfactory by the public.		
7	The Japanese civil justice system is designed to fully realize (or protect) the rights of the people.		

Q6. Please describe your experiences of being involved in a lawsuit seeking an injunction against the coal-fired power plant (optional).

Finally, please tell me about yourself.
(Responses are anonymized and kept strictly confidential.)

F1. Please mark your gender.

1. Male	2. Female	3. Prefer not to answer

F2. Please mark your age group.

1. Under 20	4. 40s	7. 70s or older
2. 20s	5. 50s	
3. 30s	6. 60s	

F3. Do you have children or grandchildren?

1. Yes	2. No

F4. Please state your occupation.

Thank you for your kind cooperation.

Bibliography

Abreu, Catherine. 2023. "Carbon Capture and Storage is a Dangerous Distraction. It's Time to Imagine a World Beyond Fossil Fuels." *Reuters*, December 11, 2023. https://www.reuters.com/sustainability/climate-energy/comment-carbon-capture-storage-is-dangerous-distraction-its-time-imagine-world-2023-12-11.

Adler, Dena, P. 2019. *Litigation in the Age of Trump: Year Two*. Sabin Center for Climate Change Law, Columbia Law School.

Alogna Ivano, Christine Bakker, and Jean-Pierre Gauci, eds. 2021. *Climate Change Litigation: Global Perspectives*. Brill.

Arahata Kanson. (1970) 1999. *Yanakamura Metsuboushi* [History of the destruction of Yanaka village]. Iwanami Shoten.

Arai Makoto, Sogabe Masahiro, Sasaki Kumi, and Yokodaido Satoshi. 2021. *Kenpo I Souron Touchi* [Constitution I: Overview and governance]. 2nd ed. Nihon Hyoronsya.

Awaji Takehisa. 2012. "Kenri no Fuhenka, Seido Kaikaku no tame no Kogai Kankyo Sosyo" [Antipollution and environmental litigation for universalization of human rights and system reform]. In *Kogai Kankyo Sosyo no Arata na Tenkai: Kenri Kyusai kara Seisaku Keisei he* [New developments in antipollution and environmental litigation: From redress of rights to policymaking], edited by Awaji Takehisa, Teranishi Syunichi, Yoshimura Ryoichi, and Okubo Noriko. Nihon Hyoronsya.

Baird, J. Christopher. 2004. "Trapped in the Greenhouse? Regulating Carbon Dioxide after FDA v. Brown & Williamson Tobacco Corp." *Duke Law Journal* 54, no. 1: 147–178.

Bernstein Research. 1994. "Tobacco Litigation: Turbulence Ahead, But Stocks Still Overdiscounting Risks." Reiterate outperforms [memorandum], October 12, 1994. Sanford C. Bernstein & Co.

Boutcher, Steven, A., and Holly J. McCammon. 2019. "Social Movements and Litigation." In *The Wiley Blackwell Companion to Social Movements*, edited by David A. Snow, Sarah A. Soule, Hanspeter Kriesi, and Holly J. McCammon. Wiley.

Burns, William C.G., and Hari M. Osofsky, eds. 2009. *Adjudicating Climate Change: State, National, and International Approaches*. Cambridge University Press.

Butterfield, Bridie. 2018. "The Potential Role of Climate Change Litigation in Furthering the Mitigation Objectives of the Paris Agreement." *Asia Pacific Journal of Environmental Law* 21, no. 1: 29–49.

California Environmental Protection Agency. 2010. "Enforcement Reports – Citizen Suits." https://www.waterboards.ca.gov/water_issues/programs/enforcement/rpts_citizensuits.shtml#a.

Carlarne, Cinnamon Piñon. 2010. *Climate Change Law and Policy: EU and US Approaches*. Oxford University Press.

Carnwath, Lord. 2016. "Climate Change Adjudication After Paris: A Reflection." *Journal of Environmental Law* 28, no. 1: 5–9.

Cairney, Paul, Donley T. Studlar, and Hadii M. Mamudu. 2012. *Global Tobacco Control: Power, Policy, Governance and Transfer*. Springer.

Canadian Press. 2014. "Energy Firms Warned Over Communication About Climate Change." CBC, May 28, 2014. https://www.cbc.ca/news/science/energy-firms-warned-over-communication-about-climate-change-1.2657185.

Centers for Disease Control and Prevention (CDC). 1999. "Achievements in Public Health, 1900–1999: Tobacco Use -- United States, 1900–1999." https://www.cdc.gov/mmwr/preview/mmwrhtml/mm4843a2.htm.

Emissions Database for Global Atmospheric Research (EDGER). 2023. *GHG Emissions of All World Countries: 2023 Report*. https://edgar.jrc.ec.europa.eu/report_2023.

Environmental Protection Agency (EPA). 2025. *Inventory of U.S. Greenhouse Gas Emissions and Sinks, 1990–2023*. https://library.edf.org/AssetLink/145ky510ew61fk1tq5c2klp5kq5yp33j.pdf.

European Business Council in Japan. 2024. "Renewable Energy Support, Coal Phase Out." July 22, 2025. https://ebc-jp.com/digital-white-paper/issues/business-fundamentals/sustainability-social-responsibility/renewable-energy-support-coal-phase-out.

De Fazio, Gianluca. 2012. "Legal Opportunity Structure and Social Movement Strategy in Northern Ireland and Southern United States." *International Journal of Comparative Sociology* 53, no. 1: 3–22.

Feng, Danyang. 2021. "Certification, Lawsuits and the Role of Epidemiology in the Yokkaichi Asthma Episode in the 1960s and 1970s: Lessons and Legacy." *Social History of Medicine* 34, no. 1: 118–140.

Fujimoto Ryo. 2006. "Sosho Riyou Doki no Inshi Bunseki" [Factor analysis of motivations of initiating legal proceedings]. In *Riyousya Kara Mita Minji Sosho* [Civil proceedings from the perspective of users], edited by Sato Iwao, Sugawara Ikuo, and Yamamoto Kazuhiko. Nihon Hyoronsya.

Fujita Masahiro. 2006. "Sosho Riyou ni Tomonau Hiyou to Jikan" [Required cost and time to initiate legal proceedings]. In *Riyousya Kara Mita Minji Sosho* [Civil proceedings from the perspective of users], edited by Sato Iwao, Sugawara Ikuo, and Yamamoto Kazuhiko. Nihon Hyoronsya.

Fujita Masahiro. 2010. *Sosyo wo Tamerau Gen-in ha Nanika* [What makes people hesitant to litigate?]. In *Riyousya ga Motomeru Minji Sosyou no Jissen* [Practice of civil proceedings required by users], edited by Sugawara Ikuo, Yamamoto Kazuhiko, and Sato Iwao. Nihon Hyoronsya.

Fujita Tokiyasu. (1980) 2004. *Gyo-sei Hou 1* [Administrative law 1]. Seirin Shoin.

Fukui Shizuka. 2011. "Doitsu no Bengoshi wo Torimaku Jokyo" [Situation surrounding attorneys in Germany]. *Jiyu to Seigi* [Freedom and justice] 62: 62–64.

Galanter, Mark. 2000. "America Tabako Sosho no Tenkai" [Development of tobacco litigation in the United Stated]. In *Tabako Sosho no Ho Shakai Gaku* [Sociolegal study of tobacco litigation], edited by Tanase Takao. Sekai Hyoronsya.

Galanter, Mark, and Tanase Takao. 1998. "Beikoku no Tabako Sosho ni Tsuite" [Tobacco litigation in the United States]. Speech delivered to the Yasuda Fire Insurance Memorial Foundation, Tokyo.

Garner, Bryan A., et al., eds. 2014. *Black's Law Dictionary*. 10th ed. Thomson West.

Gerrard, Michael B., and Jody Freeman. 2007. *Global Climate Change and U.S. Law*. American Bar Association.

Goguen, David. 2022. "Tobacco and Cigarette Litigation: History & Trends." Nolo. https://www.nolo.com/legal-encyclopedia/tobacco-litigation-history-and-development-32202.html.

Haley, John, O. 1979. "The Myth of the Reluctant Litigant." *Journal of Japanese Studies* (October): 359–390.

Harada Masazumi. 1972. *Minamatabyo* [Minamata disease]. Iwanami Shoten.

Hashiba Noriko. 2023. "Chousa Kekka no Gaiyou" [Overview of the survey]. In *Tetsuzuki Riyousha kara mita Minji Sosho no Jissai – 2021 nen Minji Sosho Riyousha Chousa* [The reality of civil litigation from the perspective of users: 2021 Civil Litigation Survey], edited by Sugawara Ikuo and Kakiuchi Shusuke. Shoji Houmu.

Hatakeyama Takemichi. 2008. *America no Kankyo Sosho* [Environmental litigation in the United States]. Hokkaido Daigaku Shuppankai.

Heinrichs, Heidi Ursula, and Peter Markewitz. 2017. "Long-Term Impacts of a Coal Phase-Out in Germany as Part of a Greenhouse Gas Mitigation Strategy." *Applied Energy* 192: 234–246.

Henry, Tanya Albert. 2020. "Lawsuit on FDA's Tobacco, Nicotine Regulation Policy Dismissed." American Medical Association. https://www.ama-assn.org/health-care-advocacy/judicial-advocacy/lawsuit-fda-s-tobacco-nicotine-regulation-policy-dismissed.

Hilson, Chris. 2002. "New Social Movements: The Role of Legal Opportunity." *Journal of European Public Policy* 9, no. 2: 238–255.

Hirano. 2005. *Kiso ko-su Minpou Saikenhou* [Basic course: Civil Law – Law of Obligation]. Shinseisya.

Hiratsuka Masatoshi, ed. 1941. *Besshi Kaiko Nihyaku Gojunen Shiwa* [Historical story of 250 years since the opening of Besshi Mine]. Sumitomo.

Hori Kiyofumi. 2023. "Chousa Kekka no Gaiyou" [Overview of the survey]. In *Tetsuzuki Riyousha kara mita Minji Sosho no Jissai – 2021 nen Minji Sosho Riyousha Chousa* [The reality of civil litigation from the perspective of users: 2021 Civil Litigation Survey], edited by Sugawara Ikuo and Kakiuchi Shusuke. Shoji Houmu.

Humphreys, Stephen. 2009. *Human Rights and Climate Change*. Cambridge University Press.

Ichihara, Masako, and Grace Nishikawa. 2024. "First Youth Climate Lawsuit Brought in Japan." *Climate Law* [Sabin Center blog], August 15, 2024. https://blogs.law.columbia.edu/climatechange/2024/08/15/guest-blog-first-youth-climate-lawsuit-brought-in-japan.

International Atomic Agency (IEA). 2021. *Global Energy Review: CO2 Emissions in 2021.* https://www.iea.org/reports/global-energy-review-co2-emissions-in-2021-2.

IEA. 2023. "New Policy and Business Approaches are Needed to Support Scaling Up of CCUS to Help Reach Net Zero Goals." November 27, 2023. https://www.iea.org/news/new-policy-and-business-approaches-are-needed-to-support-scaling-up-of-ccus-to-help-reach-net-zero-goals.

Intergovernmental Panel on Climate Change (IPCC). 2007. *Fourth Assessment Report.* https://www.ipcc.ch/assessment-report/ar4.

IPCC. 2014. *Fifth Assessment Report* [series of reports published between 2013 and 2014]. https://www.ipcc.ch/assessment-report/ar5.

IPCC. 2018. *Special Report on Global Warming of 1.5 °C.* https://www.ipcc.ch/sr15.

IPCC. 2019. *Special Report on the Ocean and Cryosphere in a Changing Climate, Summary for Policymakers.* https://www.ipcc.ch/srocc/chapter/summary-for-policymakers.

IPCC. 2023. Sixth Assessment Report [series of reports published between 2021 and 2023]. https://www.ipcc.ch/assessment-report/ar6.

International Bar Association. 2024. "50:50 by 2030: A Longitudinal Study into Gender Disparity in Law." *Republic of Korea Results Report,* https://www.ibanet.org/document?id=IBA-Gender-Report-Korea-2024.

Isayama Yohiro. 1983. *Ken-en-ken wo Kangaeru* [Considerations on non-smokers' rights]. Iwanami Shoten.

Isayama Yohiro. 2000. "Nihon ni Okeru Tabakobyo Sosho no Tenkai" [Development of Japanese tobacco-related disease litigation]. In *Tabako Sosho no Ho Shakai Gaku* [Sociolegal study of tobacco litigation], edited by Tanase Takao. Sekai Hyoronsya.

Ishiwata Higai Kyusai Seido Kenkyu-kai. 2021. "Asubesuto Higai no Kanzen Kyusai ni mukete" [Toward full relief for asbestos victims]. https://kenasu.jp/news/20210616-499 (in Japanese).

Ito Hiroshi. 2007. "Shohisya Dantai Sosho no Kadai" [The Challenges for consumer groups of collective litigation]. *Rikkyo Hogaku* 73: 161–182.

Japan Climate Initiative. 2024. "Japan Needs 2035 Emissions Reduction Target of 66% or Higher!" May 23, 2024. https://japanclimate.org/english/news-topics/jci-message-2035ndc.

Kaji, Masanori. 2012. "Role of Experts and Public Participation in Pollution Control: The Case of Itai-itai Disease in Japan 1." *Ethics in Science and Environmental Politics* 12, no. 2: 99–111.

Kawashima Takeyoshi. 1967. *Nihon-jin no Ho-ishiki* [Legal awareness of the Japanese]. Iwanami Shoten.

Kawabata Kazuharu. 2000. "Shimin no Shiho no Jitugen no Tameni: Hoso Ichigen, Bai Sanshin in seido to Kokumin Syuken" [Toward judiciary for citizens: Legal unification, the jury-referee system, and democratic sovereignty]. *Gakujutu no Doko* 27–32.

Kidder, Robert, and Setsuo Miyazawa. 1993. "Long-Term Strategies in Japanese Environmental Litigation." *Law & Social Inquiry* 18, no. 4: 605–627.

Kinoshita Manako. 2006. "Toujisya no Sosyo heno Kitai to Hyoka" [Expectation and evaluation of parties toward legal proceedings]. In *Riyousya Kara Mita Minji Sosho* [Civil proceedings from the perspective of users], edited by Sato Iwao, Sugawara Ikuo, and Yamamoto Kazuhiko. Nihon Hyoronsya.

Kitagawa, Tetsuzo. 1984. "Cause Analysis of the Yokkaichi Asthma Episode in Japan." *Journal of the Air Pollution Control Association* 34, no. 7: 743–746.

Kolstad, Charles D. 2017. "What is Killing the US Coal Industry?" Institute for Economic Policy Research, Stanford University. https://siepr.stanford.edu/publications/policy-brief/what-killing-us-coal-industry.

Koyama Hitoshi. 1973. *Senzen Syowa-ki Osaka no Kogai Mondai Siryo* [References to pollution problems in Osaka during the early Showa era]. Kansai Daigaku Keizai Seiji Kenkyu-jo.

Kranz, Kenneth D. 1998. "Tort Reform 1997–98: Profits v. People?" *Florida State University Law Review* 25, no. 2: 161 *et seq*. https://ir.law.fsu.edu/lr/vol25/iss2/4.

Ku Hyun-ju and Kim Joo-young. 2023. "At a Glance: Class Action Formation in South Korea." https://www.lexology.com/library/detail.aspx?g=fd23db84-917a-4806-996f-062a33176511.

Kyodo News. 2019. "Japan Given 2nd 'Fossil' Award Over No Change in Coal Push." December 12, 2019. https://english.kyodonews.net/news/2019/12/0c381e715a51-japan-given-2nd-fossil-award-over-no-change-in-coal-push.html.

Kyodo News. 2021. "Japan Raises 2030 Emissions Reduction Target to 46%." April 22, 2021. https://english.kyodonews.net/news/2021/04/21d433ecc75c-japan-set-to-decide-more-ambitious-2030-emissions-reduction-target.html.

Laposata, Elizabeth, Richard Barnes, and Stanton Glantz. 2012. "Tobacco Industry Influence on the American Law Institute's Restatements of Torts and Implications for Its Conflict of Interest Policies." *Iowa Law Review* 98, no. 1: 1.

Law Library – American Law and Legal Information. n.d. "Tobacco Litigation." https://law.jrank.org/pages/10805/Tobacco-Tobacco-Litigation.html.

Lin, Jolene, and Jacqueline Peel. 2024. *Litigating Climate Change in the Global South*. Oxford University Press.

Linden, Daniel. 2023. "Climate Change Litigation in Japan: A Short Overview of Japanese Characteristics within International Trends with Focus on Administrative Cases." *Zeitschrift für Japanisches Recht* 28, no. 55: 181–204.

Littlecott, Chris. 2016. *UK Coal Phase Out: The International Context.* E3G Briefing Paper, 9.

Lord, Richard, Silke Goldberg, Lavanya Rajamani, and Jutta Brunnée. 2011. *Climate Change Liability: Transnational Law and Practice.* Cambridge University Press.

Mabane Kana. 2000. "Nihon no Ken-enken Sosho" [Japanese legal cases of no-smoking rights]. In *Tabako Sosho no Ho Shakai Gaku* [Sociolegal study of tobacco litigation], edited by Tanase Takao. Sekai Hyoronsya.

Markell, David, and J.B. Ruhl. 2010. "An Empirical Survey of Climate Change Litigation in the United States." FSU College of Law, Public Law Research Paper 433. https://doi.org/10.2139/ssrn.1585341.

Mashaw, Jerry L., Richard A. Merrill, and Peter. M. Shane. 2009. *Administrative Law: The American Public Law System-Cases and Materials.* 6th ed. Thomson Reuters.

Matsui Yoshiro. 2010. *Kokusai Kankyo-Ho no Kihon Gensoku* [International law of the environment: Fundamental principles]. Toshindo.

McCormick, Sabrina, et al. 2018. "Strategies in and Outcomes of Climate Change Litigation in the United States." *Nature Climate Change* 8, no. 9: 829–833.

McCurry, Justin. 2020. "Japan Will Become Carbon Neutral by 2050, PM Pledges." *Guardian*, October 26, 2020. https://www.theguardian.com/world/2020/oct/26/japan-will-become-carbon-neutral-by-2050-pm-pledges.

McGovern, Francis E. 1986. "Toward a Functional Approach for Managing Complex Litigation." *University of Chicago Law Review* 53: 440–493.

Minji Sosyou Seido Kenkyu-kai. 2007. *2006 nen Minji Sosho Riyousha Chousa.* Shoji Homu. Original Japanese edition of the 2006 Civil Litigation Survey.

Minji Sosyou Seido Kenkyu-kai. 2012. *2011 nen Minji Sosho Riyousha Chousa.* Shoji Homu. Original Japanese edition of the 2011 Civil Litigation Survey.

Minji Sosyou Seido Kenkyu-kai. 2018. *2016 nen Minji Sosho Riyousha Chousa.* Shoji Homu. Original Japanese edition of the 2016 Civil Litigation Survey.

Miyamoto, Kenichi. 2010. "The Brief History of Japanese Environmental Problems: Lessons from Experiences and the Remaining Problems." *Narise Tatuo Hakushi Taisyoku Kinen Ronbun shu* 382: 1–26.

Miyamoto Kenichi. 2012. "Kogai, kankyo Saiban no Rekishiteki Igi" [Historical implications of antipollution and environmental litigation]. In *Kogai Kankyo Sosyo no Arata na Tenkai: Kenri Kyusai kara Seisaku Keisei he* [New developments in antipollution and environmental litigation: From redress of rights to policymaking], edited by Awaji Takehisa, Teranishi Syunichi, Yoshimura Ryoichi, and Okubo Noriko. Nihon Hyoronsya.

Miyamoto, Kenichi. (2014) 2017. *Sengo Nihon Kougaisiron* [Postwar Japanese pollution history theory]. Iwanami Shoten.

Miyamoto, Kenichi. 2017. "The Historical Lessons from Japanese Environmental Pollution Problems." *Shiga Daigau Kankyo Sogo Kenkyu Center Kenkyu Nenpo* 14, no. 1: 3–19.

Mori Michiya. 2013. "Kogai Kokkai no Mitorizu" [A sketch of the pollution diet]. *Ritsumeikan Daigaku Jinbun Kagaku Kenkyujo Kiyou* 101: 27–64.

Morinaga Eizaburo. 1982. *Ashio Kodoku Jiken (Jou)* [The Ashio Copper Mine case, vol. 1.] Nihon Hyoronsya.

Nagashima Koichi. 2014. "Doitsu ni okeru Kankyo Dantai Sosho no Tetsuzukihoujou no Mondai no Kentou" [Examination of procedural issues in German environmental group litigation]. *Hougaku Kenkyu Ronju* 40: 161–182.

Nanda, Ved P., and William R. Ris Jr. 1975. "The Public Trust Doctrine: A Viable Approach to International Environmental Protection." *Ecology Law Quarterly* 5: 291.

National Cancer Institute and World Health Organization (WHO). 2017. *The Economics of Tobacco and Tobacco Control.* NCI Tobacco Control Monograph Series 21. https://www.who.int/publications/m/item/nci-tobacco-control-monograph-series-21-the-economics-of-tobacco-and-tobacco-control.

Nikkei. 2019. "Only 20% of Bills Proposed by Members of Parliament are Passed, While Opposition Bills Are Not Debated and 90% of Bills Submitted by the Government Are Passed" [in Japanese]. March 26, 2019. https://www.nikkei.com/article/DGXMZO40626780Z20C19A1SHA000 (members only).

Nikkei. 2020. "High Hurdles to Using Civil Courts" [in Japanese]. August 19, 2020. https://www.nikkei.com/article/DGKKZO62585750T10C20A8TL3001 (members only).

Nishikawa, Yumeno Grace. 2023. "Japanese Climate Litigation and the Development of Personal Rights." *Chinese Journal of Environmental Law* 7, no. 2: 214–226.

Normann, Håkon Endresen. 2019. "Conditions for the Deliberate Destabilisation of Established Industries: Lessons from US Tobacco Control Policy and the Closure of Dutch Coal Mines." *Environmental Innovation and Societal Transitions* 33: 102–14.

Norr, Roy. 1952. "Cancer by the Carton." *Reader's Digest* (December). Condensed version of an article originally published in the *Christian Herald.* Available via https://csts.ua.edu/files/2019/01/1952-12-Readers-Digest-Cancer-by-the-Carton.pdf.

Oei Pao-Yu, Hauke Hermann, Philipp Herpich, Oliver Holtemöler, Benjamin Lünenbürger, and Christoph Shult. 2020. "Coal Phase-Out in Germany: Implications and Policies for Affected Regions." *Energy* 196: 117004.

Okubo Noriko. 2013. "Konmei suru Doitsu no Kankyo Dantai Sosho: Kankyo, Hoteki Kyusaiho 2013 Hokaisei wo Megutte" [German environmental group litigation in confusion: Legal revision in 2013 on environmental legal remedy]. *Shin Sedai Hoseisakugaku Kenkyu* 20: 227–55.

Okubo, Noriko. 2016. "The Development of the Japanese Legal System for Public Participation in Land Use and Environmental Matters." *Land Use Policy* 52: 492–500.

Okubo Noriko. 2017. "Kankyo Minsyusyugi Shihyo (EDI) no Igi to Kadai" [The significance and challenge of the Environmental Democracy Index (EDI)]. *Kankyo to Kogai* 46, no. 3: 38–43.

Olszynski, Martin, Sharon Mascher, and Meinhard Doelle. 2017. "From Smokes to Smokestacks: Lessons from Tobacco for the Future of Climate Change Liability." *Georgetown Environmental Law Review* 30, no. 1: 1–46.

Osawa Shusuke. 1988. *Gendaigata Sosyo no Nichibei Hikaku* [Japan–US comparison on modern litigation]. Kobundo.

Otomo, Hideaki, and Tsuyoshi Nihei. 2014. "Shichizunshippu Kyoiku to shiteno Ho-Kyoiku no Jissen to Kadai: Mogi Saiban no Jugyo" [Practice and Problem of Law-Related Education as Citizenship Education: Lesson of Moot Court]. *Saitama Daigaku Kyoiku Gakubu Kyoiku Jissen Sogo Center Kiyo* [Journal of Faculty of Integrated Center for Clinical and Educational Practice] 13: 1–7.

Otsuka Tadashi. 2020a. *Kankyo-Ho* [Environmental law]. Yujikaku.

Otsuka Tadashi. 2020b. "Kiko Sosho ni Kansuru Oboegaki: sono Kanousei to Konnansei" [A memorandum of climate cases: Possibilities and challenges]. In *Jizoku Kanou na Sekai he no Hou* [Toward global sustainable law], edited by Nakamura Tamio. Waseda Daikaku Hikakuhou Kenkyujo.

Otsuka Tadashi. 2023. "Climate Litigation in Japanese Law: The Possibility to File Suits in Japan." In *Mensch – Technik – Umwelt: Verantwortung für eine sozialverträgliche Zukunft. Festschrift für Alexander Roßnagel zum 70. Geburtstag*, edited by Anja Hentschel, Gerrit Hornung, and Silke Jandt. Nomos.

Park, Hai Jin. 2020. "Class Action Scarcity: An Empirical Analysis of the Securities Class Action in Korea." *European Business Organization Law Review* 21, no. 3: 665–708.

Peel, Jacqueline, and Jolene Lin. 2018. *Transnational Climate Litigation: The Contribution of the Global South*. Draft paper presented at the American Society of International Law Mid-Year Research Forum, November 9–10.

Peel, Jacqueline, and H. Martin Osofsky. 2015. *Climate Change Litigation Regulatory Pathways to Cleaner Energy*. Cambridge University Press.

Perlman, Care R. 2009. *Environmental Litigation: Law and Strategy*. American Bar Association.

Preston, Brian J. 2016. "The Contribution of the Courts in Tackling Climate Change." *Journal of Environmental Law* 28, no. 1: 11–17.

Preston, Brian J. 2021. "Climate Conscious Lawyering." *Australian Law Journal* 95: 51–66.

Ramsden, Michael, and Kris Gledhill. 2019. "Defining Strategic Litigation." *Civil Justice Quarterly* 4: 407–438.

Ramseyer, J. Mark. 1988. "Reluctant Litigant Revisited: Rationality and Disputes in Japan." *Society of Japanese Studies* 14, no. 1: 111–123.

Ramseyer, J. Mark. 1990. *Hou to Keizaigaku* [Law and economics]. Kobundo.

Rabin, Robert, L. 1992. "A Sociological History of the Tobacco Tort Litigation." *Stanford Law Review* 44: 853–855.

Reuters. 2020. "Japan Seeks to Suspend or Retire 90% of Dirty Coal-Fired Plants - Yomiuri." July 2, 2020. https://jp.reuters.com/article/japan-powerstation-coal-idINL4N2E907A.

Rodrigo, González Quintero. 2010. "Judicial Review in the Republic of Korea: An Introduction." *Revista de Derecho* 34: 1–17.

Rowling, Megan. 2021. "U.N. Chief Urges Wealthy Nations to Phase Out Coal Use by 2030." Reuters, March 2, 2021. https://www.reuters.com/article/us-global-energy-coal-climate-trfn-idUSKCN2AU29W.

Salmon, Jack, and Patterson Tanner. 2024. *Growth of the Nonprofit Sector: More Charities, Better Solutions*. Philanthropy Roundtable, September 30, 2024. https://www.philanthropyroundtable.org/resource/growth-of-the-nonprofit-sector-more-charities-better-solutions.

Salzman, James. 2019. "United States of America." In *The Oxford Handbook of Comparative Environmental Law*, edited by Emma Lees and Jorge E. Viñuales. Oxford University Press.

Sanders, Joseph. 1992. "The Bendectin Litigation: A Case Study in the Life Cycle of Mass Tort." *Hastings Law Journal* 43: 301–418.

Sato Koji. 2021. *Nijonkoku Kenpo-ron* [Theory of the Constitution of Japan]. 2nd ed. Nihon Hyoronsya.

Sato Iwao, Sugawara Ikuo, and Yamamoto Kazuhiko, eds. 2006. *Riyousya Kara Mita Minji Sosho* [Civil proceedings from the perspective of users]. Nihon Hyoronsya.

Schall, Christian. 2008. "Public Interest Litigation Concerning Environmental Matters Before Human Rights Courts: A Promising Future Concept?" *Journal of Environmental Law* 20, no. 3: 417–453.

Schmit, Joan T. 1994. "The Role of the Work Place, Business Plaintiffs, and Mass Torts in Products Liability Litigation." *Journal of Insurance Regulation* 12, no. 4: 530–553.

Schreurs, Miranda A. 2004. "Assessing Japan's Role as a Global Environmental Leader." *Policy and Society* 23, no. 1: 88–110.

Seki Tenshu. 1963. *Hitachi Engai Mondai Mukasibanasi* [An old story about Hitachi air pollution]. Kyodo Hitachi Bunka Kenkyu-kai.

Setzer, Joana, and Lisa Benjamin. 2019. "Climate Litigation in the Global South: Constraints and Innovations." *Transnational Environmental Law* 9, no. 1: 77–101.

Setzer, Joana, and Rebecca Byrnes. 2020. *Global Trends in Climate Change Litigation: 2020 Snapshot*. Grantham Research Institute on Climate Change and the Environment.

Setzer, Joana, and Rebecca Byrnes. 2019. *Global Trends in Climate Change Litigation: 2019 Snapshot*. Grantham Research Institute on Climate Change and the Environment.

Setzer, Joana, and Catherine Higham. 2023. *Global Trends in Climate Change Litigation: 2023 Snapshot*. Grantham Research Institute on Climate Change and the Environment.

Setzer, Joana, and Catherine Higham. 2024. *Global Trends in Climate Change Litigation: 2024 Snapshot*. Grantham Research Institute on Climate Change and the Environment.

Setzer, Joana, and Lisa Vanhala. 2019. "Climate Change Litigation: A Review of Research on Courts and Litigants in Climate Governance." *Wiley Interdisciplinary Reviews: Climate Change* 10, no. 3: e580.

Setzer, Joana, and Michael Nachmany. 2018. "National Governance: The State's Role in Steering Polycentric Action." In *Governing Climate Change*, edited by Andrew Jordan, Dave Huitema, Harro van Asselt, and Johanna Forster. Cambridge University Press.

Setzer, Joana, and Rebecca Byrnes. 2020. *Global Trends in Climate Change Litigation: 2020 Snapshot*. Grantham Research Institute on Climate Change and the Environment.

Sher, Vic. 2020. "Forum Versus Substance: Should Climate Damages Cases Be Heard in State or Federal Court?" *Stanford Law Review* 72: 134–144. https://www.stanfordlawreview.org/online/forum-versus-substance.

Shiho Seido Kaikaku Shingikai [Judicial System Reform Council of the Ministry of Justice]. 2001. *Minji Sosho Riyousha Chousa Houkokusho* [Report of Civil Litigation Survey]. https://www.kantei.go.jp/jp/sihouseido/tyousa/2001/survey-report.html (in Japanese; accessed on August 4, 2024, no longer active).

Shimamura Takeshi, Sugita Shunsuke, Ikeda Naoki, Asaoka Mie, and Wada Juta. 2021. *Nihon ni okeru Kikou Sosyou no Houteki Ronten: Koube Sekitan Sosyou wo Rei tosite* [Exploring the possibilities of expanding the scope of the Japanese Group Action by Anti-Organized Crime Law through interpretation]. Kobe University Repository. http://www.lib.kobe-u.ac.jp/handle_kernel/81012970.

Shiomi Yoshio. (2005) 2020. *Library Hogaku Kihon Kougi 6–2: Saiken Kakuron 2 Fuhou Koui Hou* [Basie Lecture of Legal Studies 6–2: Tort law]. 3rd ed. Shinseisya.

Shoji Hikaru and Miyamoto Kenichi. 1975. *Nihon no Kogai* [Japanese pollution]. Iwanami Shoten.

Shoji, Hikaru, Takeo Yamamoto, and Konosuke Nishida. 1966. "Studies on the Air Pollution Due to Automobile Exhaust: The Gas Chromatographic Analysis of the Hydrocarbons in the Air in the Highway Tunnel and Its Vicinities." *Transactions of the Japan Society of Civil Engineers* 132: 34–41.

Sindico, Francesco, and Makane Moïse Mbengue. 2021. *Comparative Climate Change Litigation: Beyond the Usual Suspects*. Springer.

Society for the Study of the Civil Procedural System. 2014. *Report on Japan's 2011 Civil Litigation Survey* [English translation of 2011 Civil Litigation Survey].

Sugai, Masuro. 1983. *The Development Process of Mining Pollution at the Ashio Copper Mine*. Institute of Developing Economies, Japan External Trade Organization.

Sugawara Ikuo. 2010. "Motomerareru Minji Sosyo no Jitsumu to Riron wo Shirutameni" [Learning practice and theory of required civil proceedings]. In *Riyousya ga Motomeru Minji Sosyou no Jissen* [Practice of civil proceedings required by users], edited by Sugawara Ikuo, Yamamoto Kazuhiko, and Sato Iwao. Nihon Hyoronsya.

Sugawara Ikuo, Yamamoto Kazuhiko, and Sato Iwao, eds. 2010. *Riyousya ga Motomeru Minji Sosyou no Jissen* [Practice of civil proceedings required by users]. Nihon Hyoronsya.

Sugawara Ikuo, Yamamoto Kazuhiko, Kakiuchi Syusuke, and Ishida Kyoko. 2021. *Minji Sosho no Jitsuzo to Kadai-RIyousha Chousa no Tsumikasane ga Shimesu Mono* [The reality and actual state of civil litigation: What accumulated user surveys reveal]. Yuhikaku.

Sugawara Ikuo and Kakiuchi Shusuke, eds. 2023. *Tetsuzuki Riyousha kara mita Minji Sosho no Jissai – 2021 nen Minji Sosho Riyousha Chousa* [The reality of civil litigation from the perspective of users: 2021 Civil Litigation Survey]. Shoji Houmu.

Sweda, Edward L. Jr., Mark Gottlieb, and Christopher N. Banthin. 2007. *Light Cigarette Lawsuits in the United States: 2007*. Tobacco Control Legal Consortium.

Takahashi Hiroshi. 2010. "Riyousya ha Donoyouna Doki de Sosho wo Okonaunoka" [What motivations cause users to initiate legal proceedings?]. In *Riyousya ga Motomeru Minji Sosyou no Jissen* [Practice of civil proceedings required by users], edited by Sugawara Ikuo, Yamamoto Kazuhiko, and Sato Iwao. Nihon Hyoronsya.

Takahashi Shigeru, eds. 2013. *Kaisei Gyoseihou no Sekoujoukyou no Kensyo* [Verification and implementation of the revised Administrative Procedure Act]. Shoji Houmu.

Takahiro Takenouchi. 2024. "Japan Tagged 'Fossil of the Day' For Not Fighting Global Warming." *Asahi Shimbun*, December 4, 2024. https://www.asahi.com/ajw/articles/15074438.

Tanaka Hideo. (1991) 2008. *Eibeihou Jiten* [Dictionary of Anglo-American law]. Tokyo University Press.

Tanaka Shigeaki. 2005. *Hou heno Shiza Tenkan wo Mezashite* [Toward a shift of legal perspective]. Yukikaku Gakujutu Center.

Tanase Takao. 2000. "Tabako Sosho no Ho-shakaigaku: Gendai no Ho to Saibann no Kaidoku ni Mukete" [Sociolegal studies of tobacco litigation: Toward an interpretation of modern law and litigation]. In In *Tabako Sosho no Ho Shakai Gaku* [Sociolegal study of tobacco litigation], edited by Tanase Takao. Sekai Hyoronsya.

Tilly, Charles. 1984. *Big Structures, Large Processes, Huge Comparisons*. Russel Fage Foundation.

Tonami Koji. 2015. "Judicial Review in Japan and its Problems." *Waseda Bulletin of Comparative Law* 33: 1–11.

Trencher, Gregory, Adrian Rinscheid, Mert Duygan, Nihi Truong, and Jusen Asuka. 2020. "Revisiting Carbon Lock-In in Energy Systems: Explaining the Perpetuation of Coal Power in Japan." *Energy Research and Social Science* 69: 101770.

Tsuru Shigeto, ed. 1968. *Gendai Shihon Syugi to Kogai* [Modern capitalism and pollution]. Iwanami Shoten.

Uga, Katsuya. 2006. *Gyo-seihou Gaisetsu II: Gyosei Kyusaihou* [Overview of administrative law II: Administrative Relief Act]. Yuhikaku.

United Nations Development Programme (UNDP) and University of Oxford. 2021. *People's Climate Vote: Results*. https://www.undp.org/publications/peoples-climate-vote.

United Nations Environment Programme (UNEP). 2020. *Global Climate Litigation Report: 2020 Status Review*. UNEP Publications.

United Nations Environment Programme (UNEP). 2023. *Global Climate Litigation Report: 2023 Status Review*. UNEP Publications.

United Nations Framework Convention on Climate Change (UNFCCC). 2023. "COP28 Agreement Signals "Beginning of the End" of the Fossil Fuel Era" [press release]. December 13, 2023. https://unfccc.int/news/cop28-agreement-signals-beginning-of-the-end-of-the-fossil-fuel-era.

Upham, Frank K. 1975. "Litigation and Moral Consciousness in Japan: An Interpretive Analysis of Four Japanese Pollution Suits." *Law & Society Review* 10: 583.

Upham, Frank K. 1979. "After Minamata: Current Prospects and Problems in Japanese Environmental Litigation." *Ecology of Law Quarterly* 8, no. 2: 218–268.

Upham, Frank K. 1987. *Law and Social Change in Postwar Japan*. Harvard University Press.

Upham, Frank K. 1989. "What's Happening in Japan, Sociolegalwise." *Law & Society Review* 23, no. 5: 879–889.

Urabe Noriho. 2016. *Kenpougaku Kyoshitsu* [Lecture on constitutional studies]. 3rd ed. Nihon Hyoronsya.

Vanhala, Lisa. 2012. "Legal Opportunity Structures and the Paradox of Legal Mobilization by the Environmental Movement in the UK." *Law and Society Review* 46, no. 3: 523–556.

Vanhala, Lisa. 2013. "The Comparative Politics of Courts and Climate Change." *Environmental Politics* 22, no. 3: 447–474. https://doi.org/10.1080/09644016.2013.765686.

Vanhala, Lisa. 2018. "Is Legal Mobilization for the Birds? Legal Opportunity Structures and Environmental Nongovernmental Organizations in the United Kingdom, France, Finland, and Italy." *Comparative Political Studies* 51, no. 3: 380–412.

Vanhala, Lisa. 2020. "Legal Mobilization." Last reviewed November 23, 2021. *Oxford Bibliographies*. https://doi.org/10.1093/OBO/9780199756223-0031.

Vélez-Echeverri, Juliana, Catharine Higham, and Joana Setzer. 2024. "Climate-Washing Litigation: Towards Greater Corporate Accountability?" Grantham Research Institute on Climate Change and the Environment. https://www.lse.ac.uk/granthaminstitute/news/climate-washing-litigation-towards-greater-corporate-accountability.

White Paper on Attorneys. 2018. *Comparison of the Total Number of Attorneys, Judges, and Prosecutors with Other Countries* [in Japanese]. https://www.nichibenren.or.jp/library/ja/jfba_info/statistics/data/white_paper/2018/1-3-5_tokei_2018.pdf.

White Paper on Attorneys. 2020a. *Attorneys' Population* [in Japanese]. https://www.nichibenren.or.jp/library/pdf/document/statistics/2020/1-1-1.pdf.

White Paper on Attorneys. 2020b. *Civil Legal Aid* [in Japanese]. https://www.nichibenren.or.jp/library/pdf/document/statistics/2020/6-2-2.pdf.

White Paper on Attorneys. 2024. *Number of Attorneys* [in Japanese]. https://www.nichibenren.or.jp/library/pdf/document/statistics/2024/1-1-1.pdf.

Yamamoto Hajime. 2020. "Naze Ima Sekitan Karyoku ga Mondainanoka?: Kikou Kiki to Datu Sekitan heno Taiou wo Motomeru Shimin no Uttae" [Why is coal problematic now? Citizens' plea for countermeasures against climate crisis and decarbonization]. *Agenda: Mirai heno Kadai* 68: 65–73.

Yu Fujinami. 2021. "Switching to Renewable Energy Without Increasing Costs? Decarbonization for Small and Medium-Sized Enterprises" [in Japanese]. *Asahi Shimbun*, April 2, 2021. https://www.asahi.com/articles/ASP3V3V8QP3DULBJ00X.html.

Zhao, Yue, Lyu Shuang, and Wang Zhu. 2019. "Prospects for Climate Change Litigation in China." *Transnational Environmental Law* 8, no. 2: 349–377.

Index

Case names are in italics. Page numbers in italics refer to figures, page numbers followed by *n* indicate footnotes, and page numbers followed by *t* indicate tables (59*t*).

www.ingramcontent.com/pod-product-compliance
Lightning Source LLC
LaVergne TN
LVHW010659300926
849161LV00005B/1167